The Test

The Test

My Autobiography

BRIAN O'DRISCOLL

with Alan English

PENGUIN
IRELAND

PENGUIN IRELAND

Published by the Penguin Group
Penguin Ireland, 25 St Stephen's Green, Dublin 2, Ireland
(a division of Penguin Books Ltd)
Penguin Books Ltd, 80 Strand, London WC2R 0RL, England
Penguin Group (USA) Inc., 375 Hudson Street, New York, New York 10014, USA
Penguin Group (Australia), 707 Collins Street, Melbourne, Victoria 3008, Australia
(a division of Pearson Australia Group Pty Ltd)
Penguin Group (Canada), 90 Eglinton Avenue East, Suite 700, Toronto, Ontario, Canada M4P 2Y3
(a division of Pearson Penguin Canada Inc.)
Penguin Books India Pvt Ltd, 11 Community Centre, Panchsheel Park, New Delhi – 110 017, India
Penguin Group (NZ), 67 Apollo Drive, Rosedale, Auckland 0632, New Zealand
(a division of Pearson New Zealand Ltd)
Penguin Books (South Africa) (Pty) Ltd, Block D, Rosebank Office Park,
181 Jan Smuts Avenue, Parktown North, Gauteng 2193, South Africa

Penguin Books Ltd, Registered Offices: 80 Strand, London WC2R 0RL, England

www.penguin.com

First published 2014
006

Set in 13.5/16 pt Garamond MT Std
Typeset by Jouve (UK), Milton Keynes
Printed in Great Britain by Clays Ltd, St Ives plc

A CIP catalogue record for this book is available from the British Library

ISBN: 978–1–844–88291–5

www.greenpenguin.co.uk

For Amy & Sadie
and in memory of my pal Barry

Contents

Prologue

The day begins like any other. I'm awoken by the sound of chat coming from across the landing, just a mumble at first but then rising in pitch to a full-blown call to action.

Get up, get up, wherever you are. I want my bottle!

I check the time on my phone. It reads 7.02 a.m., but it's three minutes ahead, the leeway I give myself after a lifetime of trying never to be late.

Beside me, my wife Amy is still sleepy after working into the early hours of the morning. No point in two of us not getting any more shut-eye: I throw back the covers and answer the call.

The nursery door is open, and as I peek around the corner, Sadie, aged fifteen months, is standing up at the near end of her cot, the soother still in her mouth.

'Hello!' I say.

She smiles, pleased to see me. She spits out the soother, because she knows it stays in the cot, alongside Audrey the rabbit and Merle the bear.

Gently, I pull her out of her sleeping-bag and she points, as she does every morning, to the creature stencilled in green on the opposite wall.

'Will we give Ernie a kiss?'

I hold her up. She plants a smacker on the owl, perched on his tree, who watches over her.

It's breakfast time on the morning of my final day as a rugby player.

I turn on the coffee machine and make Sadie's bottle – five ounces, enough to keep her happy for now, with room left for the main course of Weetabix and Readybrek mixed with fruit purée.

When I was a boy, my parents drilled good manners into me. Now, as a father myself, I find myself almost wrestling the food back from my little one if I don't hear the magic word, or challenging some of the kids who come up to me on the street . . .

'Give us a picture!'

'Sign this!'

'Selfie!'

It's the bee in my bonnet.

'I'll give you another go. Now try asking nicely . . .'

In the kitchen, I hand Sadie her bottle.

'Ta-ta,' she says.

That's my girl.

We hang out for a couple of hours, just the two of us, while Amy sleeps. I pick up my iPad, type 'nursery rhyme songs' into Google as she lies on my chest and before each one ends I know what's coming up next . . .

'Baa Baa Black Sheep', 'Happy Birthday', 'Row Row Row Your Boat', 'Old MacDonald' . . .

On my phone there are emails from the night before. Near the top of my inbox is one sent by Johnny Sexton at 20:55.

He has never mailed me before, but I've been expecting it. A few days have passed since he called me from Paris, the place he calls home now, the city where we played our last game together, in the Six Nations a couple of months ago. He was looking for my email address. 'And I don't want the one for BOD Inc,' he said. 'I don't want your mum or your sister reading it first, like it's fan mail.'

Me and Sexto, we shared some special times. Like everyone at Leinster, I was desperately disappointed to see him leave, but I completely understood his decision.

We had shouting matches on the training field in our day, but they were always about what was better for us as a group of players. You need that in a team, sometimes. He wore his heart on his sleeve and the fierce competitive streak burning inside him sometimes boiled over.

There were times when I smiled and tried to reason with him: 'Johnny, you don't always have to have the last word!'

But it was hard to penetrate the wall of certainty he built around himself, the conviction that he had to be right, all the time: '*Says you!*'

Now, as I read his email, I feel moved by the generous sentiments.

And I wish he was here, still wearing the Leinster number 10 jersey, alongside me in our backline. One last time.

*

There is a picture I love, a favourite memory from my Leinster days. It shows us on the pitch at the Millennium Stadium in Cardiff, a few minutes after we've lifted our second Heineken Cup.

We are huddled in a circle, and the trophy is in the middle. The Black-Eyed Peas are booming from the loudspeakers.

I gotta feeling that tonight's gonna be a good night . . .

The stadium is full of Leinster fans who have willed us to victory. Our families are all there, the loved ones who have supported us all our rugby days. Our coaches are close by, the men who have guided and helped shape us.

But we still had to do it.

We still had to pull it back.

Sixteen points down to Northampton at half-time, 11 ahead at the finish.

And what's in the picture is *us*, just us.

Enjoying each other's company, celebrating an unforgettable achievement.

Happy and proud and together for a perfect moment in our lives.

And every time I see that photograph I can't help but smile. I look at it and think: *Nothing beats winning with good friends.*

Because I know what it took to make it happen, the disappointments we went through before success came our way, the criticism we shipped for being bottlers, chokers, mentally weak.

I remember the time, back in 2005, when we were taken to an adventure centre on the side of a mountain in the deep west of Ireland, the kind of place where businesses send their employees to bond over some compulsory fun. I remember it pissing rain for two days, the lads being fed up: *What are we getting out of this?*

And, most of all, I recall the knowing looks of the camp leaders in the debrief room afterwards – the presumption in their words.

'We've seen your weaknesses . . . We know where they lie.'

I stood up and let them have it.

'You don't know us. You can't judge us on what you've seen today. You haven't seen these guys in training, running until they puke their ring and then running some more. Taking the kind of impacts you'd only get in a nasty car crash – and then getting back up and taking some more.'

In fifteen years as a player I saw our sport move on

massively, the better for professionalism in almost every respect. But the best team-building experiences of my career had nothing to do with making rafts or climbing hoardings. They were about good nights out, about friends getting closer while having fun together. Old school.

If some of us went a little overboard on the conviviality in the early days, then we learned as we went along.

Fifteen seasons and I can draw a line almost down the middle. From 2008 onwards I became a better all-round pro: less reliant on the ability I was born with, more determined to get every last ounce out of my career and what was left of it.

At Leinster we saw Leo Cullen and Shane Jennings come back to us from Leicester with different mindsets. We came to recognize – late in the day, but not too late – that success against the best sides in Europe was going to take more than we were giving.

Better diet.

Better rest.

The things you do – or don't do – on your days off.

The way you live your life.

The small margins that make the difference.

Professional rugby offers you a test. Talent isn't enough to pass it: you need to go deeper and find the desire to keep proving yourself. And if you can combine those qualities with a professional approach – the extras after training, the stretching at home – then it goes a long, long way.

Even during the work-hard, play-hard days there was satisfaction in getting through the tough training sessions without holding back, in driving the last residues of the weekend's enjoyment out of the system. But when we had three stars on our jerseys – one for each Heineken Cup – I looked back and wondered how things might have been different in the earlier years.

Maybe, though, the best days would never have arrived if our ambition hadn't been built on the back of failure.

And maybe the reason we got there in the end was because when we picked ourselves off the ground in the final minutes of the biggest games we looked up and saw friends.

Without that bond when the going gets tough, why would you dig in?

*

The Pro12 final against Glasgow Warriors has a 6.15 p.m. kick-off and the pre-match nerves – the hours when I become a slightly weird, silent person – are a while away yet.

I had a word to myself last night: *Carry really hard! Choose not to be tackled!*

I had two fairy-tale games in the space of a week back in March and I'm pushing my luck big-time hoping for a third, but it would be nice to pull out a performance that leaves people wanting a little bit more.

Amy gets an unreal welcome from Sadie when she comes down to join us around nine, and we float around for a while as texts start arriving, wishing me luck. First some special words from Ferg McFadden, then a lovely one from Leo, who is bowing out with me.

The long goodbye has dragged on painfully and I feel ready for the end, relieved that I'm nearly done, with a second Six Nations championship on my record. It was nice to finish on a high with Ireland, after a few decent personal performances – *possibly* not deserving man of the match at the Stade de France – but I haven't really got going since.

Maybe in a perfect world, to spare myself the digs about the longest farewell tour since Frank Sinatra, I'd have walked off into the sunset after we beat France in Paris. But seeing out the season with my club is the right way to go – hopefully with a trophy on the pitch when it ends.

I feel proud of what I've achieved in the game, but I've been on the wane for a couple of years now. As an older player you're forced to reinvent yourself, but every time you do it you're losing another trait. I can still make the half-breaks and the offloads, I can still put other people through holes. I've evolved and learned new skills, but I look at how I used to change direction and accelerate and that has been leaving me. I've begun feeling a bit blunt . . .

When you know you're going to retire it's difficult not to switch off, at least a little. 'Just stick in there for the next couple of months,' I told myself back in March, and I tried to work as hard as ever, to give my preparation the same focus. But it's been hard to fight the reality that I'm not where I want to be physically, that I'm a lesser player than I was.

I used to go out and think, Just give me the ball and there's every chance I'll cause someone trouble. Not out of arrogance, I hope, but pure confidence. I saw the gaps and the opportunities and I backed myself to exploit them. And now the head still sees it all happening but the body just doesn't respond like it used to: there's isn't as much juice in the legs. They feel heavier than they once did and eighty minutes seems a long time.

When I saw the zip in the younger guys' legs I wanted that feeling back. I remember being their age and seeing the older guys take longer to get themselves warmed up – almost laughing as they worried about the tightness in their hamstrings and the creaking in their knees. And then eventually you become that person. The sense of camaraderie in being part of a squad never dissipates, but you don't enjoy the game itself quite as much.

*

I'm wired very simply. I don't dwell on the negative, and the quality I value most in my friends is loyalty. Like most people, I'm someone who wants an easy life, as free from stress and hassle as possible. I enjoy having the spotlight on me when I'm playing rugby, because I'm in my comfort zone then, but away from the game I like simple things, like a quiet weekend at home. I love the release that a good time out with friends brings, but I couldn't think of anything worse than going out every night.

Talk to any international rugby player and he'll say the same thing: the vast majority of the people we meet out and about are genuinely nice, but sometimes we don't get to spend as much time as we'd like with the friends whose company we're there to enjoy. And not all of the conversations with people we don't really know are guaranteed to make us smile.

'Congratulations on your wedding!'

'Thanks.' *It was two years ago but we'll let that pass.*

'How's that working out? You're not divorced yet, are you?'

'No, no! Still hanging in there.'

'Come to me if you need a good lawyer. Ha ha!'

Hilarious.

At the kitchen table, I flick through Twitter. It's mostly how I find out what's going on in the world. One of the things I like about it is that it gives you a voice if you need one. Unless the lads hijack your phone, you can't be misquoted. They're your words and nobody can twist them.

What I choose to put out there reflects, to some extent, the person I really am. But not entirely: I have to be careful sometimes. I've hesitated over many a tweet, worrying about how it'll be perceived. I live by a rule: 'Am I happy seeing this in the paper tomorrow?' Certain opinions – perhaps a touch outspoken, but no more than the next guy's – I've rubbed out when they were ready to go.

Because you're opening yourself up to abuse.

Because it's not expected of you.

The problem with being in the public eye is that the public believe they know you. They judge your behaviour through the lens of their own preconceptions.

That's typical!

That's so unlike him!

If you stick around long enough and you do enough of the right things, you get seen in a largely positive light. It's a nice way to have it because most of us are some way sensitive about how we're perceived as people – but it can stifle you. Just a little, but enough to make you second-guess yourself every so often.

After a certain amount of success you can be put in a kind of category, held up as a role model, attractive to sponsors and the people behind good causes, pushed into behaving in a slightly different way than you might ordinarily do, every now and then, because people have put you on a pedestal.

As long as you're not living a lie, it's just a tweak here and there, a small concession. Even when you're not in the best of form, it should never feel like any kind of hardship to smile for a picture or sign a few autographs. And it's a whole lot better than fighting the perception that you're a clown, years after you've handed people the ammunition – such as appearing on your country's top-rated television show with yellow hair.

Sometimes the things you do early in your life – when you're young and still finding your way – are not easily forgotten or forgiven. But the mistakes you make along the way are part of your story too. And so, offered the chance to put that story out there – in your own way, like one long string of tweets – you'd like to think you might change one or two minds.

*

For a while now, my match-day ritual for our home games has included brunch with the Kearney brothers, Rob and Dave, at a café in Donnybrook, The Greenery. We like to sit at a window table just inside the door and watch the passing traffic.

There's a beautiful waitress and Rob enjoys it when it's his turn to pay. But every time we go I take great pleasure in hitting him with the unpalatable truth: she has a soft spot for Dave; Rob's playing second fiddle to his younger brother.

Today, though, Dave is laid up. He's just about to come out of hospital after knee surgery. He sends me a text: *Have pancakes for me. Best of luck later.*

He's a great lad, known to his team-mates as Dreamboat, the good-looking Kearney.

It kills Rob.

After a shower I drive to Donnybrook, skipping through the radio stations, looking for a song I like. I don't want to listen to anything serious – not in the mornings, and not today. 'Happy' by Pharrell Williams nails my mood.

There's a couple making their way towards the café as I look through the window and see our favourite table's free. I quicken my step and throw my keys and sunglasses down to claim it, but end up sitting at a table outside when I spot our back-row forward Rhys Ruddock.

Kearns rolls up and I go with the pancakes for Dreamboat instead of my usual eggs Benedict.

There's a brief mention of the match –

'So this is it?'

'This is it. The end.'

– but they're probably just as sick of all the hoopla as I am, so we talk about anything and nothing. The usual.

After an hour I head to Riverview, our training base, for my pre-match stretch – getting a few cracks out of my back with a foam roller, loosening my glutes by lying on a hockey ball, throwing a few passes to Gordon D'Arcy when he shows up, then stretching the calf that tightened up in training at the beginning of the week. I haven't trained on it since, on the advice of the physios, but it feels absolutely fine.

Back at the house, I potter around the kitchen for half an hour while Amy and Sadie are upstairs. They come down with flowers.

'We got you these,' Amy says. 'You got your balloons, yeah?'

'Balloons?'

'The ones in the middle of the kitchen? The big round things?'

'Really?'

I've walked past them at least twenty times and not seen them, which can only mean that my pre-match routine has already moved on – a little earlier than normal – to phase two. The weirdness.

After some lasagne in mid-afternoon I'm picked up by Shane Jennings and his wife, Cliona. We head down the Clonskeagh Road to Beaver Row, onto Anglesea Road, then Simmonscourt Road and through the gates of the RDS. Jenno isn't one for rushing and we arrive insanely early – two and a quarter hours before kick-off.

For years before Leinster home games some of us have killed time by going straight to the Spot the Difference page in the match programme. An action shot from the week before, two versions of the same picture, always eight differences – stripes missing on boots or socks, Canterbury logos missing on shorts, a one-legged man somewhere in the distance.

It started off ridiculously easy. We complained: 'Where's the challenge here?'

They made it crazily difficult, next to impossible. We complained again: 'Come on, give us some chance! It's got to be realistic!'

I'd walk in and some of my biggest Spot the Difference rivals, like Isa Nacewa, would already be hard at it.

'How many have you got?'

'Two.'

'I'm on the case.'

Now I pick up the programme for my swansong, but there's no sign of Spot the Difference because the programme's been produced on behalf of the tournament sponsors, RaboDirect.

Whoa! I'll have to chat to the lads instead!

Since I was twenty years old I've had numbers 12 and 14 on either side of me in the Leinster dressing room. On 3 September 1999 Darce and I appeared on a team sheet together for the first time, and I can't imagine anyone else under the number 12 peg alongside me today.

'I'm not doing the whole sentimental thing, but it's been a pleasure,' he says.

Ferg is on my right, in the spot mostly filled by Shane Horgan until injury forced him to retire a couple of years back. Good lads, special friends.

I get my thumb strapped up by our physio Karl Denvir and start feeling a touch of nostalgia coming on. 'That's the last time you'll be doing that,' I tell him. 'Thank you for your considerable expertise in the strapping field.'

Ours is a friendly dressing room. Everyone shakes hands with everyone, every day – something brought in by Joe Schmidt, our former coach. We take the piss out of one another endlessly – from the day I first walked in we always have – but as a group we're tight.

The thing about rugby players is that we spend huge amounts of time in each other's company. For Leinster, for Ireland and for the Lions, I have spent much of my adult life in training. In certain seasons we've spent a third of the year in hotels, away from family and friends, all working from the same schedule with the same time off, so that we often end up getting together for coffee or dinner in our down time, even holidaying together when summer comes or there's a chance to unwind for a few days mid-season.

Spending as much time as we do in camp might seem boring, but it rarely is. There are always entertaining personalities to help pass the hours when you're not training. Table tennis, pool, the odd game of cards or the annual interest in the Cheltenham Festival brings out the sharks among us. The competitive edge is never put to one side, and many's the table-tennis bat that's been flung in anger during a tense five-set thriller.

Running hills, refuelling, socializing: we're together for such sustained periods of time that it's really only those who are part of camp, and the family members and close friends who are in touch with our everyday lives, who really understand what goes into those eighty minutes of rugby. The outcome on match day will affect our mood until the next game, and the difference between success and failure can be a borderline decision from a television match official or a puff of chalk rising from a boot that has nicked the touchline.

We win together, we lose together. That feeling of contentment, sitting in a dressing room with a trophy resting on the floor and no need for words, is not really something that the world beyond sport can offer you.

And as the end comes for me, it's the feeling that I'll miss most: that silent understanding. I'll miss, too, the palpable pride – on the best days – of the people close to me.

*

Eoin O'Malley comes in and speaks. A year retired, forced by a knee injury to quit at just twenty-five, Chubbo was one of the unlucky ones.

There's emotion in his voice but he holds it together well. The professional game gave him only four seasons, but he was a young player with the kind of talent at outside centre that once made me fear for my place in the team.

Sometimes you forget that talent and desire aren't always enough: you need luck, too.

The rest of it plays out like any other game: two co-codamol tablets and an anti-inflammatory exactly an hour before kick-off, for the niggles that never leave you when you're in the over-thirty club; a few words from our coach Matt O'Connor; a rub from our massage guy Tommo, a.k.a. Michael Thompson, that ends with a double slap on the arse ('Right! That's you!'); four pieces of caffeine chewing gum, which give me a little edge, at least in my head; then warm-up number 186 in Leinster senior colours.

Jamie Heaslip, captain on the day, comes over as we're about to leave the dressing room.

'D'you want to lead the team out, Briano?' he asks.

'Absolutely not!' I tell him. 'That's all done. Let's just get on with it.'

Our manager, Guy Easterby, is at the door as we come back in from the warm-up, counting us down: 'Six minutes!'

I towel myself, put on my sleeveless vest, then my jersey. Good to go.

Our out-half Jimmy Gopperth kicks off, into the breeze.

For six minutes and twenty seconds I don't touch the ball, or make a tackle, or hit a ruck. Then, inside their 22, we go with a play off a lineout and I run up hard, the first time I've gone balls-out all week. Jimmy sees me coming but our timing is fractionally off. He throws it to Zane Kirchner instead and I carry on running, trying to sit someone down or open up a hole for Zane.

I feel a pop in my calf and I know straight away I'm in trouble. With knocks and bangs, the power of the mind can get you over them, but a soft-tissue injury doesn't listen.

The doc, Arthur Tanner, comes over for a word. Garreth Farrell, our physio, runs on and rolls his eyes to Heaven. We've both known all week that the calf wasn't quite right but neither of us had remotely expected this.

I'm 99.9 per cent certain it's game over, but I hold out for the 0.1. I don't want it to end like this, seven minutes into a final I've contributed nothing to.

'Just give me a minute to see if I can get by.'

A Glasgow scrum forms fifteen metres from their line and I swap with Jimmy because I feel less vulnerable at 10.

As their scrum-half Chris Cusiter fires the ball back, I run at the receiver, Finn Russell, but after a couple of yards there's another big bite in the calf.

Walking off the pitch, I start pulling the strapping off my

thumb. I don't feel any big emotions coming over me: I'm just annoyed that this is how it ends.

I sit with the subs for a few minutes but I could do without the cameras being pointed at me, trying to pick up whatever I'm feeling, and I don't fancy the prospect of seeing myself come up on the big screen during a break in play.

When we score a really good team try, I slip away – past the diehard fans still celebrating in the Pit, and towards the dressing room.

The strangest things can come into your head at unexpected moments. As I go through the door I get a flashback to a brief conversation at Windsor Castle seven weeks ago. Amy and I had been invited to a state banquet in honour of the President of Ireland, Michael D. Higgins.

I'd spoken to the Queen first. I was last in the queue to be announced, behind Amy: 'Brian O'Driscoll – ex Irish rugby captain.'

'Oh, yes,' she'd said, 'you're retiring, aren't you?'

'Yes, ma'am.'

'You look relatively unscathed. Certainly your nose looks as though it's in slightly better condition than Mike Tindall's.'

I smiled at the quickness of her wit and agreed. My old rival, the England centre, who married the Queen's granddaughter Zara, wasn't around to defend himself. 'Maybe a little . . .'

Prince Philip was alongside Michael D. and his wife, Sabina. 'No doubt you'll get injured in your final game,' he piped up.

I forced a smile and thought, *Jaysus, how shit would that be? Surgery the week after I finish?*

But now, pulling off my jersey, I find it difficult to feel hard done by. Instead, there's relief that it has ended with only a soft-tissue injury and not a break, or anything serious enough to put me out of commission for the first five or six months of my retirement.

There's relief, too, that I'm finally done – out of the game pretty much intact.

I never thought I'd still be playing in my mid-thirties. After ten years as a pro I looked ahead to the 2011 World Cup in New Zealand: it seemed like the right stage to depart on. I wanted to enjoy the rest of my life. I wanted to play golf, take holidays at the time of my choosing, not dictated by the rugby calendar.

But when the time came I wasn't ready to go. I didn't know what else I wanted to do with my life. I'd been looking for something but it wasn't suggesting itself.

Even when they told me I needed a fusion operation on my neck to stop the pain I kept getting from the heavy impacts, I didn't feel ready to let it go. I looked ahead and saw a new target in the distance, another reason for another season or two: the chance finally to be part of a winning Lions tour.

I gave serious consideration to retiring last summer, but I would have left with doubts. Now, as I sit on a bench with an ice pack strapped to the calf that has given me trouble for half the season, I have none. I've been hanging in there, hanging on for this day. It hasn't ended the way I hoped, but the disappointment leaves me when I think about what the game has given me.

That was a good run.

If someone held a gun to my head, then maybe I could just about manage one more pre-season. There's another World Cup not much more than a year away and perhaps I could get myself into a certain condition that would put me in the mix. But I feel I'd struggle to hold down my place, with the quality of players available to Ireland now. I could do without the worry of being smoked by the new kids on the block, or the misery I know I'd feel if I found myself sitting on the bench, feeling like I'm undoing – just a little, but enough to matter – whatever reputation I managed to build in my best years. For fifteen seasons I made the Ireland team whenever I was fit to play and I wanted to be in control of taking that away. I didn't want someone else taking it from me.

Our bag man, Johnny O'Hagan, is the only other person in the dressing room. We watch the game unfold on TV and I'm anxious, frustrated by the five-second delay that means cheers or groans echo from outside while we wonder what's about to happen.

I stay there through half-time and on into the second half, happy for Leo as he comes off the bench to a big reception twenty minutes from time with the game still in the balance, relieved when Zane's second try makes it safe for us. By the time Darce puts the icing on the cake and jumps for joy, I'm back with the subs and the guys who've come off after me, ready to enjoy the moment.

It's our seventh trophy in seven years, but for a few of the lads it's a first big win and seeing what it means to them makes me very happy. I'm already alongside Darce and Jenno on the podium when Leo – our skipper since 2008 – is called up for his medal.

We've played rugby together since schooldays. As he walks past me and heads – ever modest – to the very back, I give him the old big-up from our days at Blackrock College, where he was revered: 'Leo! Leo! Leo!'

Jamie is the last man up. The Pro12 trophy is nestling on a table and he gestures for me to come down. 'Briano?'

I'm not having it, but somebody pushes me down off my step.

I'm still not having it.

Leo is hustled down from the back. He asks me to lift it with him.

I put a token couple of fingers on the bottom as he raises it high.

Another good night lies ahead.

*

The following Wednesday, with Amy away in London, I drive across town to Clontarf with Sadie in the car seat behind me. I spoke to Mum and Dad after the game but we haven't caught up properly. The conversations you have with your family in the blare of a post-match function aren't real because there's always someone listening in over your shoulder or trying to catch your eye and you can never talk naturally.

Sometimes you forget that your loved ones are living every moment of the journey with you — stressing about the big games, struggling to eat properly, worrying about the injuries that inevitably come your way. For eighteen years, since my first game of representative rugby outside the country — for Leinster Schools in Halifax, Yorkshire — Mum and Dad have flown all over the world to support me.

'Will you miss it?' I ask Mum, at the house.

'No,' she says. 'We feel like we had a great ride, but we're ready for the end.'

Four days after the endgame, she has captured completely what I'm thinking.

They're already moving on, with plans in place for a holiday during which rugby won't get a look-in. She'd told me about it before, but I'd almost forgotten: a ferry trip to Cherbourg, then two weeks' driving around France. Back to some of the places where we spent our family summers long ago.

'Janey,' I say, 'old school!'

At seven o'clock I get Sadie into her Babygro, slip on her jacket and put her into the car seat, knowing there's a big chance she'll KO on the way home.

I keep a good eye on her in the rear-view mirror and she closes her eyes just as we're coming up to the East Link toll bridge.

1. What Am I Doing Here?

I'm eight years old and I'm sitting in the back of my father's Renault Louisiane as he pulls out of our drive in Park Lawn, Clontarf, and turns onto Mount Prospect Avenue. It's July 1987 and we're off on our summer holidays to France.

My sister Julie is on one side of me. She's thirteen, the eldest. She gets to sit beside a window because she threw up in the car once and nobody wants to see that again. Sue is ten but nearly eleven. She always gets a window too.

So that leaves me. Forever in the centre.

Mum's from Cork and Dad's from Dublin. Both of them are doctors. Maybe they think I'll turn out to be a doctor too. In the history of our family, nearly everyone's a doctor.

In the back seat, Sue is doing what she usually does: annoying me, making me lose my temper, forcing me to give her an elbow into the side.

'Mum, Brian's after hitting me!'

'Brian! Don't hit your sister!'

'But she – !'

'It doesn't matter!'

Sue chalks up another victory at my expense, but I can't allow her to enjoy it. 'I wish you'd just jump in a lake and drown . . .' Straight away I know I've gone too far. I try to rescue myself. 'A fish! I wish you'd drown a fish!'

Sue doesn't fall for it. She's outraged. 'Dad! Brian said he wants me to drown! You can't let him get away with that!'

'Brian!'

'I said drown a fish!'

Dad's car has a Philips cassette player. He puts on his favourite tape and Christy Moore's voice comes out of the two speakers mounted on the dashboard.

Summer comes around each year
We go there and they come here.

Our boat sails at half five, and Dad looks like the happiest man in Ireland when he pulls into the car park of Kelly's hotel in Rosslare at one o'clock, with plenty of time for a big family lunch.

'The holiday begins now!' he says.

When we're hungry again, on the ferry to Le Havre, we watch the other kids walking back to their tables with burgers, sausages and greasy-looking chips.

Mum opens her cooler box and takes out a roasted chicken with stuffing, fresh salad in Tupperware boxes, coleslaw and a loaf of sliced bread, already buttered.

We'd like to tell her and Dad that we don't want to be different from everyone else, that we'd much prefer the burger and chips, but we don't want to hurt Mum's feelings.

As we drive across France she keeps us entertained in the back by offering a cash prize for the winner of her educational quizzes.

'Who knows what product this part of France is famous for?' she asks.

We haven't a notion. 'Give us a clue.'

'Look out the window. What can you see?'

We're in the middle of nowhere. There's nothing to see apart from cows grazing in the fields.

'Milk!'

'No.'

'Beef!'

'No.'

'Cheese!'

'No.'

We rack our brains and fall silent: peace and quiet for the price of a few francs.

We give up.

'Leather,' she answers.

'Clever one, Ger!' says Dad.

*

For three or four years I've worn glasses. According to Mum, I have astigmatism.

'What's astigmatism?'

'It means your eyeball is shaped a bit like a rugby ball.'

It was Julie who noticed I couldn't see very well, the day I asked her what the time was.

'Read the clock yourself!'

'What clock?'

But sometimes I don't wear my glasses, especially at my school, Belgrove.

One day Mr Cleary writes some sentences in Irish on the blackboard and leaves a word out of each one. He tells us to write down the sentences and fill in the blanks.

Without my glasses, I can't make out the words. I try to look at the copybook of the boy next to me but that's a blur too. I'm afraid to put up my hand and tell Mr Cleary that I've forgotten my glasses, so I squint at the board and guess.

Mr Cleary collects our copybooks, and when he hands them back the following day he starts giving out to me. 'This is absolute rubbish! Drivel!'

I feel the tears coming.

'Get out of this classroom and show your aunt that work –
it's appalling!'

My auntie Anne is a teacher in the next classroom. I knock
on the door and tell her, through sniffles and tears, that I left
my glasses at home.

My auntie is lovely, just like my old teacher, Mrs Cox. She
dries my eyes and sends me back to the class.

'Well?' says Mr Cleary. 'What did she say about that awful
work?'

'She gave me a packet of jellies because my handwriting
was so nice.'

*

When you've two doctors for parents, you have to work a bit
harder to pull the wool over their eyes when you feel like a
day off school.

'Time to get up, Brian.'

'I don't feel well.'

'What's the matter?'

Out comes my trump card, picked up while listening to
them talk around the house about chickenpox and chilblains,
fevers and flu.

'I'm cold, but I'm sweating.'

'Really? I'd better take your temperature.'

Usually what gives me away is I'm an unbelievably bad liar.
Often I fib to cover my tracks after helping myself to some
chocolate I'm not supposed to have. I absolutely love chocolate but Mum never puts any bars in our lunchboxes so
every time I get invited to someone's birthday party I nearly
make myself sick stuffing my face with it.

Over the course of a week I steal a full bar of cooking
chocolate, sneaking a few squares at a time until it's all gone.

There's trouble when Mum wants to bake a cake. I'm the chief suspect, the first child accused.

I deny all responsibility.

A week before Christmas I rip the cellophane off a box of Mikado biscuits, help myself to a couple of rows, then seal it back up.

'Who opened these?' Mum asks on Christmas morning, when half the contents are found to be missing.

'Not me,' says Jules.

'Not me,' says Sue.

'It wasn't me either,' I say. 'It must have been a dodgy box.'

'It wasn't a dodgy box,' Mum says. 'Was it you, Brian?'

'No!'

'Are you sure?'

'It wasn't me!'

'Tell the truth, Brian.'

'Okay, it was me.'

'I knew it was you,' she says, cool as a breeze. She never loses her temper. She never has to, because she knows how to get me where it hurts. 'I'm not angry, Brian. I'm just really disappointed in you for not telling the truth.'

*

My best friend in Park Lawn since the age of three is Donovan Rossi. We call him Dunny. He says that when he makes his Confirmation and gets to have another name, he's picking Paolo, after the Italian soccer player. Then he'll be Donovan Troy Paolo Rossi.

Dunny never backs away from anyone or anything. He's got a serious temper and sometimes I'm the one in his firing line. We play nearly every game going and there's not much between us in any of them, apart from tennis. His Dunlop racket gets so bashed up from being slammed into the road that it ends up more square than round.

'Stupid bloody game!' he says.

We run for our parish in the Community Games at Santry Stadium, trying to beat one another to the top step on the winners' rostrum. Apart from the times when he wants to beat me to a pulp, Dunny has my back. When we're playing soccer or Gaelic and somebody starts on me, he doesn't just stand off or wait for the referee to deal with it – he gets his retaliation in early.

Clontarf is a great place to grow up, a lovely part of the northside. When I'm not playing on the road I'm kicking a football around in St Anne's Park, or in the back garden with my dad. Over on Castle Avenue there's a rugby club he once played for, but we never go there. He prefers to let me play whatever the rest of the lads are into and rugby isn't on their radar.

We play Gaelic football for the school and soccer for Clontarf St John, alongside lads from Coolock and Killester, Donaghmede and Donnycarney. When they ask me where I'm from I put on my best northside Dub accent . . .

'Clon*taaarf.*'

When they ask me what I want to be when I grow up I say a fireman.

In our house there's a picture of Dad playing rugby for Ireland against Argentina in 1970, nine years before I was born. Now, with his rugby days long in the past, his favourite game is golf. We watch Seve on the telly in the majors, and when Dad takes me out to caddie for him at Royal Dublin on Sunday mornings I get to hit a few balls with my 7-iron once we're out of sight of the clubhouse.

Mum and Dad know they haven't got a genius for a son.

And if there's a little part of them holding out some hope that I might somehow muster the points for medicine, then it's probably just as well that I set them straight good and early. When they put me forward for the entrance exam to Belvedere College, a private school on the northside, I don't get in.

The following year I resit the exam and it doesn't go much better, but this time there's a stroke of luck. A boy pulls out and they offer me his place.

Then a letter arrives at home with the Belvedere crest on the envelope. *Dear Mr and Mrs O'Driscoll – It is with regret that I have to inform you . . .* The boy wants his place after all.

'He will never, *ever* go to Belvedere,' my dad says to my mum.

They come up with a new plan, a different school. The only problem with Blackrock College is there's a waiting list and I'm never getting in, unless I leave Belgrove a year early and do sixth class at Willow Park Junior School first. You can't get turned down by Blackrock once you're a Willow Park boy: it's the rule.

It's eleven miles across town.

It's on the southside, another world.

Dunny won't be coming with me. None of my Clontarf friends will.

I say okay, I'll go. If they think it's for the best, I'll do it.

Mum drives me there on my first day, but the next morning she drops me down to the DART station in Killester for the train that leaves at twelve minutes past eight. It's already packed when it arrives, full of workers heading into town. There's no chance of a seat. There's pushing and shoving and people giving out. There are eight stops and it takes twenty-seven minutes, out past Clontarf Road, across the

Liffey, down by the side of Lansdowne Road and into Black-rock. After that it's a six-minute walk to Willow Park.

Some kids stroll along, messing and joking; I go whizzing by them, pretending I'm in a race. The idea of being late, of not being there when the bell rings at five to nine, makes me panic.

I don't know anybody. Someone asks me where I'm from. I put on my poshest accent. 'Clon-*torf.*'

He does a double-take. '*On the northside?*'

When word gets around, one of them calls me a northside knacker. They're always talking about rugby, about playing for Blackrock in the Junior Cup.

'Do you play rugby?'

'No.'

'Have you never played?'

'No.'

'Wouldn't you like to?'

'I suppose.'

Every day the train is full. One morning I'm standing on the platform when there's an announcement over the loud-speaker: the next train is delayed by thirty minutes.

Thirty minutes! I can't wait thirty minutes!

I run out of the station and down to the phone box in Kil-lester. I phone Mum but there's something wrong with the line and I can't get through.

I charge back up the road, pick a house at random and ring the bell. A friendly-looking lady opens the door.

'Excuse me! Could I use your phone? I really need to call home!'

She invites me in. By the look on her face, she thinks some-thing is seriously wrong. She points to the telephone on the hall table. 'There you are,' she says. 'Are you all right, love?'

'I just need to phone my mother.'

She answers straight away.

'Mum, it's me. Listen, panic! The DART isn't working. You'll have to give me a lift!'

When the 8.12 train is delayed again, a few weeks later, I run off and call her from another house.

'You can't keep getting yourself into a state,' she says. So when the 7.27 pulls into Killester station the next morning, I'm waiting for it. I have four seats all to myself and I arrive at Willow Park an hour early. In the yard I am thirty seconds away from my classroom and nothing can happen to stop me being on time.

For the next twenty years and more, the prospect of being late for anything stresses me out.

*

Sport is the best thing about Willow Park. Running, basketball, PE – I'm decent, and faster than most. Everyone says they're going for the rugby trials and I want to fit in, so Dad takes me there on a Saturday morning.

'Are you looking forward to it, Brian?'

'I don't know the rules.'

'You'll be grand.'

'I don't even know what I'm supposed to do.'

'Get your hands on the ball, run fast and avoid being tackled. That's the secret.'

In Willow Park rugby, there are the As and Bs, then the Cs and Ds.

The coach has never seen me on a pitch before. He puts me in the second row, for the Ds. He doesn't tell us we're the Ds, but any team with a midget in the second row has to be the fourth string.

I get the ball once and run, just like Dad told me. I run and nobody can catch me. I score my first try, and one of the few things I know about rugby is that after a try comes a conversion.

I've kicked a lot of frees in Gaelic football. I run over to the ref. 'Can I have a go at this?'

'You might as well.'

When the Under-12 squads go up on the board, I see my name among the As and Bs, who are listed together.

I'm no longer a second-row. I'm a wing.

For our first match of the season, we go on the bus to Lakelands to play Terenure. We take to the pitch in our brand-new blue-and-white hooped jerseys and socks, with white shorts.

When the ball comes to me I'm afraid that some of their forwards are going to smash me, so I put the foot down and sprint as fast as I can. I score in the corner. Then I get the ball again and the fear of getting hurt makes me take off and I score another one.

When the coaches say they're looking for parents to help out on Saturday mornings, I volunteer my father. 'He played for Ireland.'

'Really?'

'Against Argentina.'

'Seriously? So you'll ask him?'

'I'll ask him.'

So Dad starts doing some coaching and refereeing, and at every rugby match he's the loudest parent there. I don't want to hear him, but I've no choice. Everyone hears him.

'Great running!'

'Great pass!'

'WELL DONE!'

After four or five games he has a word with one of the coaches, Hugh McGuire. He's been wondering, he says, would it be an idea to give me a run at out-half?

So I'm put in at 10 against the Under-13 B team and it's a different world from running fast and not being caught. I'm brutal. I'm barely aware that there's anyone outside me, that it's up to me to link the play. In my head it's all about making things happen on my own.

But maybe Hugh sees something. He keeps faith in me and slowly I start falling for the game and getting better at it.

Anyone who knows anything about Under-12 rugby in Dublin knows that Belvedere are the team to beat. We play them once and we lose. We take them on again and we hockey them on a Wednesday afternoon.

Dad is beside himself with happiness, until something occurs to him. Not enough people have borne witness to our triumph. In particular, not enough Belvederians.

'The only shame about today was that it wasn't a Saturday,' he says. 'But, anyway, that was great! Belvo didn't know what hit them! WELL DONE!'

*

In that summer of 1991 Bryan Adams is never off the radio and I get into Royal Dublin Golf Club as a youth member.

One morning I'm down on the practice ground hitting a few balls on my own when a guy I've never seen before walks over. He's about seventy. He looks me up and down. 'Let's see your swing there,' he says.

I'm not exactly revelling in the attention. I'm thinking . . . *Jaysus! Who's this old-timer?* I hit a couple of shots for him and he gets me to change this, change that. I hit a few more.

'Better,' he says. 'What do you play off?'

'Eighteen. What's *your* handicap?'

'Old age.'

As he's wandering away, my next-door neighbour from Park Lawn arrives on the range and salutes him. 'Christy! How are ya?'

The penny finally starts to drop.

Christy O'Connor Senior, the greatest Irish golfer of the twentieth century, says he's doing grand, thanks.

Now that I'm twelve Dad reckons I'm ready for the world of work, so he gives me a shovel and a summer job digging up the back garden at the surgery he and Mum have on the Clontarf Road. He has great plans for vegetables, flowers, all sorts. I put my back into it for weeks on end, getting it ready for planting, but by the end of the summer the only thing we've got growing is a new crop of weeds.

The following year, on the afternoon of my uncle Fin's funeral, I'm playing football with my cousins on the green and there are thirty people in our house when everyone suddenly pours out onto the road: the house is on fire. By the time the fire brigade arrives the place is practically gutted. We have to take refuge in the flat above the surgery while the builders put it back together.

*

At the first training session of the season for the Willow Park Under-13s, I see the future of the Blackrock College rugby team and his name is Ciaran Scally.

We've seen him once before, wearing the light blue jersey of St Michael's the previous school year. But nothing we saw then prepared us for the shock of how good he is now, how much better he is than the rest of us.

We stand in line, waiting our turn in a tackling drill.

Defenders lined up on one side, attackers on the other. One against one, no hiding place. Take your man on, then get back in line to go again.

Ciaran Scally reaches the front of the queue on the attacking side. He looks across the tackle zone and sees Paul Grehan. They walk to the single cone placed in the middle, then sprint in opposite directions towards cones six metres away. When they turn, the contest begins. *Mano a mano.*

Scally has five metres of space to play with. Up to this moment, any attacker who has beaten his man has done it with footwork, with a sidestep or a late burst of pace, after taking the defender left and right and back again.

Scally never checks his stride once he rounds the cone. He runs straight at his man. Grehan braces himself and hunkers down, ready to make the hit. Scally literally runs over the top of him.

We watch Paul Grehan flying backwards in a double somersault. While he's still stretched across the turf, Scally is jogging back into the line of attackers. He doesn't say a word. He doesn't have to. We look at each other and we're all thinking the same thing: *Oh my God! Who's he up against next?*

I start counting the boys in the queue on the opposite side. He's a few places away from pairing up with me, but I'm not taking any chances.

I bend down to examine my left bootlace and find that it's nicely tied. I pull it open and glance back at the boy behind me. 'Go on ahead there. Just tying my lace.'

*

Ciaran Scally is a Booterstown boy, which means he can walk to Willow Park. Nobody calls him by his proper name – he's Skiddy Kiddy. Everyone has to have a nickname. Somebody says Mark Quinlan looks like Michael Lynagh, the Aussie out-half who has just broken Irish hearts in the World Cup quarter-final, so Mark becomes Mick. Skiddy comes up with a nickname for me, and once they hear about it back in Clontarf, Dunny and the lads run with it too. I'm Fathead.

By the time we start at Blackrock, me and Skiddy are good pals. He's a proper messer but he's bright as a button with it. He has this incredible ability in class to go from laughing his head off one second to being deadly serious the next.

He lashes a squashy rugby ball off the back of Gareth Quinn's head as he's reading from our textbook in the middle of Cozy Powell's geography class. It ricochets across the room like a missile. He throws it so fast that the only witness is me. Then Skiddy just sits there like nothing has happened while I'm in stitches.

Cozy storms down to the back of the class and doesn't bother asking questions.

Detention for me; Skiddy walks free.

Nobody is surprised when he makes the Junior Cup team as a second-year and plays a starring role when Blackrock beat St Mary's out the gate in the final. The rest of us have to wait for the following season. When I make it onto the panel, Skiddy is scrum-half, captain and our best player by a mile.

I'm on the edge of the team: too small and too timid to be a certain starter. Fast, but not physical. Talented, but not trusted to make the tackles that win matches.

It's unbelievably serious at training. At Blackrock College, Junior Cups matter. Three or four thousand people turn up at Donnybrook to see us take on Newbridge in the quarter-final. We're strongly fancied and our coach Alan McGinty tells us not to show our best moves to the opposition spies from the other big Dublin schools.

With five minutes left, it's over as a contest and I still haven't been called off the bench, which is doing nothing for my self-belief.

I mustn't be any good, if they're not bringing me on.

Mr McGinty has a word in my ear as I'm standing on the touchline, ready to go in at scrum-half. 'Don't show them anything!'

I burst onto the pitch, terrified. There's a scrum in mid-field. Somebody calls one of our top training-ground plays – one dummy switch followed by another. I'm barely on the pitch and I'm not about to argue, so I roll with it.

The move comes off perfectly and I run thirty metres into the corner. Our supporters appreciate the moment, but the coaches are less than impressed.

'The game was over and there you are giving away our good plays!'

A few days later, I see my name printed in a newspaper for the first time. There's even a headline about my big moment, in the *Evening Herald*:

SUPER SUB'S TERRIFIC TRY

Blackrock super sub Brian O'Driscoll got a brief opportunity to show his worth in last Tuesday's 31–7 AIB Junior Cup quarter-final defeat of Newbridge at Donnybrook and grasped it with both hands. His supreme confidence was a little out of the ordin-ary for a substitute and it comes as no surprise to hear that he is the son of Frank O'Driscoll, a brilliant centre who narrowly failed to win a full cap in the 70s. Frank played on the St Paul's team beaten by Rock in the first round of the Senior Cup back in 1965.

My mum cuts out the article and pastes it into a new scrap-book. Maybe she's hoping there'll be more coming to fill it up, but I'm an unused sub in the semi and it's hard to know what hurts more on the day of the final: Belvo beating us or not being given a run, again.

The following year, Skiddy moves on to the Senior Cup team and wins another medal. I spend the season at number 10 with the Clontarf Under-16s, playing with old friends and making new ones.

Most of the team play schools rugby with St Paul's in Raheny, where my father went. Dunny, our full-back, is in the middle of everything, with guys like Robbie Ryan and Paul Ryan – good fellas and nice players. Conor Redmond – a.k.a. Redser – is someone I've seen around but never gotten to know, after five years at school on the southside. We become pals and the friendship grows when we go off on tour to Aberystwyth. We're a hell of a team having a whale of a time but there's never anything in the newspapers for Mum to cut out because nobody's too excited about the Leinster Under-16 League, except the guys who end up winning it.

Which turns out to be us.

By the end of the season I'm a different proposition from the boy left sitting on the bench in the Junior Cup, doubting himself and wondering if the game is for him. I've been trusted in a pivotal position with a team playing winning rugby and having fun along the way. It feels like a spark has been lit.

Once the trophy is won a long summer stretches ahead. There are girls on the scene, parties and free houses. It's not a world that comes naturally to me and I'm slow enough to come out of my shell, but I'm sixteen years old and it's all about fitting in, about acceptance. And, like everyone else around me, I want to be accepted.

*

When the Senior Cup comes round again, in the first week of February 1996, I'm back in the fold and better equipped for the physical side of the game.

We're billed as the Dream Team. We have Ireland Schools internationals everywhere.

I'm named on the wing in the team to play Monkstown in our first cup match. I'm thrown a terrible pass but I catch the ball around my ankles, step a couple of defenders, then off-load it around the back of another guy, directly into the path of Leo Cullen, who is running a hard line behind me.

It isn't just the supporters who rate our number 8. If you asked the coaches to nominate one schoolboy in the country as a certainty to make the senior Ireland team, they wouldn't hesitate. They'd put their house, their car and all their wives' jewellery on Leo Cullen.

He's an icon in the school.

He's six foot six inches, a massive polar bear of a back-row.

He's five yards from the try line with nobody near him.

He drops my pass.

Ten seconds later, I hear the chant going up: '*One Leo Cullen! There's only one Leo Cullen!*'

Even when he's spilling ball, Leo can do no wrong.

For me, it feels like a turning point. I've shown them something and won a little respect, but it turns out to be a case of one step forward and another step back.

Skiddy's injured for round two and they switch me to scrum-half, where I haven't played all year. We're expected to put a cricket score on St Michael's but we barely survive and

I'm identified as the weakest link. They don't just put me back on the wing when Skiddy returns, they drop me altogether. For the rest of the campaign, I'm not trusted with another minute on the pitch.

The Dream Team marches on to glory.

*

Eleven months later, there's a big picture of me in a mud-splattered Blackrock College jersey, surrounded by three Newbridge College defenders, with both feet off the ground and my right arm wrapped around the ball. On the cover of the *Irish Times*.

My mother buys five copies.

The picture shows a more confident, more physically powerful kid. I'm wider, I'm wirier, I'm five inches taller, a running number 10. I'm so fit I could run all day, alongside Skiddy in a team that's going places.

I'm boarding at Blackrock, not studying as much as I should be in my Leaving Cert year but less tired from the travelling and more energetic at training. We don't just throw a ball around in the yard during lunch break, we're running full moves, building up a sweat, giving everything because, for most of us, this is our last crack at the Senior Cup.

The boarders live in a two-hundred-year-old castle, supervised by a couple of teachers. We like it best when Mr Wynne is on duty. He's a bit of a pushover because he's new.

When somebody pulls a pipe off a wall under the stairs, Mr Wynne has a complete shit-fit while we're waiting for the fire brigade to arrive, with water gushing everywhere.

Skiddy strips down to his boxer shorts and does a little dance in the pool of water while 'Freed From Desire' by Gala is pounding from a ghetto-blaster and Mr Wynne is running around the place, shouting, '*Where's the water mains?*' over and over.

On the rugby field it swells my chest to make a big tackle, to dish out some pain. And if my man stays down after the hit, if someone comes running towards him with a magic sponge, then all the better.

That was me. I did that.

On 5 March 1997 we run out at Lansdowne Road for the semi-final, fully expected to kick on and claim the school's sixty-third Senior Cup. But the game turns when their prop-like full-back Gordon D'Arcy cuts through us and sets up a try. With time running out the scoreboard reads Blackrock College 14, Clongowes Wood College 16.

Our forwards keep rumbling to within drop-goal range and I have two cracks at a winning kick.

Wide and wide.

We come again and I stand back in the pocket. When Skiddy fires it straight at me I pull the trigger and it's the sweetest strike of my life. It sails directly over one of the posts.

Wide.

Three minutes into stoppage time there's another scrum near their posts, another chance for me to put them away. The ball leaves my boot on target but then it drifts and clips the upright.

Wide.

The whistle goes. We're out.

*

Four years later, I'm recognized late at night on Grafton Street by three Blackrock College boys with pints on board.

Two of them are full of the joys of spring. The third guy says nothing, until he sticks a hand behind the buttons of his shirt.

'You know what?' he says. 'I've got something that you will never, *ever* fucking have.'

'Yeah? What's that?'

'A Junior Cup winner's medal.' It's resting against his chest, hanging from a chain. He pulls it out and shoves it at me. 'Take a good look! You're never going to have one of these!'

By this time I've got fifteen full international caps. I'm a couple of days away from being named in the Lions squad touring Australia. But none of this counts for much, when judged against a Junior Cup medal for Blackrock College. He hits me with his killer line: 'I've achieved more than you.'

Maybe he's expecting to hear that it eats me up every day, not having a medal like his. That there'll always be a void, no matter what happens in my career.

There's a part of me that would like to set him straight . . .

You, my friend, are an arch clown.

And remind him of his unfortunate affliction . . .

I know you're jarred — but you were sober when you put that medal on.

And maybe offer him some friendly advice . . .

Let it go, son! Move on! It's only a school!

But I just smile, because he's drunk and it's late and I want to get on my way.

And, anyway, I'm still too young to adequately explain what I'll come to feel further down the road. That, for a fifteen-year-old kid playing rugby, sheer enjoyment should always trump medals. That even if I did have one of his precious pieces of metal, I wouldn't feel like I'm part of a special club, because Belgrove was just as important as Blackrock in the shaping of my character and the values I try to live by.

And that I enjoyed my schooldays, on the northside and the southside, but not as much as the rest of my life.

*

The selectors for the Ireland Schools team see something in me beyond the failed drop-goal attempts. With Andy Dunne of Belvedere nailed on as the number 10, I'm named at inside-centre against a massive England side on a Saturday night at Lansdowne Road. That the centre is an option for me in the first place is down to John McClean, the Leinster Schools coach who picked me outside Andy at 12 back in the autumn.

The date is 29 March 1997 and the occasion is deemed sufficiently prestigious to merit an eight-page match programme. The era of the professional rugby player has dawned. The country's first elite pros are getting thirty grand a year, plus a car and match fees. Of the England players who come from behind to beat us by a couple of scores, nine will go on to play for the senior international team. Three will captain their country: Mike Tindall, Steve Borthwick, Jonny Wilkinson.

You don't need to be much of a student of the game to see that the England out-half has something about him. And the match programme makes it clear that he already knows where he's going.

JONATHAN P. WILKINSON (Lord Wandsworth College & Hampshire): He hopes to read Sport in the Community at university and become a professional rugby player.

Nobody in the Ireland squad has the bottle to go public with that kind of ambition, and some of us are stuck for any kind of answer.

BRIAN O'DRISCOLL (Blackrock College): He is undecided about his career.

Next up, we beat Wales by two points and Scotland by 37. After a decent campaign, me and Skiddy are among those awarded scholarships on the new rugby programme at University College Dublin to be run by John McClean. But the offer is subject to a respectable Leaving Certificate, and once the rugby is done and dusted for the season I've got too much study time to make up.

For the rest of April and all May I'm in the horrors. Stressed about what's coming, embarrassed that I'm not where I need to be, or even close.

Fail to prepare, prepare to be disappointed.

It doesn't help that I've got no clue about what I want to do in life, no target to aim for that might focus the mind. When I make a mess of my favourite subject – English – I'm filled with a sense of impending doom.

With a couple of exams to go, I sit down with Mum and review my performance to date, trying to work out how I'm going to get the points I need for UCD – commerce, arts, whatever.

Every way we look at it, I'm short.

She comes up with an idea. I'm officially desperate so I run with it.

Biology is supposed to be my last exam but once it's over I head home to Clontarf. When I arrive Mum has been through the syllabus and written me a bunch of notes on the honours paper in home economics, a subject I abandoned in fourth year. After a four-hour crash course I sit the exam the following morning, then spend the rest of the summer fearing the worst.

In the third week of August, Mum drives me down to the gates of the school and I see my classmates streaming out, mostly smiling. I collect my results and walk straight past the lads.

'Well?'

'I dunno yet.'

I'm not opening the envelope until I'm safely back in the car with Mum. When I do, the grades hit me like a slap from a wet fish: E, F, F, NG, E . . .

Ordinarily I try not to swear in front of Mum, but this is no time for manners.

'*Fuuuuuuuck!*'

Three-quarters of the way down, I see my first pass in the shape of an Ordinary Level D2. It's good for ten points. This leaves me about three hundred and fifty short for anything at UCD.

I turn to Mum. 'I'm definitely repeating!'

I'm holding my head in my hands, trying to absorb the nightmare. I take another look at the sheet of paper and notice the name printed at the top. It's not mine.

The relief is indescribable.

'They've given me someone else's!'

I bolt back out of the car and go past the lads for a second time. My heart is still pounding when I explain the situation.

'Sorry about that,' says Brother Gaul.

'Sorry is right!'

Compared to the car crash of a few minutes previously, my actual results are halfway decent.

Skiddy's big smile tells me all I need to know about his

results: next stop commerce at UCD. He's one of the select few with an A1 in honours maths, but he makes my day when he tells me he failed home economics.

My D2 is good for fifty points.

When the offers come out the following week I miss arts by five points, but I'm not overly bothered because I barely know what it's about. Instead, I sign up for a new course at UCD: a diploma in sports management. It's not rocket science, but when anyone asks what I hope to get out of it, at least I have a vaguely plausible answer, thanks to Tom Cruise and his new hit movie. 'I want to be Jerry Maguire,' I tell them.

Meanwhile, the IRFU offer me a place in their part-time academy. It pays three grand a year.

Show me the money!

*

Barry Twomey is on the periphery of the UCD Under-20s. A scrum-half and a laugh. Infectious company. At training he cracks a lot of one-liners and everyone finds them funny. He lives on the same estate as my cousins in Cabinteely and we've come across each other before, years ago, on a train heading for Cork.

'You followed me around,' I tell him. 'When I got chips, you got chips. When I went to the loo, you went to the loo. You were acting like a psychopath.'

He denies everything. A few months later, on one of our nights out, he finally cracks. 'In fairness, you were probably right about the thing on the train,' he says.

The way he owns up is funny. Pretty much everything about Barry Twomey is funny. He tells me he made a dog's dinner of his Leaving Cert and he doesn't have a clue what he wants to do with his life, which is why he's ended up on the same kick-for-touch course as me. Sportsman Dip, we call it, even though the eighteen students in our class include women with full-time jobs.

We're in our own building, separated from our fresher friends, and the two of us feel like student frauds. We avoid the main college bar where all the action is. We hang out at the Sports Bar, sticking some tunes on the jukebox and shooting the breeze.

Detachment from the more legit students on campus doesn't mean we're averse to the lifestyle, especially when we're fully paid-up members of University College Dublin RFC.

At Hartigan's on Lower Leeson Street, hours after my first senior away game for the college, and with a bunch of tins already on board, I'm up for a few rounds of Tequila Stuntman.

We sniff some salt, throw the liquor down the hatch, then squirt lemon in our eyes, like proper UCD jocks, blind drunk on a Saturday night.

My eyes are bad enough already so I blink when the lemon juice shoots out, but nobody's any the wiser as I stagger blindly about. When they finally put me into a taxi to Clontarf, I jump out at Dollymount House and make for the bar.

The bouncers know me and they also know what's good for me. 'Not tonight, Brian.'

'But my sister's in there.'

'No, she isn't.'

'But –'

'Go home, Brian.'

My mate Dave Murray, a.k.a. Bubbles, comes out of the pub. He calls another cab, gets a pint of water into me and takes me home. My folks get me upstairs and into bed but when I wake up I'm on a mattress on the floor in their room and I have no memory of how I got there.

Not my finest hour.

*

John McClean, UCD's new director of rugby, runs an impressive operation. Lee Smith is head coach, another progressive thinker, a Kiwi who makes a major impression on me. He talks about rugby in a way I've never heard before.

Me and Skiddy establish ourselves in the college senior team. Division Three of the All Ireland League feels like the big time: we have a dietitian, fitness advisers, hopes for promotion. But there is no part of me that thinks the life of a professional rugby player might lie ahead, even when the number of mentions I'm getting in the newspapers means Mum has to go out and buy a second scrapbook, or when I'm picked for my country in the Under-19 World Cup.

'Why can't *we* win it, lads?' asks our coach, Declan Kidney. 'Why not us?'

The New Zealanders and the Australians haven't entered. England aren't playing either.

'They think they're too bloody good for it, don't they?' says Kurt McQuilkin, the fired-up assistant to our fired-up manager, Harry McKibbin.

Nobody bothers sending a journalist to report on our progress. On the day we fly out from Dublin airport we get two paragraphs in the paper and our names in small print.

Three along from me in the list, there's a force to be reckoned with.

D. Rossi (Clontarf).

*

We find ourselves in the village of Samatan, fifty kilometres west of Toulouse in the middle of nowhere. Population: 1,832. Things to do: zero.

Declan gets us pumped up for our first match, against the US. He pulls me aside at training and tells me to stop spitting into the huddle when he's talking. I'm not even aware I'm doing it.

'Please don't spit into the middle of it.'

'Okay, sorry!'

'If you have to spit, then spit out, not in.'

I don't spit into a huddle again. Ever. For the next sixteen years I notice it whenever anyone does.

Declan doesn't play me in our win over the Americans, but I'm back in for the big one. Dunny is picked at full-back and we're pumped leaving the dressing room, but at half-time we're staring down the barrel of humiliation.

Why not us?

Because South Africa are murdering us 17–0.

We fight our way back and when the final whistle blows the score is 17–17. Our pack, drilled by Bart Fannin, is blowing them away. There's only one winner if extra time is played, but it's not in the rules and a penalty shoot-out is called. Five kicks each.

I'm our number-one kicker. I've already knocked over a conversion from the touchline and a forty-yarder to draw us level. I'm first up. The kicks are from twenty-two metres out, straight in front of the posts.

I yank it wide, bottle it.

We lose 4–3 and we're out.

As we're walking off the pitch one of our supporters spots that an unused South Africa sub has kicked one of their penalties.

47

We lodge an appeal. We're asked to withdraw it. Harry McKibbin refuses. We are awarded the match and a semi-final against the defending champions, Argentina. We beat them 18–3 in a blustery wind.

The final against France is fixed for three days later at Les Sept Deniers, Toulouse.

Declan's siege mentality goes into overdrive. He tells us that, as far as the French are concerned, we might as well not bother turning up. 'Are we supposed to lie down in front of these guys, just because we're Irish?' he asks. He starts looking for slights and insults. Real or imaginary, it doesn't matter. 'Have you noticed,' he goes on, 'how the quality of our team bus is getting worse and worse? Do you realize what they're at?'

The final is a rout. With thousands watching we hold France scoreless. Paddy Wallace sends us on our way with a phenomenal try eight minutes in and we never take our foot off their throat. We win 18–0 and they present a handsome shield to our captain, Shane Moore.

My parents are there. My granny is there. Dunny's folks are over.

Back home we're the biggest sports story of the week and there are TV cameras waiting for us at the airport. We're on the front page of all the sports sections, and a couple of weeks later two of us even make the *St Gabriel's Parish Newsletter*, Volume 3, Number 8.

WORLD CHAMPIONS!!!

Congratulations to Donovan Rossi and Brian O'Driscoll on being part of the Irish Under-19 rugby team who won the world championship. It is rare to have two young men from the same area on such a team, but to have them from the same road – Park Lawn – must be something exceptional. Well done, lads!!

*

Along with Skiddy and some other students, I'm invited into the Leinster camp once pre-season training starts in the summer. I've got zero expectations and a fortnight in Tenerife booked, but after a few weeks they ask me to cancel, reimburse the money I've paid over and pitch me into the A team.

Leinster's head coach is Mike Ruddock. When he says he's excited about the talent coming through, Shane Horgan is probably the first guy he's got in mind. He's an outside centre – five inches taller than me, two stone heavier and on a fast track to the first team.

He starts at 13 when Leinster get the better of Munster in Limerick with three hundred people watching. I'm named at 12 in the Leinster A team beaten at Dooradoyle the following day. The best player on the pitch is wearing red: David Wallace scores a hat-trick from the back row and keeps our pack away from Munster's influential number 10, Ronan O'Gara.

The following week I sit down with a journalist for the first time and hedge my bets when Peter O'Reilly of the *Sunday Tribune* asks me where I see myself going.

Maybe a sports agent, I tell him.

The paper photographs me in the gym, lifting a dumb-bell. The closest thing to the camera is the chunky bracelet on my left wrist, which jumps out at me when I open the paper on Sunday morning. I imagine the reaction of the *Tribune*'s readers. *Look at this guy and his bracelet – what an absolute prick!*

*

49

Warren Gatland is the new Ireland coach and he's not slow to recognize the country's best young scrum-half: C. Scally is listed among the replacements for the World Cup qualifier against Georgia in November. Skiddy comes off the bench and scores. Gatland starts him the following week against Romania. He scores again.

Maybe to keep Skiddy company, I'm called into an Ireland training camp before Christmas, alongside Gordon D'Arcy, who, unlike me, has already broken into the Leinster first team.

I look around and see Keith Wood, Paul Wallace, Jeremy Davidson and Eric Miller – four of the British and Irish Lions who beat the Springboks in 1997. It's exciting and intimidating, and there's a question in my head that doesn't go away for the week.

What am I doing here?

To nobody's surprise, Leo Cullen is given the captaincy of the Ireland Under-21s and I make it into the centre. We're bigged up for a potential Grand Slam, but I'm hauled off when we're beaten by Wales after missing a couple of tackles. It hurts like hell.

We're better against England, and there's talk of some of us being promoted to the Ireland A team for the final Six Nations game of the championship, against Italy.

When the A squad is named on April Fool's Day, I'm not in it. That's because I'm listed among the substitutes for the senior team to play the Italians at Lansdowne Road on 10 April 1999.

At home, the announcement generates enough newsprint to warrant a third scrapbook.

'Versatile UCD back Brian O'Driscoll,' opens the report in the *Evening Herald*, 'is a big step closer to winning the full Irish cap which narrowly eluded his father Frank almost thirty years ago.'

2. Waltzing

Fifteen hundred quid is what the IRFU pay me after we beat Italy at Lansdowne Road. That's my win bonus. I didn't play a minute, but I still get the money. It's almost half my academy income for a whole year. There's lots I can do with fifteen hundred nicker.

Then Warren Gatland tells me I'll be going on the summer tour to Australia, and when the squad is announced the cards start coming thick and fast. The first is from my granny in Cork on my mum's side, Noël Barrett. She married an engineer called Niall, who played rugby for Munster, and gave birth to four daughters – three of them doctors.

'Have a really wonderful time,' she writes. 'We will be eagerly watching the papers for the latest news.'

Somehow I've been parachuted in over Shane Horgan's head. Shaggy has been playing centre for Ireland A and how I'm in and he's not is beyond me. But I don't ask any questions: I just turn up at the airport with Skiddy and try to blend in.

We're in the departure lounge in Dublin when I see Colm Murray, from RTÉ, coming towards me with a cameraman. A lovely man, Colm. I think the only reason he wants to interview me is because he lives in Park Lawn.

'A couple of questions for the six o'clock news, Brian?'

'Uhm, grand, yeah.'

Keith Wood is milling about. Colm points to him and asks what it's like to be among all these big names, these legends of Irish rugby. When he thrusts his big TV microphone towards me I haven't got a single thought in my head. So I say the first thing that comes into it.

'Ah, yeah, there's a great squad turnout here today!' As if this was the Clontarf Under-16s on a rainy night in Castle Avenue. Nice of everyone to show up. No doubt Warren is delighted.

The lads watching this at home absolutely love it. They never let me forget. For years afterwards they plead with me to get it into speeches. Mick Quinlan makes it his catch-phrase. The whole Quinlan family follows suit. There's barely a situation they can't squeeze it into.

'Ah, yeah, a great squad turnout from the potatoes here at Sunday dinner, fair play!'

In our team room at the hotel in Sydney there are drinks and snacks: Powerade, Jaffa Cakes, jellies, all free. Trevor Brennan empties a load of swag into a bag and disappears off to his bedroom, cool as a breeze. I grab a fistful of sweets and drinks and do the same, trying to make it look like it's no big deal.

We beat New South Wales Country 43–6 in the first game of the tour. I'm picked at 13 and I go pretty well. The Saturday before the first Test at Ballymore in Brisbane I get a dead leg against the New South Wales Waratahs and I'm off at half-time, but again I've done myself justice and I'm talked up as a likely Test starter. I wrap my leg in ice and go to bed early while the rest of them head out on the town.

I'm woken during the night by the sound of two people giggling. My room-mate has pulled. He's single, so it's not exactly front-page news. I close my eyes and keep them closed. I could do without being branded a perv before my first cap.

Three days later I'm passed fit and Warren names me in the team, alongside Kevin Maggs in the centre, with Skiddy on the bench.

At the Parkroyal hotel in Brisbane, faxes start pouring through from back home.

'Well, well, well,' writes my sister Sue. 'If it isn't the famous, capped Brian – can I have your autograph?!'

'The phone has been hopping all day,' reports Jules. 'All the rellies are really excited.'

There are lovely faxes from coaches past and present – John McClean, Lee Smith, Declan Kidney, Mike Ruddock; from my old schools, from the neighbours on Park Lawn, from Royal Dublin Golf Club, Clontarf Rugby Club and so many more.

From Manchester, my dad's first cousin John O'Driscoll – who, like his brother Barry before him, played rugby for Ireland – offers his encouragement. 'I am sure that everything will go well on Saturday,' he writes. 'Most of all make sure that you enjoy the day to the full. There is absolutely nothing in the world that is as much fun as playing international rugby!'

Everyone keeps telling me to enjoy it, that it'll be over before I know it. I'm fine until we run through the tunnel and fireworks start exploding all around me.

I have it in my head that Tim Horan is a smallish, stumpy guy, until I see him up close.

I watch Joe Roff and Ben Tune flashing a ball around and I've never seen backs built like them.

I look for Daniel Herbert, the man I'm marking, and he's not hard to find. I'm giving him four inches in height and almost a stone and a half in weight.

Australia beat us by nearly 40 points without ever hitting top gear, but I'm not exactly hurting inside when I walk off the pitch. When I'm collared by a couple of journalists I try to sound a bit rueful about the result but inside I'm still buzzing. I've just played a full international match against one of the best centres on the planet and I haven't disgraced myself.

I see my folks waiting for me as I come out of the post-match function. They're not remotely bothered by how much we've been pumped – they just give me a big hug and tell me they're proud.

'Yeah, I *am* delighted,' I tell them. 'But we lost . . .'

They're not having any of it. 'Don't worry about that!'

We're a lot better a week later at the Subiaco Oval in Perth. We outscore the Aussies by three tries to two in a 32–26 loss that feels like some kind of semi-victory.

In eight days I have played for Ireland twice, just like my father. The difference is that my appearances are in the record books, but three decades on he's officially uncapped. They flew him seven thousand miles to Buenos Aires, and even though he played six of the seven games on the tour, including the two internationals alongside Willie John McBride and Tom Kiernan, he came home without a cap. The excuse they gave him was that Argentina weren't considered good enough opposition – a standard not applied years later when weakened touring parties came home with full caps from matches against lesser rugby nations. For most of the 1970 team it didn't matter too much, but for a few of them it mattered a lot because they never got to wear the green jersey again. Like Dad. It's an injustice done to him – and to others like him – that should be put right.

After we get home, our manager, Donal Lenihan, rings me up. 'We're offering you a national contract,' he says.

*

Life as a fully fledged member of Team Leinster starts promisingly on a midsummer's day in Dublin. We load our golf clubs into the back of a van parked outside Donnybrook, board the team bus and head out on the Stillorgan Road, bound for Wicklow and some team bonding.

The itinerary isn't so much sketchy as non-existent, but with a day's golf in prospect nobody's too pushy about whether the destination is the scenic Druids Glen or the majestic European Club at Brittas Bay. The bus turns right on Foster's Avenue and heads inland. Somewhere deep in the Wicklow hills we turn into a car park. Wherever we are, it's a long way from the first tee.

'Everyone off,' Mike Ruddock says. 'We're here for the night.'

We are greeted by some guys acting like army commandos. They point to a row of tents in the trees: our sleeping quarters. We're told to line up for a run just as the skies empty. I've got no boots, no trainers – nothing but my street shoes and a brand-new pair of FootJoys. When darkness falls and the commandos leave, we climb into the tents.

At half four in the morning there is shouting outside.

'Everybody up!'

'Up! Up! Up!'

'We're on a mission!'

I put on my golf shoes and head off into the night. I don't have my glasses so I take hold of the jacket-tail of the guy in front of me and don't let go. He's my eyes as we trawl through trenches like thirty Andy Dufresnes breaking out of Shawshank State Prison.

We're taken back to civilization at three o'clock the next day, collect our golf clubs from the back of the van at Donnybrook and go home. Cold, wet and broken.

A few weeks later I make my Leinster debut and we find that a night of yomping through the Wicklow hills doesn't prepare you for a full-blooded contest against the coming force that is Munster. They beat us easily.

Maybe they put down two nights in the wilderness to our one.

Or maybe not.

*

Skiddy's upset after the Munster defeat. It was a big game for him to start and he didn't do himself justice. He says his knee came at him again, a legacy from the time he did his cruciate playing for Ireland Schools. He can't run flat out, he's at 80 per cent tops and he's got to get it sorted.

He makes an appointment to see Ray Moran, the country's leading expert on knee injuries.

Later that day, I phone Skiddy.

'Well?'

'Not good news.'

'What did he say?'

'I'm goosed. My knee isn't going to get better. I'm going to have to retire.'

I can hear the emotion in his voice. I'm too shocked to respond properly. I tell him we'll meet up, then put the phone down.

He's twenty years old. He's got four caps, a fraction of what his talent would have brought him if it wasn't for this.

I head for my bedroom and there are tears for my good friend. I'm upset for Skiddy but also for myself. The two of us were on a journey together and it was supposed to take us into our thirties.

Some people get lucky in sport and others get robbed blind.

*

My first game in the World Cup is against the USA at Lansdowne Road on a Saturday evening in October. Playing opposite me is Juan Grobler, out of Denver, Colorado.

For a while Juan does a number on me, physically and mentally. I can't get around him, I can't get through him, I feel like I'm out of my depth. The anxiety only starts to ease when Keith Wood takes charge and scores some tries. He ends up with four in a 53–8 win. I get one and almost butcher it. Running across the try line I circle round behind the posts, just to make things easier for David Humphreys' conversion. I'm still running when I see the dead-ball line right in front of me, like a cliff edge I'm about to topple over. With a foot to spare I touch the ball down. My first try for Ireland.

Next up, Australia. My fifth cap and the third against the Wallabies. It's also the first time I've been properly frightened on a rugby field. After half an hour, Daniel Herbert empties Kevin Maggs in the tackle and Maggsy goes down like he's been hit by a truck. When he gets up his legs wobble, buckle, and down he goes again.

I'm shaken just watching it. If Herbert can do that to a bruiser like Maggsy then what could he do to me? As Maggsy is helped from the field I make a couple of mental notes.

1. Never be the type of player who runs straight and looks for contact.
2. Never serve yourself up on a plate to the Daniel Herberts of this world.

We're outclassed from beginning to end. We score three points, they score 23. In my innocence I try to do Tim Horan for pace at one point by smoking him on the outside. He tracks my run and hunts me down. When the tackle comes, I spill the ball. He picks it up and he's away. Man against boy.

Nobody expected us to beat Australia, but Argentina is a different story. For the first time in the tournament we leave the comfort of Dublin and head for Lens in northern France to play the Pumas in a play-off for a place in the quarter-final. Back in August we beat them in a warm-up match at Lansdowne Road and we're hot favourites to beat them again.

Gonzalo Quesada is Argentina's goal-kicker. He takes half the night to kick a goal but every time he does, the ball sails straight between our posts. You lose the will to live waiting for him to kick, then he bangs them over from everywhere. The guy can't miss.

We're ahead, but we can't shake them off because of Quesada's lethal boot. Then, disaster strikes. They run a simple move out the line and our defence can't cope. They score in the corner and Quesada pops over the conversion as if he's playing in a club match back in Buenos Aires.

Now we're officially in the shit.

I still think we'll win, though. I have good memories of that August game, of cutting them open a couple of times. Even when the crisis comes I'm confident I can do damage, if only the ball comes to me.

But it doesn't come. A few minutes from the end we get a lineout deep inside Argentina's 22. Thirteen of us pile in. We've practised this before, but in training you can't simulate Argentina's obsessive defence. We bang away and go precisely nowhere. Phase upon phase of nothing. This is how it ends.

On the sliding scale of devastation I'm at the lower end compared to most in our dressing room. I'm twenty years old and I'll get another chance. Others won't.

*

England do us in cold blood at Twickenham in the first week of the Six Nations. Fifty points and six tries. It's no surprise, because we have no defensive system worth the name. Defence coaching at the highest level has moved up a couple of gears but we're still stuck in neutral, without a specialist in our set-up. When England attack us we splinter, each of us doing our own thing.

Warren Gatland is under pressure. He picks five new caps for our next match against Scotland in Dublin – John Hayes, Simon Easterby, Peter Stringer, Ronan O'Gara and Shane Horgan. Peter Clohessy is back in the team a year after winning his last cap. Denis Hickie returns after twenty months. And it works, big-time.

We win 44–22. Shaggy scores on his debut and there's even one for me. All of a sudden the wheels are back on the bike and a fortnight later we put 60 points on Italy, 30 of them from Rog.

The weekend before we play France I'm on the town in Dublin, in Buck Whaley's on the Leeson Street strip. It's two o'clock on Sunday morning and I'm with a friend of my sister Jules, one Oran Malone. He likes to be called the Big O.

He's in flying form. He leans in and hits me with his big idea. 'Listen,' he says, 'the next time you score a try for Ireland . . .'

'Yeah?'

'You gotta give a shout-out to the Big O.'

'After I score a try?'

'Yeah.'

'In an international match?'

'Yeah. Send a message to the Big O.'

'Riiiiight . . .'

I'm cloudy about how long it's been since Ireland won in

Paris, but I know I wasn't born at the time. Journalists keep talking about baggage, but I'm travelling light – all that ancient history means nothing to me.

The Stade de France is like no other stadium I've played in. Pristine changing room. Huge warm-up area. Everything is perfect, and out on the pitch the French hit the ground running. They attack us with a pace and a fury that's jaw-dropping, but we hang on in there, build some phases. Malcolm O'Kelly finds me with a pass five metres short of the posts, in acres of space. David Bory comes across but it only takes a slight sidestep to put him on the wrong side of the goalpost padding and I slide in to score.

It's bizarre how the brain works. In the split second between the time the ball is grounded and the moment Paul Honiss raises his left arm, an image flashes into my head from right out of nowhere.

I see Oran Malone leaning across the bar table in Buck Whaley's.

Give a shout-out to the Big O.

I haven't thought of him for a single second since that night, but with sixty-five thousand people in the stadium watching me, I shape an O with my thumbs and index fingers. Only two people on earth know what it means.

France come back at us, running hard and in waves. They're 16–7 ahead when their hooker, Marc Dal Maso, goes steaming downfield, looking certain to score. If he makes the line, the game is over. Denis Hickie hunts him down from somewhere south of Toulouse and crashes him to the ground, within touching distance of our posts. Technique goes out the window: it's pure desire to stop him. Den gets a split head for his trouble, but he's made the most impressive and important tackle I've ever seen.

The gap is 12 points when Rob Henderson's power and vision set me up for a second try, and a second shout-out goes winging its way back to the Big O.

We keep handing back the momentum and Gérald Merceron inches them eight points clear with his goal-kicking. Six minutes from the end I'm loitering around the back of a ruck when Peter Stringer gets whacked and the ball goes free. I scoop it up and bolt for their line. I'm waiting for the full-back Émile Ntamack to come across and nail me, but for reasons unexplained he doesn't bother. He doesn't even chase me into the corner to make the conversion harder, so I cut back inside and steal a few metres before the touchdown.

This time there's no shout-out – it's getting way too serious for any more Big O stuff – and when Humps slots the conversion, we're one behind. Then, with three minutes on the clock, he puts us ahead: a nerveless penalty from forty-five metres, beautifully struck and fatal for the French.

The final whistle sounds and everyone goes ballistic. Trevor Brennan and Frankie Sheahan get me up on their shoulders. I'm no sooner down than I'm back up, with Mal and Andy Ward hoisting me again. An Irish Tricolour comes flying my way. People are crying. When I get back to the dressing room I switch on my mobile and there are shedloads of texts. For the rest of the night the phone is radioactive. It never stops beeping.

Practically every message in my inbox is about the three tries, but the satisfaction I feel is more about my all-round game . . . and the fact that I've never had a better one.

*

I get changed into a tux and hit the post-match dinner. The food is incidental – it's all about the craic. I'm sitting with

Craig White, our fitness instructor, and we're on our own buzz. We head for Kitty O'Shea's, around the corner from place Vendôme.

A few of the players are already there. We get a spot in the corner near Mick Galwey and his wife, Joan. It's pushing 1 a.m. when Gaillimh and Joan get up to go.

'Come on, Drico, we're leaving – and you're coming with us.'

We get our taxi driver to stop at a kebab place for some soakage on the way back to the hotel. Joan stays in the car and we're waiting at the counter when we notice five French guys eyeballing us from the end of the shop.

We ignore them, pick up our grub and climb back into the taxi. We're about to take off when my door is pulled open. I turn to see what's going on just as a fist comes flying through the window and catches me flush on the side of the head.

'What the fuck?'

When I look up, one of the guys from the kebab shop is standing there, fists clenched. I'm about to get back out of the taxi to have a cut off him when Gaillimh reaches across and drags me back. Joan pulls the door shut and tells the driver to step on it.

The Galweys head for bed while I stick my head around the door of the hotel bar and find the stragglers. Whitey's still going, fair play to him. So – *quelle surprise* – is my trusty partner in the centre.

Hendo tells me we're heading out again, just the two of us. 'Let's go. I know this great place,' he says. 'How often are you going to score a hat-trick in Paris?'

He calls another cab and gives the driver his instructions. 'VIP Room, *s'il vous plaît.*'

The cab pulls up on the Champs-Élysées and Hendo

walks confidently up to the bouncers guarding the entrance, sifting the VIP types from the nobodies.

Whatever the French for 'not tonight' is, they come out with it pretty pronto. When Hendo raises a protest we're dismissed with Gallic contempt.

'Pas possible.'

We shuffle over to a dingy restaurant across the road. I've already had the kebab but I go for an omelette and chips so Hendo's not eating alone, plus a bottle of some poison they're passing off as wine.

We hoover up the food and the booze and go looking for another cab. As soon as we hit the early-morning air, I puke my ring up on the cobbles of the Champs-Élysées.

Hendo just stands there and laughs. 'Jesus, this is some comedown,' he says.

It's after four in the morning by the time we get back to the Trianon Palace, close by the Palace of Versailles on boulevard de la Reine.

I'm asleep for what feels like a minute when Anthony Foley gives me a shake. 'Come on, kid, get packed. Downstairs in five.'

I shove everything into my bag and add the hotel dressing gown for good measure.

On the way back, our PR man, John Redmond, tries to prep me for what awaits us in Dublin, but my head doesn't feel great and I'm not taking it in.

'There'll be television, radio, newspapers. They'll all want something from you. Okay?'

'Yeah, yeah. Grand.'

I'm signing autographs in the arrivals hall when the RTÉ camera crew comes across and I get hit with questions.

I have no answers. My brain is fudge.

John yanks me away before I make myself a national embarrassment. He puts his arm around my shoulders. 'We're going to have to get you ready for some of this stuff,' he says.

*

For days the papers go crazy about my O in Paris. They have lots of theories, all wrong.

I meet the Big O and he's buzzing, except nobody believes his story. He says he got laughed out of Dollymount House by the regulars when he saw me give the shout-out.

'Did you see that? That was for me! The Big O!'

'Yeah, right!'

Three days after the France match I arrive late at Lansdowne Road to watch Blackrock in the Schools Junior Cup final. I'm heading over to join some fellow past pupils when, all of a sudden, half the stand gets up and starts chasing me *en masse* across to the North Terrace – kids looking for autographs.

By the time I finally get to my pals I'm feeling weird: it's like something has just changed in my life. I even notice a difference in the way people look at me.

It's an uncomfortable feeling.

Ten days later the hype is still on the go. We play Wales on a manky day in Dublin and Carphone Warehouse puts up a prize of a million pounds for the player who beats the Paris hat-trick and scores four tries. As publicity stunts go, it's not a bad one. It's such a lousy afternoon there isn't a chance in hell of them having to part with the prize.

Fifty-six minutes in, Shaggy gets a try in the corner. When he touches it down he shows four fingers to the crowd. It's his fourth try for Ireland but every man, woman and child in the ground takes his little signal as a declaration of intent.

Three more of those and I get the million!

As soon as he realizes what he's done he wants to crawl into a hole, and the embarrassment only gets worse when Wales go on to beat us.

Later, we tear him to ribbons. After ending the Six Nations on such a downer, the only thing we can do to lighten the mood is take the piss out of Shaggy, his imaginary four tries and his invisible million quid.

*

The summer of 2000 brings change at Leinster. Mike Ruddock stands down as head coach and Matt Williams steps up. He's been on the coaching ticket for a season, so we know him well. But when he starts running the show himself, everything is different.

Matt tells us stories about the great Australian players he has worked with and the things they do to make themselves better professionals. He opens our eyes to a whole new world.

He tells us we're like Ragball Rovers coming into training, one guy arriving in a Welsh tracksuit top, another wearing Old Belvedere and somebody else turning out in a maggoty old Scottish jersey picked up years before. Matt says if we're going to be a team then we have to look like one. He orders us to wear Leinster kit to training and fines us if we forget.

His assistant is Alan Gaffney, another Australian with new ideas and a great rugby brain. We respect them to the hilt, but some things are slow enough to change and we have no problem enjoying ourselves away from the training ground through Christmas and into the new year.

On the second Friday in January we play Edinburgh at Donnybrook. Beat them, and we're as good as in the Heineken Cup knockout stages.

We're 24–9 ahead at half-time and it's 34–17 as the game enters the final quarter.

We're coasting.

Then we're panicking.

Then it ends: 34–34.

The following week we get destroyed in Biarritz and miss the quarter-finals by a point.

We've taken out a gun and emptied the barrel into our own feet.

*

Two weeks later the Six Nations begins. I'm at home with a tweaked hamstring when Ireland wallop Italy in Rome. This time it's Hendo who gets a hat-trick. I'd take him out to celebrate if only I could – omelette and chips and a bottle of piss in some downtown fleapit. It's tradition.

In the second round we sneak past France in Dublin and that's it for the season. Foot-and-mouth disease is threatening to spread from Britain to Ireland and the country goes into lockdown. Our remaining three games are postponed until the autumn. The Six Nations carries on without us.

We're short of opportunities to impress, but still six of us get picked for the Lions tour to Australia – myself, Rog, Hendo, Mal O'Kelly, Keith Wood and Jeremy Davidson.

Graham Henry, the New Zealander coaching Wales, heads up the touring party. It feels surreal hearing my name called out. When the Lions toured South Africa in 1997 I was still a child, in the middle of my Leaving Cert. Martin Johnson was a colossus at the heart of that trip and now he's my captain.

I head for Heathrow with another big man, Mal O'Kelly, the only other Leinster player selected. I'm stressed to the gills at Dublin airport, waiting for him to show, when he finally breezes up sixty seconds before the gates close. I've brought a massive bag full of gear. He's carrying a tiny backpack, which contains nothing but a toothbrush.

'Are you not a bit light on the old packing there, Mal?' I say.

'Ah, no, bud,' he counters. 'This is all we're going to need. They're giving us everything.'

In London, Woody swings by in a cab and we head for Tylney Hall, the plush Hampshire estate where the Lions are meeting up. When I get to my room there are three massive bags with my name on them, packed solid with Lions gear. One up for Mal.

Woody is so at ease it's almost like he's running the show. He knows everybody and everybody knows him. His kind of confidence is a different world for me. All I want to do is settle in and disguise the fact that I'm just a giddy kid in this company. I'm way out of my comfort zone.

I have Jason Robinson as a room-mate. He tells me the story of how he became a born-again Christian. He's not trying to convert me: he's just a great guy who shows me a world that I know nothing about.

Jonny Wilkinson provides a different kind of education. He's the youngest guy in the squad but you'd never guess. Nobody I have ever met analyses the game like Jonny. He lives it. He dissects it like a surgeon with a scalpel.

Every change of room-mate is an awakening.

Things are tipping along nicely. Then, on the Saturday

before the first Test, we play the Waratahs in Sydney and they try to do a hatchet job on us. Three seconds into the match Tom Bowman elbows Danny Grewcock in the face and gets sin-binned, a curtain-raiser for Duncan McRae's unprovoked assault on Rog.

The first I know about it is when I look over and see blood coming from Rog's battered eye. McRae gets a red card but red is too good for him. There was a worse fate waiting if he'd stayed on the pitch.

*

On the Wednesday night before the first Test I join some of the boys from the midweek team and we head for the City Rowers, a bar on Eagle Street Pier overlooking the Brisbane river. I have some snappy bottles of beer, then call it a night as the lads kick on for more.

As I walk back to the team hotel, the city is dancing to the beat of an occupying Lions army. When Saturday comes they take over the Gabba like it's their own. They bedeck the place in red and fill it with their noise. It feels like a home match.

Jason scores a mesmeric try down the left wing, then I make a break down the right and Dafydd James goes over for another try.

A minute into the second half I see an opportunity in front of me. Ten metres short of the halfway line there's a gap between Nathan Grey, the Australian centre, and Jeremy Paul, their hooker. It's not big, but it's big enough if I get the ball in my hands pretty lively.

I scream at Jonny. He sees the opening and I run onto his pass. I'm a foot inside their half when Grey sticks out his right arm, but I carry on through it. Paul tries to make a tackle but he just slides off me. George Smith comes across but he's too late getting there and I've broken the first line of defence.

I look outside for support but the only option is a second-row forward, Danny Grewcock, and the decision to drive on myself takes a tenth of a second. When I straighten up Matt Burke is coming right for me, ready to hit me with his best shot.

There's no decision this time: either I get out of his way or he knocks me into next week.

I skip to my left and drive on while Burke goes flying past me. The posts are thirty metres up ahead and the only one who can stop me reaching them is Joe Roff, who's been tracking me hard from the opposite wing. He's got serious gas and he gets hold of my legs three metres short, but I've already dived for the line and momentum carries me across it.

We win by 16 points, 29–13. Nobody saw it coming.

Later on, I head back to the City Rowers to celebrate. Barry Twomey is in there with his brother and his father. His dad isn't a small man but the lads have given him a tight-fitting Slim Shady T-shirt and a new nickname that sticks: from that night on he's no longer Cormac, he's Slim. Paul Ryan from Clontarf has flown over and my folks are there too, looking euphoric. They tell me they were on a bus heading back from the stadium when the Lions fans broke into song.

Dad can hardly contain himself. 'Waltzing O'Driscoll! The whole bus was singing it!'

There are a lot of good things about being a Lion, and the pride it brings to my family is right at the top of the list.

The second Test is in Melbourne and the Australian Rugby Union have learned their lesson from Brisbane. They counteract the sea of Lions red by spending a fortune on T-shirts and scarves, which they give away for free outside the stadium.

The stadium might be a Wallaby gold-fest but we're ahead 11–6 at half-time, having butchered a couple of golden opportunities. We're forty minutes away from winning the series. Then the wheels come off.

Thirty-two seconds into the second half Jonny floats out a pass that gets plucked from the air by Joe Roff. I see it happening, almost in slow motion. Roff is heading for the left corner. I pin my ears back in midfield and try to make up the ground.

He's a metre short when I wrap myself around him. It's like the first Test all over again with the roles reversed. I try to bundle him into touch but he fires his left arm forward and brings the ball down on the line a millisecond before he crashes into the corner flag.

Jonathan Kaplan, the referee, goes upstairs to the TMO. Try.

The momentum in the series switches there and then. Roff is on fire and he scores again. Matt Burke adds a third try and kicks penalties with his eyes closed. We're beaten out the gate, 35–14. It's 1–1 going into the final Test in Sydney.

*

We check into a hotel overlooking Manly beach and there are hordes of Lions fans all around, so we spend most of our time in the team room. We're a little weary from the non-stop training load, in need of a few laughs.

Austin Healey picks up some boxing gloves provided for fitness work and puts them on. He's not short of confidence, our Austin. He starts prancing around the room, throwing shapes, feigning punches.

He goes up to Rog and pretends to give him another dose of what Duncan McRae dished out in the Waratahs match. Just about enough time has passed for the piss-take to be allowable, but Rog has no interest in taking the bait.

'Anyone else fancy a go?' says Austin.

I'm a terrible boxer but for some unknown reason I take him up on it.

Maybe I fancy giving him a few clips on Rog's behalf, maybe it's because even a half-chance to make Austin Healey look silly is not one that's easily passed up.

He starts with the fancy footwork while I'm putting my gloves on and hits me with a cheap jab. By this stage about twenty of the lads have gathered around in hope more than anticipation that Austin might cop a smack or two.

He's dancing around, cocky as you like, ready to throw his first big punch.

I'm afraid of getting the head knocked off me so I figure attack is the best form of defence.

I pick him off with a couple of good shots.

I land a few combinations.

He hasn't put a glove on me, and if there's anyone more surprised than me by how the fight is playing out, it's Austin.

As every blow lands flush there are raucous cheers – louder and louder – from the boys gathered round us.

I get in about ten unanswered punches and decide to quit while I'm ahead as the lads start firing napkins into our imaginary ring.

'I can't give you any more of a hiding,' I tell Austin. 'You might have a Test match to play at the weekend.'

At Stadium Australia we're losing 23–20 eleven minutes into the second half when Daniel Herbert clotheslines me and gets ten minutes in the bin. Jonny kicks the penalty; 23–23. With a minute and a half left on the sin-bin clock, we get a scrum midway inside Australia's 22.

We call a move called World Class. It's the perfect play with the opposition one man down. Jonny's pass is laid on a plate for me. If I take it we score, but I take my eye off it and spill it backwards. I'm disgusted with myself as I get off the floor.

Shiiiiiit!

The game is over after Justin Harrison pinches a lineout from Martin Johnson, and when our manager, Donal Lenihan, makes a speech in the dressing room he's so emotional he can hardly get the words out.

For a Test and a half we had the series in our hands. We're left with the mental torture of knowing we let it go.

*

I holiday on Hayman Island, a luxury resort in the Great Barrier Reef far too fancy for a twenty-two-year-old, then it's on to Beachcomber Island, a party spot off the coast of Fiji. There's me, my girlfriend Suzanne Meenan . . . and Barry.

I'm not sure how he muscled in on the trip but I'm glad he's around. I get on really well with Suzanne, but three weeks on my own with any girl is still a daunting prospect.

The three of us eat together, drink together, and when we hit Fiji we even lie down in the same room.

Barry takes the single bed and justifies the sleeping

arrangements on financial grounds. 'I'm not getting caught for a room on my own! No bloody way!'

Suzanne is very fond of him but I've never, ever seen a girl happier than the day she hooks up with some of her mates on Beachcomber Island. She is euphoric.

As she's hugging them and jumping around the place, myself and Barry head off for a beer.

3. Captain

I come out of the bank in Clontarf, get in my car and turn on the radio. A reporter on RTÉ is talking about a plane crashing into the World Trade Center in New York.

At home I watch the second plane hitting the second tower. It's mid-afternoon and I have to get my shit together to play a Celtic League game. There's a weird feeling at Donnybrook, an eeriness in the ground. We beat Pontypridd 52–14. For some unknown reason we've chosen this surreal day to produce a top performance.

Eleven days later the Six Nations resumes after the foot-and-mouth delay. We're two from two after the spring fixtures and now we have three games in four weeks.

Our Grand Slam chance evaporates when we're annihilated 32–10 in Murrayfield. It's a 44-point turnaround from the last time we played them. But just when the knives are being resharpened for Warren Gatland, we post a record victory against the Welsh: 36–6 in Cardiff.

We are rugby's Jekyll and Hyde.

England arrive in Dublin with four wins from four and a Grand Slam in their sights. They're not just beating teams, they're rewriting record books as they go. They've scored 43 points against Scotland, 44 against Wales, 48 against France and 80 against Italy. They're on an average of seven tries per match. White hot.

Our training goes shockingly. There's a fear that England

will wipe the floor with us, and from this panic comes intensity on match day. We beat them 20–14, thanks to a Woody try and a Peter Stringer tap-tackle on Dan Luger that prevents a certain score and certain defeat.

We're as unpredictable as the weather.

In November we're looking good against New Zealand at Lansdowne Road. We're leading 13–0 after half an hour. Less than two minutes into the second half I get an offload to Den and he scores in the corner: 21–7.

It's ninety-six years since Ireland first played New Zealand and we've never beaten them. Here's our chance. History beckons.

The All Blacks decide that we've had far too much fun. In the next eighteen minutes they score four tries and 26 points. They work a move that leaves Jonah Lomu one-on-one with me in the midfield. I've read the play, I know exactly what's happening, but he runs over the top of me as if I don't exist. They score again. We lose 40–29.

A few weeks later Warren Gatland is sacked and replaced by Eddie O'Sullivan. I hear about it on the radio and it's news to me. There are theories about what's gone down, and there's bad blood between Eddie and Gats. There are players who have their ear to the ground on this stuff. Gossip finds some people but I'm not one of them.

I write Gats a letter to thank him for giving me my first cap. I've a fair bit to thank him for. He brought a decent edge to the team. Brought us to the next level. He was never afraid to take risks on young, unproven players. Under him we had our highest finish in the championship in fourteen years, beat France for the first time in seventeen years and won in Paris for the first time in twenty-eight.

He raised the bar, but I'm not losing sleep over him leaving. It's business. Coaches come and go. It's the nature of the game we play. Brutal, at times.

*

Along with my fellow Lions, I'm invited to the BBC Sports Personality of the Year awards. Before the cameras roll I stand around feeling awkward in a big room full of big names.

There are people who know they belong in this kind of company and there's the rest of us, wondering why we're here and doing a double-take whenever someone really famous walks in.

Christ! Boris Becker!

Audley Harrison, Olympic boxing champion, makes a big entrance, looking like Diddy without the shades, in a get-up of patchwork brown leather. People are scanning the room for the bookies' favourite, the nation's hero, but David Beckham is nowhere to be seen, because elsewhere at the BBC Television Centre there's another green room, another level of celebrity.

I'm expecting a seat in Row Z, but the rugby players are all split up and I'm ushered down to the front. Second row, dead centre. I've got Becker directly in front and Alex Ferguson in the seat alongside him.

Two along from Fergie there's an empty seat. People start craning their necks as Beckham suddenly emerges, the most striking man I've ever seen, all gangstered up in two-tone shoes and sparkling from every angle – the bling watch, the diamond earrings, the dazzling ring, the sheer, mesmerizing presence. He's got Michael Owen in tow but they part company coming down the steps and Beckham heads for the front-row seat four feet away from me, beside Lawrence

Dallaglio. Every time he glances behind he catches me staring at him.

*

At Leinster we win thirteen in a row, including four out of four in the Heineken Cup, and make the Celtic League final, where we play Munster at Lansdowne Road ten days before Christmas 2001. Thirty thousand people turn up. It's unheard of for a match between two provinces, so unexpected that thousands are let in for free over safety concerns when there aren't enough turnstiles open.

After twenty-five minutes our flanker Eric Miller gets sent off for aiming a boot at Anthony Foley. Early in the second half, Munster go into a nine-point lead. There can't be a soul inside the ground who likes our chances, but Gordon D'Arcy and Shaggy score tries and we win 24–20.

As soon as the whistle goes I look to the touchline and Matt Williams is going ballistic. He's running and jumping and punching the air. He was reared in the western suburbs of Sydney but has the passion of a man who's never set foot out of Leinster.

Afterwards Matt praises our work ethic and the intensity of our training. But away from the hard grind we're rocking it harder than ever. Most of our home games are on Friday nights, and Kiely's in Donnybrook is the launch pad for our weekends.

Further down the road, when we're a team with trophies to our name, we'll look back at that time and wonder how we ever hoped to conquer Europe. But the penny takes quite a few years to drop.

On Saturdays and some Sundays we mix it up between Bruxelles on Harry Street, Kehoe's on South Anne Street and maybe a nightclub that's flavour of the month. There's even – on occasion – a Monday-night food and beverage club, which meets at a good restaurant and invariably ends up in Rí-Rá off Dame Street, far from your typical rugby haunt, which suits us down to the ground.

A pint bottle of Bulmers with ice is usually my beverage of choice. Nobody tells me it's heavy on the calories, but I don't look like someone who's counting.

Bob Casey comes up with a name for the guy who occasionally stares right through his closest friends as if they weren't there, after the cider has kicked in. He calls me Bobby Bulmers.

There are times – probably too many times – when I do a right job on myself. I'm a man of extremes and at twenty-two years of age I don't see the need to behave in a certain way just because I'm starting to become well known as a rugby player. And maybe there's a part of me that enjoys getting away from that side of my life, the escapism that comes from getting heavily jarred after a week of hard training and eighty minutes of giving it everything on the field.

On the mornings after a big night I give myself a cold shower and some eye drops and I stay as far away from the fitness coaches as I can. If some of us aren't always feeling 100 per cent, it doesn't stop us putting ourselves through the pain barrier. The work always gets done, which is probably why Matt doesn't come down heavy. Work hard, play hard. Some mornings, among certain players, there's a form of admiration for the late-night revellers.

'Jeez, fair play! You did well to hang in there after a monster one like that!'

Live and learn. That sort of thing will be unthinkable in years to come.

With the Celtic League trophy won and Christmas coming up, Matt thinks back to our implosion at the same time last year.

He knows the damage that a heavy Christmas can do to us early in the new year, in the business end of the Heineken Cup pool stages. He coins himself a catchphrase.

'I've got one message for you guys,' he tells us. 'D-N-F-U-J!'

We look at each other and he spells it out.

'Do Not Fuck Up January!'

We beat Newcastle to make the knockout stages with a game to spare and head for the south of France to play a non-vintage Toulouse, looking to nail down a home quarter-final. With a record of three defeats from five pool games – including a 30-point drubbing in Donnybrook – the aristocrats of French rugby draw fewer than seven thousand fans.

They destroy us, 43–7.

Our home quarter-final becomes a trip to Welford Road, where Leicester knock us out on the final weekend of our F-U-J.

Europe's big boys carry on without us. Again.

*

The Maples is a quiet cul-de-sac development off Bird Avenue in Clonskeagh, Dublin 14. This is where I buy my first house, early in 2002. And Barry Twomey is my first and only house-mate.

Easy company. A perfect fit. We call each other 'Face' and from the first day of living under the same roof we get on famously.

We've got completely different work schedules, but I'm never stuck for company if I fancy something other than a night in front of the telly.

'Will we go out for a look, Face?'

'Nah, it's all right for you! I'm working in the morning.'

'Ah, come on! You're only young once.'

'True. Go on so.'

Barry's a bit of a modern-day Del Boy. When we move in he's working in his father's SuperValu in Deansgrange. He's also got a sideline in bed linen, delph and other household goods. His rent comes in the form of the food he brings home from the shop. When he leaves the job there's no food and no rent but I'm not bothered because the laughter that comes from his company is payment enough.

We go to Arnott's department store and buy a couple of La-Z-Boy chairs for the sitting room, along with a giant television.

We order our fair share of takeaways and gladly avail ourselves of the free Coca-Cola a sponsor gives me by the pallet-load.

We play golf in the dark and blast balls over our back wall, into the grounds of the Catholic University School.

We bring hordes of people back with us from Club 92 in Leopardstown for house parties. We have an arrangement with the barman. He gets a black sack and sticks in some bottles of liquor and buckets of ice. We haul the cargo into a taxi. Later in the week I'll pop in and replace the booze, no questions asked.

It's not the social life of a model professional, but I'm far from alone in cutting myself some slack and I pride myself on the work I get through on the training ground once Monday morning comes.

I'm not the most naturally fit guy in the squad, but I've got a high enough pain threshold and a willingness to push myself out of the comfort zone, never to take the easy option if I'm carrying a niggle.

I try to be first in the drills, the best player on the training pitch, the one who wins the most compliments from the coaches.

I do it because I absolutely enjoy it, because it's no hardship to train well and put the effort in.

I'm a young guy living in the moment, learning from my own mistakes but still clued-in enough to see the big picture. To realize that – unless you're unlucky, like Skiddy – what you get out of the game is decided by what you're prepared to put into it.

If you're paying attention you come to learn – the earlier the better – that the players who earn the most respect are the ones who bring a high work ethic onto the training ground. The guys always doing extras, working on the weaker parts of their game, trying to understand the principles behind the training drills. The leaders who hold themselves to high standards and expect the same from everyone else. Not the ones blessed with a rare talent but unwilling to graft and get the most out of it.

*

January 2002. Eddie and Woody have their own little relationship going on. They're tight. There's a new dynamic and new people all over the place.

Declan Kidney is Eddie's assistant and Niall O'Donovan is forwards coach. Mike McGurn is our new conditioning coach and Mike Ford is another new hire from rugby league, brought in to revolutionize our defence.

Fordy hammers it home in training. Structure. Accountability. Who are the pillars at this ruck? What's *your* job? And *yours?* And *yours?* He's relentless. My mind boggles as to how we survived without knowing this stuff before.

The day before we play Wales at Lansdowne Road, in the first match of the Six Nations, I leave our base at the Berkeley Court Hotel and meet Barry at Eddie Rocket's in Stillorgan. We sit in the corner and order club sandwiches and cheese fries, buffalo wings and chocolate malt. Chilling out with Barry becomes a pre-match ritual.

On the field, we are a work in progress. Against the Welsh, it seems like we've cracked it. It's Paul O'Connell's debut. He scores a try, gets concussed and goes off. We beat them 54–10. But over in Twickenham it doesn't seem so straightforward. When we tire, our system vanishes. England pick us off with ease and hockey us 45–11.

Two weeks later we play Scotland in Dublin and continue the Jekyll and Hyde act by beating them 43–22. I score a hat-trick. Three tries guarantees you good reports even when two are Mickey Mouse run-ins through gaping holes.

The night after, I go to the Meteor Ireland Music Awards at the Point Depot in Dublin. It's a plus-one invite, but I'm without a one. Suzanne and I are no longer together so Skiddy comes with me. What do you wear to a bash like this? It's not hard. I have one suit. I find a shirt and off we go.

Our seats are directly in front of U2. I feel a tap on my shoulder and when I turn around it's Larry Mullen. 'Well done yesterday, Brian. A hat-trick. Fair play!'

'Ehh, thanks, Larry!'

Bono is sitting next to him, wearing his customary shades. I didn't have him down as a rugby supporter but he pays me another compliment. 'Yeah! Well done, man!'

'Cheers, Bono!'

I'd like to keep the conversation going but what are you supposed to say to U2?

We beat Italy handily but finish our Six Nations in Paris and it's a very different experience this time. We lose 44–5 and France take the Grand Slam.

We travel to New Zealand with a depleted squad and lose both Tests, but the tour is a personal milestone. Eddie holds a meeting in a coffee shop off the high street in Dunedin and invites Woody, Mike Ford and me. It's the point when I start feeling like I'm a senior player. We're ratcheting up for the 2003 World Cup and Eddie makes me feel I can bring plenty to the party.

*

There's a price to be paid for losing to Argentina at the last World Cup: it means we have to qualify for the next. We make our way to Krasnoyarsk, the third-largest city in Siberia.

Eddie sends one of the IRFU's top operations guys out on a reconnaissance mission. His verdict is grim.

The hotel is horrible.

The food is awful.

The locals are dangerous.

It's horrifically cold.

When we get there, we reckon the IRFU guy must have been on the vodka.

The hotel is grand.

The food is fine.

The people are lovely.

And it's hot.

We get the job done on a postage stamp of a pitch. On the endless trek home Woody aggravates a neck injury and is missing when we beat Georgia a week later and officially qualify for World Cup 2003.

Woody's struggling. He's talking about a disc problem. It doesn't sound good.

Five weeks later the phone rings in my room at the Glenview Hotel in Wicklow and Woody's on the line, asking if he can come around.

This is unusual. He's as sociable as they come but he's not in the habit of stopping by to pass the time of day.

Which he doesn't.

All week there have been doubts about whether he'll be passed fit to captain us against Australia, but he tells me the decision has now been made: he's resting up, he's being saved for bigger days ahead.

He cuts to the chase. 'I've been talking to Eddie,' he says. 'He thinks you're the right man to take over while I'm out.'

I'm shocked. Captain of Ireland? The only team I've ever captained is the UCD Under-20s – maybe twice. 'Really? Me?'

'Yeah.'

'What about Axel?'

Anthony Foley is one of the three new vice-captains picked by Eddie, along with Humps and – by far the least experienced of the trio – me.

But Woody says Eddie thinks I'm ready for it. He doesn't explain why he's been sent as an emissary and it doesn't occur to me to ask.

'Just think about it,' he says.

But in my head there's no decision.

Woody tells me to keep it under wraps, but after calling

my parents I just have to tell Shaggy. I'm still in shock when he calls round. 'Woody said I should think about it,' I tell him.

'Are you kidding?' he says. 'What's there to think about? Captain of your country! This is unbelievable!'

Shaggy's almost more excited about it than I am, but then I was never a jump-through-hoops type of person. And Eddie doesn't exactly lose the run of himself either when I talk to him.

'Woody spoke to me,' I say. 'I'd be very interested in that.'

'Right so. We'll do that, for the time being. Good man.'

Five days before we play Australia, on the Monday morning before training, he announces it to the team. As he says it, I look around for the reaction, hoping I won't catch any eyes shooting up to Heaven.

There's nothing. Everyone's very nice about it. And then all I can think about is that at 6.15 p.m., on the night before a game against the world champions, they will walk into the team room, sit around in a circle and expect me to sound like an international captain at twenty-three years old.

My carefree Fridays with Barry are over. I spend the afternoon completely stressed, making notes, panicking about the meeting – worrying about what to say, how to say it, what they'll think of me.

At half five I walk in there on my own and write my bullet points down on a board. I go through them in my head one by one, over and over, until the first guys walk in.

The following day the rain pelts down all afternoon, and Rog out-kicks them in a slog-fest. It's our first win over Australia since 1979.

'That was just absolute shite – not proper rugby,' Matt

Burke says to me, at the post-match dinner. He's got a point, but I'm ready to chalk it down as a good day once I get my speech over and done with.

I've got it all written out but I make a brutal job of reading it.

'Well done, you were good,' says a kind-hearted liar at the table, once I sit back down.

*

Dublin 4 in springtime. The clocks go forward and England are back in town, looking for the Grand Slam they left behind them two years before.

I sit at the back of a bus moving slowly towards Lansdowne Road. Den is opposite me. We look out the window in silence and see the crowds milling about. Green everywhere, as usual on match-day. But this is different. We, too, are four from four in the Six Nations, eighty minutes away from a Slam.

Woody's still injured so I lead the team out. As we finish our warm-up, President Mary McAleese is making her way down onto the pitch and Martin Johnson already has his team lined up to shake her hand. He's got his game face on and his players on the wrong side of the red carpet.

We always stand on the right: it's protocol. I'm shepherding the mascots across the pitch when the lads raise a protest.

'They're on our side!'

'Johnson's taking the piss!'

'Fucking disrespectful!'

We don't hear Johnno's reply when one of the stewards asks him to move along, but his body language tells us it's something along the lines of 'Not today, my friend.'

Anyone trying to shift him is going to need earth-moving machinery.

We've got three options:

1. Stand on their side.
2. Stand in front of them.
3. Walk past them and stand at the far end.

Option 1 is out of the question.

Option 2 means it could all kick off in front of the president.

Option 3 gets the president's shoes dirty when she runs out of red carpet.

I'm not overly pushed on protocol and I've got a quiet admiration for Johnno over standing his ground, but the contextual discussion can wait. I listen to the fury of my team and I like it.

'Let's sow it into the bastards!'

England aren't long in showing us what we can do with our fury. They go after us like it's the last game they're ever going to play. Hungry and ruthless. For three years in a row they've lost the Slam on the final weekend.

Not today.

We get annihilated 42–6. It's not merely that they want it more – they're just better than us. A lot better.

With a few minutes left, I have a despairing lash at their defence, a little show-and-go on a loop play, trying to get through a gap between Will Greenwood and Jonny Wilkinson.

Jonny reads it and cuts me in two. I know about his ability to kill people in the tackle. I've seen it and now I've felt it. I'm subbed off, barely able to walk. Injury added to insult on our big day.

*

A fortnight later I'm still not right. I'm bandaged up and hobbling ahead of Leinster's first Heineken Cup quarter-final – against Biarritz, the reigning champions of France.

With forty-five thousand people in Lansdowne Road we hang on and win 18–13. The road to glory stretches out in front of us. The semi-final and final are also in Dublin. We don't even have to cross the river, never mind the continent.

First up, Perpignan. Our record for the season against French teams is flawless. Played three, won three after two pool games with Montferrand and the quarter-final with Biarritz. We think this is our time.

Then the game starts and we're brutal. We're out-muscled. Mistakes all over the place. My hamstring goes and I limp off. I watch the rest of this industrial-scale screw-up from the sideline.

Leinster 14, Perpignan 21.

Matt gets a kicking from the press but the fault lies with us, his players. Too many errors and not enough fight. To make it worse, it's Matt's last game. Next time we see him some of us will be on opposite sides. He's moving up in the world and coaching Scotland.

His job goes to Gary Ella, another Australian.

What we know about him pretty much begins and ends with one key fact: he's Mark Ella's brother. So he must have something.

*

Woody is not your average rugby player. The 1997 Lions tour – a series win in South Africa – put him up with the greats. He has confidence, charisma, connections. He introduces me to Nigel Northridge, CEO of the Gallaher Group,

My father played rugby for Ireland, and this photo suggests that there was a child-sized rugby ball in our house when I was little – but I never played the game until I went to Willow Park for my last year of primary school

Forever in the centre: with my sisters Julie (*left*) and Susan

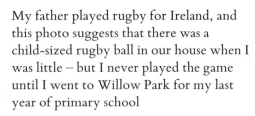

Representing the parish at the Community Games in Santry with my great friend Donovan Rossi

Playing for Blackrock College against Newbridge College, February 1997
(*Matt Kavanagh/Irish Times*)

Handing off Australia's Daniel Herbert in Brisbane on the day I won my first Ireland
cap, 19 June 1999 (*Patrick Bolger/Inpho*)

Stepping past Stéphane Glas on the way to my first of three tries against France in 2000 …
(*Tom Honan/Inpho*)

… and celebrating at the final whistle: our first win in Paris since 1972
(*Billy Stickland/Inpho*)

It was a thrill to be Daniel Herbert's partner in the centre for the Barbarians against South Africa in 2000

After bursting between Nathan Grey (*left*) and Jeremy Paul in the first Lions test against Australia in 2001, I stepped past Matt Burke en route to a try that gave us a commanding lead (*Billy Stickland/Inpho*)

In 2001, Ireland hadn't yet made a habit of beating England – in fact they had beaten us six times on the trot – and our celebration after beating them at Lansdowne Road probably reflected that (*Billy Stickland/Inpho*)

At the Monaco Grand Prix, 2003, with Bono, Ali Hewson and Eddie Jordan. That trip gave me a brief glimpse into a completely different world

With my pals Denis Hickie and Shane Horgan in our Ireland suits, ties and caps for World Cup 2003 (*Billy Stickland/Inpho*)

Scoring against Australia in the 2003 World Cup group stage; my cousin Gary O'Driscoll, the Ireland team doctor – standing and wearing a white shirt – looks on (*Morgan Treacy/Inpho*)

With Eddie O'Sullivan after winning the 2004 Triple Crown – the first of three in four years under his leadership (*Billy Stickland/Inpho*)

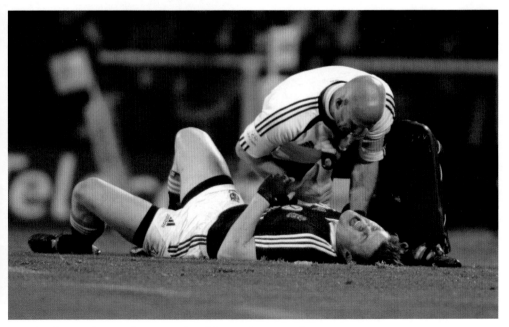

After being dropped on my shoulder early in my first Test as Lions captain in New Zealand in 2005, the pain was excruciating. What came after wasn't much better (*Hannah Johnston/Inpho*)

The build-up to our first match against England at Croke Park, in 2007, was intense. The anthems were a big deal – and John Hayes wasn't the only one who got emotional – but the main thing we knew was that we couldn't lose …
(*Dan Sheridan/Inpho*)

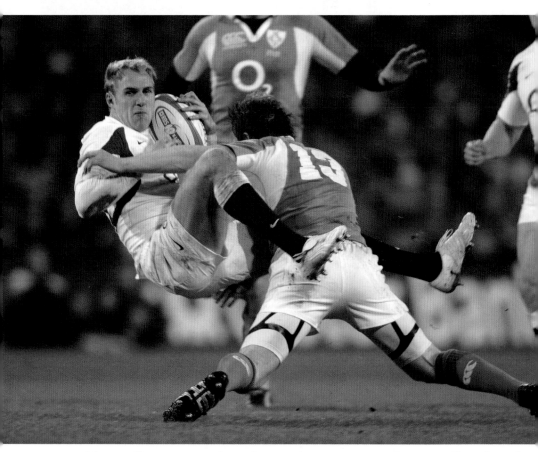

My tackle on Olly Morgan early in that match was just one indication of how hyped up we were (*Morgan Treacy/Inpho*)

sponsors of the Benson & Hedges Jordan Formula 1 team. Nigel and his friend Dave Marron send me one of the great invitations of all time – a weekend trip to the 2003 Monaco Grand Prix, a private jet into a different world.

There's a helicopter waiting for us at Nice airport and a speedboat in the water close by the helipad in Monaco. As it zooms off towards Port Hercule and pulls up to the yacht we're staying on for the weekend, I keep telling Nigel I can't believe my eyes. I am properly, jaw-droppingly wowed.

Friday night in Monte Carlo. We go for dinner, we hit a few bars. We have paddock passes for the qualifying session the following morning, and my hosts save their petrol for a big day ahead. I bump into a high roller from Dublin and we figure we have another few laps left in us. The next thing I know we're on another speedboat, heading for a super-yacht in the bay that's too big for docking and too luxurious for words. By the time we've outstayed our welcome and been ferried back to shore, the sun is up and the streets are being closed off before qualifying starts.

For a while I can't get access to the part of the marina where our boat is moored and when I eventually do they all look the same.

By now I'm so exhausted I just pick one. I'm compos mentis enough to remember the protocol about taking off your shoes. I curl up on a seat at the back of the boat and nod off, until a deck hand comes along and sends me packing. I eventually find the right boat, collapse into bed and miss the qualifying session for my first Grand Prix.

When we're invited up to the Jordan area on race day, with grid passes around our necks, the special guests are Bono, his wife, Ali, and some Middle Eastern royal.

Jordan's number 1 driver, Giancarlo Fisichella, spots Bono

as we're walking in between the cars. He's only too happy to pose for a picture with the great man and his hangers-on. He finishes tenth in the race, but nobody seems too disappointed about that at the post-race party in the Amber Lounge. It's a new hotspot run by Eddie Irvine's sister, Sonia, and on the opening weekend she pulls in the royalty of the Formula 1 world, plus Prince Albert of Monaco.

The following morning the private jet flies back into Farnborough airport and I'm driven to Heathrow for my flight home.

'So how was it?' asks Barry, back at the Maples.

He cooks us his famous roast chicken with dauphinoise potatoes and I tell him how the other half lives.

*

Summer on the seafront. I'm in Bray with my girlfriend of two months, the model Glenda Gilson, tagging along while she carries out her duties as a judge for the Face of Bray 2003.

A photographer sees us together and asks us to pose for a picture. I'm not keen but he's persistent. There's a crowd of unfamiliar people on his side and it feels churlish to refuse.

Glenda plants a kiss on my cheek. The next day the picture is on the front page of the *Sun* underneath a corny headline: *Scrum Guys Have All The Luck!*

The dressing room can be a savage place and I know what's coming next. Rog sees the picture and savours every word in the article, with its cringe-making reference to Ireland's Posh and Becks. It's an open goal for him. In the business of ripping the piss out of people, he's already world-class. He doesn't need his material served up to him on a silver platter.

At our pre-World Cup training camp he lets fly. 'You're

bloody lucky you scored those three tries in Paris!' he says. 'If you didn't play rugby you'd be sitting on the 46A with your cheese sandwiches.'

I'm the butt of the joke, but I'm laughing with the rest of them. He carries on. He isn't done painting his picture of the miserable life I've avoided.

'That's right, you'd be heading into your desk job at First Active. Data input, boy! That's all you'd be good for. You'd be hating every minute of it. You'd be fat as a fool.'

Rog's wit is like a blade. He cuts you up, but he's funny, and the funniest thing of all is that he's probably right about the 46A, although I'd have to draw a line at the cheese sandwiches.

When we get to Australia for the World Cup, Woody is back. He has patched up his body and this is his last stand. Base camp is the paradise town of Terrigal, fifty-five miles north of Sydney. When I open the curtains of my room in the morning, the sun is hitting the water of the Pacific Ocean. A place like this makes a difference to your psyche.

We ease past Romania in our first game and Namibia in our second, and kick on for Adelaide, where we play Argentina in our pivotal match in the group.

The memory of Lens is in the air. There's no escape from it. Everybody knows that we can't lose this game. We just can't. The thought of it is horrific. Another early exit and to the same team? It can't happen.

The mood becomes heavy and stressed. From Terrigal to Adelaide is like Heaven to Hell. Alan Quinlan scores a big try after twenty minutes and that settles us down, but Quinny dislocates his shoulder scoring it and he's taken off in agony.

There's niggle all over the place. Bad blood. Two of our lads are gouged. The Argentines make our lives a misery with their crazy intensity and their refusal to go away and die. And they keep chipping away at the scoreline.

We lead by seven.

We lead by four.

We lead by one.

We trail by two.

Rog comes on for Humps and kicks us back into the lead with as ballsy a penalty as you're ever going to see. Then he lands another. We lead by four.

They're still not dead. With seven minutes to go, the Grim Reaper of Lens, Gonzalo Quesada, fires over a kick and it's a one-point game.

The clock is showing eighty minutes when their full-back, Ignacio Corleto, makes a last-ditch break. He heads into open country but I bolt after him and scrag him down. The thought of missing that tackle sends a shiver through me. When it ends there's no celebration, no joy, only relief.

We're in the quarter-finals, no matter what happens against Australia in Melbourne a week later, but when they sneak home 17–16 they move on to face Scotland for a place in the semi-final while we've got France in our way.

It's not like Eddie to pull a game plan from left-field, but he comes up with something completely different. Eddie's a sharp operator but this is as blunt as a hammer.

What it amounts to is me running into brick walls where we thought there would be gaps. Our levels of deception are not exactly sophisticated. France can see us coming and they bury us every time.

It's not just the game plan, it's everything. We know France like a crossfield kick, so we practise for it. We tell ourselves we're not getting suckered by a cheeky one from Freddie Michalak. In the third minute, he's ten metres inside our half with too much time and space. Paulie recognizes the danger and pushes forward, but Michalak gets the ball away.

Imanol Harinordoquy charges after it and for a number 8 he's got serious pace. The ball bounces back towards him, and as he claims it in the air from Girvan Dempsey, he's got support runners steaming up behind. He ships it to Tony Marsh, and when Olivier Magne takes the next offload we've been busted so badly he practically saunters across the try line and under the posts.

We're not at the races. The French score at will. At half-time we're losing 27–0. In the second half Maggsy gets a try and I get two, but it's only consolation stuff. France have taken their foot off the gas. They're thinking about the semi-final and we're going home.

4. In the Wars

After the World Cup – and the daily itineraries that tell us to be there at *this* time, wearing *that* shirt – I let my hair down, literally. It's already on the long side, with a few blond streaks, but I'm not done yet.

So much of my life is controlled by others. By Leinster. By Ireland. By the need to be a good professional doing the right things every day. Everything's dictated. Be here, wear that, eat now.

The way I see it, my hair is my own and I can do what I want with it. If people don't like it, then so be it. It's my little rebellion.

There's a new name at number 10 on the Leinster team sheet for my first match under Gary Ella: Felipe Contepomi, fresh from the World Cup with Argentina, a medical student and a class act. I score a couple of tries and we're impressive in beating Ospreys away from home. We follow that up by going two from two in the Heineken Cup pool games, but we stumble in game three. I'm off with a torn hamstring in the first quarter and Sale do us by a point at Lansdowne Road.

By the time the final pool game comes around, we're four from five but I'm still not fit. A win or a draw away to Biarritz and we're through to the quarter-finals. A defeat and we're out of the competition.

I don't travel to France. The day before the match I turn up for a function at Silks Casino on Earlsfort Terrace in the heart of Dublin. It's a bash organized to drum up publicity for *Social & Personal* magazine by revealing their idea of Ireland's Top 50 sexiest men for 2004.

The new Miss World, Rosanna Davison, is one of the judges. Three more models join her on the panel: Sonya Macari, Katy French, Glenda Gilson.

They have convened at a late bar in Dublin and somehow come up with the following top four:

4. Bono. *Alas, not able to make it. Possibly recording the new U2 album. Or doing something else.*
3. Damien Duff. *Also unable to come. Busy with Chelsea FC.*
2. Colin Farrell. *Unavoidably absent. On location in Morocco with Angelina Jolie.*
1. Brian O'Driscoll.

I'm there all right. Hard to miss. The guy with the yellow hair and the uncomfortable look that says . . . *What am I doing here?*

It's a world that feels alien to me, deep down, and when the invite came my first instinct was to knock it for six. 'Sorry, this isn't for me, thanks all the same . . .'

But the whole point of the night is that they have someone standing by for a photo opportunity with the judges. Can't get Colin Farrell to turn up and accept? Then get *somebody*.

I resisted, but not enough.

In the end, trying to keep other people happy, I went against my gut and compromised myself.

At the casino I give an on-the-spot interview to Henry McKean, a guy I was at school with, a witty broadcaster with a talent for gentle, mocking humour.

'How does it feel?' He smirks. 'Do you think you deserve it?'

I laugh and tell him I don't have any illusions about what I see in the mirror.

I'm looking at the whole thing as a bit of a joke, but not everyone gets it.

A man-about-town, popular with the tabloids, comes over for a word. He tries to hide his disappointment at being over-looked, but he's not very convincing. I can't believe anyone is taking it seriously, but most of all I can't believe I've allowed myself to walk into this situation.

Before it gets better, it gets a lot worse. From Silks I go to the RTÉ television studios to appear as a guest on *The Late Late Show*, the most-watched television programme in Ireland. Woody has listened to his body and retired after a heroic last stand in Australia and Eddie has named me as captain for the upcoming Six Nations.

But the rugby will have to wait. Pat Kenny, the host, doesn't look gift horses in the mouth. He isn't even subtle about it – he full-on takes the piss as soon as I'm in my chair. 'All over the country,' he begins, 'women want to be sitting right here where I'm sitting – inches away from Ireland's sexiest man . . .'

I say nothing. I have no words to respond. In my entire life I've rarely been as uncomfortable.

'You got the award tonight. What was it like?'

'It was embarrassing, to say the least.'

'Really . . .' He arches his eyebrows and shoots me a look that says, *Too right it's embarrassing.*

He won't let it go. He can't believe I've won this thing. 'Ahm, who decided that you are Ireland's sexiest man?'

I start stuttering. 'Well, *Social & Personal*, ah, magazine, ahm, do it. They, er, run it yearly so it's the twelfth year of it.

Ahm, and they have a panel of five judges so, ahm, they were the ones that chose.'

'And who were the judges?'

He knows full well who the judges were. Glenda is sitting in the audience. He wanders off for a chat with her, leaving me sitting there on my own.

Finally, he takes me out of my misery. 'Let's move on to the other title you got this week, which is captain of Ireland. You're more comfortable, I think, with that title than with the other one.'

'A touch more comfortable with that, all right.'

We start talking rugby, but the damage is done and it colours some people's opinion of me as a person for years to come.

The guy who got above his station.

The flash lad with the dyed blond hair and the celebrity lifestyle.

After my *Late Late* appearance I talk to Den. He has watched and is horrified. 'How did this happen?' he asks.

It's a good question.

It takes me a while to figure it out. I've got a fair idea of who I really am, of who I was brought up to be, but it takes me a little longer to fully become that person. In years to come, when I see young guys making similar mistakes, there's a part of me that wants to pull them aside for a friendly word, but I figure there's really no point because they've got to live it for themselves.

All I know for sure as I'm turning twenty-five is that I don't feel comfortable with the kind of celebrity that has come my way – and I'm not very good at it either.

In a queue for Copper Face Jack's on Harcourt Street, I try

to get into the upstairs bar but the bouncer directs me towards the club down below.

I'm friendly enough with the owner, Cathal Jackson, but I don't want to cause a scene by dropping his name and I'd rather shoot myself than come out with the dreaded line . . .

Do you not know who I am?

The bouncer has seen me with Cathal more than once. Maybe he remembers me, maybe not, but it doesn't really matter. The right thing to do now is go downstairs or go somewhere else, but I decide to jog his memory.

Big mistake.

As soon as I ask the question I know it sounds bad. 'Sorry – you know me, right?'

The way it comes out jars, like I'm putting myself on a pedestal rather than reminding him that we've met before.

He's not impressed, he shows me downstairs again. Proper order.

I tell myself I'll never challenge someone in that way again. Sometimes you have to learn the hard way, but when you're in the public eye, impressions of your character can be quickly formed and not easily altered.

The general public don't do nuances. They take you at face value – what they see on TV, what they hear around and about. You get one image, one reputation. Right or wrong, good or bad, it's never a very accurate reflection of who you are.

A year later *Social & Personal* brings out its thirteenth annual list and I plummet straight out of the top fifty.

I don't take it too hard.

*

The day after my *Late Late* appearance, Leinster lose 32–21 in Biarritz. It's one defeat too many, another Heineken Cup elimination in the pool stages.

We go to Lanzarote with Ireland for a warm-weather training camp ahead of the Six Nations. In the middle of the La Santa resort in the north-west of the island there is a supermarket and some of our boys in the winter of their careers are somewhat regular customers at the booze counter. They disappear out of camp with empty rucksacks and come clinking their way back. Times may be changing but the old school hasn't closed its doors yet.

I don't make it back in time for the opening defeat in Paris, for which Paulie steps up as skipper only two years after his international debut. When the team is named to play Wales in the second weekend I'm back in as captain with a new partner in the centre – Gordon D'Arcy.

We've never played together in the midfield for Ireland, but it works a dream. Shane Byrne scores off a lineout maul after one minute and we never look back. We score four tries in the first half and six in all. I get two – the twenty-third and twenty-fourth of my Test career.

Two weeks later we travel to Twickenham to play the world champions and Eddie has an idea. 'I think we should clap them out,' he says.

I try to shoot it down straight away, but he persists. 'Listen, it's reverse psychology. It might make them complacent.'

I tell him I'm not one for reverse psychology. I'm not standing there applauding while England puff out their chests and walk on by.

Instead of deference, I offer England ammunition.

I've been captain for long enough to know better, but

maybe the prospect of taking on the world champions in their backyard scrambles my brain.

In a ghost-written column for the BBC Sport website, I come over like a prize-fighter trying to put bums on seats at a grudge match.

'They're the world champions playing their first competitive game back at Twickenham,' I say. 'That's what I call pressure. This could be our big opportunity to take them. The only way England can go now is down.' Just to be sure I'm giving my BBC paymasters some proper bang for their buck, I lodge my tongue in my cheek and borrow one of Roy Keane's better lines. 'Hopefully we can give the prawn sandwich brigade at Twickenham something to choke on.'

It doesn't go down too well with England's coach, Clive Woodward.

'I don't like prawn sandwiches,' he says in response. 'I prefer chicken and tomato.'

He then slaps me down gently. 'It's best to keep quiet. I'm surprised teams haven't learned that when they come to play England. We do our talking on the pitch.'

As we exit the dressing room and head for the pitch at Twickenham there are 22 reminders of how much of a fortress this place is. England have won that many Tests in a row here, stretching back to 1999, and there's a plaque on the wall for each and every one.

They're cock of the walk, but they're vulnerable. Jonny is injured. Johnno has retired. Neil Back is off the scene.

With fifty minutes played, Darce busts the English defensive line. At the next breakdown Strings goes up the short side with T-Bone – Tyrone Howe – then we come steaming across the field with Keith Gleeson, Shaggy, Mal and Axel Foley. After the recycle, we go back to where we came from.

Left-right-left. England are spread thin. They're short of numbers on the far wing. We can see it and England can see it too and they're scrambling like hell to recover the ground. Darce finds me with a skip-two pass. I throw a long miss pass too, to T-Bone. He slips Girvan Dempsey in for the score.

From the time Darce smashes through to the moment Girv touches down it's forty-one seconds. It's a class try and it's the difference. We shake up world rugby with a 19–13 victory. Apart from France, we are the only country to beat England, home or away, in forty-four Test matches.

It's a famous day, but I know I've put up the worst performance of my Ireland career. Stray passes. Poor decisions. Too many errors. Just downright bad.

Darce has played well. Outrageously well. I look over at him in the dressing room and I think of the journey he has taken to get here. Capped at nineteen in the 1999 World Cup, then dropped like a stone. Going nowhere fast for years. Then, the comeback.

We take care of Italy a fortnight later at Lansdowne Road and have a week to prepare for a Triple Crown game with Matt Williams's Scotland.

Darce is on fire again. A glutton for work, a constant menace to the Scots. He scores the first and last of our five tries. Silverware at last. It might not be a championship or a Grand Slam but it's an achievement – the country's first Triple Crown in nineteen years. A monkey off our backs.

At the end of the championship, Darce polls four times more votes than anybody else and wins player of the tournament, a fair old feat given that France have won the Slam.

When I'm told that Declan Kidney is bowing out as

Eddie's assistant, I'm not exactly speechless from shock. Eddie and Deccie don't get on and don't pretend to get on. It's not like it's been open warfare between them, but you can tell there's an issue. Eddie wants to be more hands-on with the coaching of the team and Deccie wants more say about the overall scheme of things.

It's been a bad marriage and there's a quiet divorce. They keep it civil for the sake of the children. The IRFU offer Deccie a desk job. He declines.

*

Three weeks after the Scotland win, Leinster play a Celtic League game at Stradey Park, home of Llanelli. We have eight of the Triple Crown winners in our team – myself, Girv, Shaggy, Darce, Mal, Reggie Corrigan, Shane Byrne and Victor Costello. We're a good side, on paper.

We're losing 13–5 at half-time. Not good, but not disastrous. After the break, we're blown to kingdom come. Llanelli score five tries to bring it to 51–8. We're a disorganized shambles. We get some points late on when they take their foot off the gas but it does nothing to take the filthy look off the final score: Llanelli 51, Leinster 20.

Having butchered the Heineken Cup semi-final the previous year we're getting stick for being bottlers, for not fronting up when things get rough.

We get a strong vibe from the Leinster branch that they want us to make it easier for them to get rid of Gary Ella. They want to hear he has lost the dressing room.

We meet up. We talk for hours. We refuse to give the Leinster branch an easy out. We send word back to them that the coach has our confidence. Gary is out of his depth and he's never going to take us to the next level. But they brought him in. If they want him out, it's a decision for them to make, not us. If they flunk it, we'll carry on.

But they know we've gone backwards since Matt Williams left. We're lacking direction, structure, a touch of ruthlessness and a game plan that gets the best out of what we have. Everyone knows there has to be change.

Declan Kidney hasn't even started in his new job as coach of the Newport Gwent Dragons, but there's a clause in his contract that allows him to come home. When the call comes, he answers it straight away.

There's a touch of paranoia in parts of our dressing room. Deccie, one of the driving forces of Munster, now coaching Leinster? It doesn't seem right to some of the lads. But with two European finals and a World Under-19 trophy on his CV he sounds pretty all right to me.

For some of us, the uneasy relationship with the men governing rugby doesn't stop at Leinster's door. Relations between the country's professional players and the IRFU are strained: a them-and-us situation. It's less than three years since we set up the Irish Rugby Union Players Association and we decide to take a stand on the issue of match fees and win bonuses. Six years have passed since there was an increase in either, while ticket prices for internationals have risen by 80 per cent.

For a couple of weeks it plays out like an industrial dispute.

We state our case.

The IRFU's management committee pleads poverty.

We ask for talks.

We're portrayed as greedy.

We're not asking for the sun, moon and stars but we would like a little more respect. As Ireland captain, and with a tour to South Africa looming, I'm in regular consultation with the IRUPA chairman, Niall Woods.

As players we are united. Through Niall we send word back to the Union: come to the table or the tour is off.

Late in the day, Niall takes a call from the IRFU's chief executive. Philip Browne agrees to talk and a compromise is reached.

For us players, it's a step forward.

Not everyone in the Union agrees, but it feels like progress for Irish rugby too.

*

Bloemfontein in June. We look out the window of the team bus as we make our way to the Free State Stadium for the opening Test of our summer tour in South Africa. It's the first time I've been here, the first time I've encountered the Afrikaner rugby man in his own backyard.

It's everything I was told it would be. Loud and aggressive. Endless cries of 'Bokke! Bokke! Bokke!' On the street, some locals gesture at us by sliding a finger across their throats.

Welcome to Bloem. You're in our place now.

We lose the first Test 36–15, then go to Cape Town and lose the second 26–17. It's hard, fast, physical and intensely disappointing. We're at the end of a long season, running on empty for the final fifteen minutes. They're fresh and it's the difference.

Eddie makes a point of promising they'll find it harder going against us in the autumn, for Act Three.

The week before the November match at Lansdowne Road Eddie gives us some time off and I take maximum advantage by going into town five nights in a row. I figure I can handle it. The way I look at it, I'll be back in camp six days before the Test, so where's the harm in a few sociables to take the edge off?

By the time I report to the Killiney Castle Hotel on Sunday evening the madness of that thinking is clear.

On Monday morning I still feel terrible, but the embarrassment over my Grand Slam of nights out is worse.

Eddie knows something is up. He comes over to me at training. 'Are you all right?'

'Fine, yeah.'

'You don't seem like yourself.'

'Bit of girlfriend trouble.'

'Ah. Okay.'

He walks away. I spend the week feeling guilty.

You gobshite!

You'd better deliver on Saturday!

In our history we've played the Springboks sixteen times. We've lost fourteen of them. The other two – a win and a draw – came long before I was born.

Twenty minutes in, still no score, South Africa are penalized five metres out from their line. John Smit, their captain, is told to have a word with his team about their discipline. While he's doing that, Rog gets the go-ahead from Paul Honiss to restart. He takes a quick tap and scampers over before the Springboks know what's going on.

Smit kicks up a fuss. He has a point, but Honiss is having none of it.

Rog ends up scoring all our points in a 17–12 victory. We survive a ferocious onslaught at the end, a full-on smashing.

I've played one of my best Tests for Ireland, a performance driven by the fear of letting people down. I promise myself I'll never compromise my preparation for a game like that again. And I don't.

We kick on through the autumn, beating America, then facing Argentina on a dire day at Lansdowne Road. It's not just the foul weather that makes it a horrible experience, it's the antics of some of the Pumas.

In the World Cup game in Adelaide, two of their team were done for gouging. And now they're at it again. We trail from the third minute to the seventy-ninth, when Rog booms over a drop goal from forty metres and wins it. Sweet.

By the end of the autumn I'm the bookmakers' favourite to get the Lions captaincy for the 2005 tour to New Zealand.

*

When I fly into Heathrow airport on 25 January 2005, Clive Woodward is waiting for me at Arrivals. He drives me to his house in Henley and we talk about the Lions tour, which he's leading as head coach.

He asks me which players I rate, what kind of game we need to win. He wonders how I'd feel about being captain. It's not an offer, it's a hypothetical question, but it still feels like a big moment. I tell him I'd try to lead by example, like Martin Johnson did. But I'd do it my own way, be my own man.

I fly home knowing that I'm bang in the frame. We beat Italy in our opening match of the Six Nations but before our second my hamstring goes again. There's no good time to be sitting at home while Ireland are playing a Test match, but a Lions season is the worst time of all. I'm drinking tea with my sister Jules on the day we put 40 points on Scotland at Murrayfield.

I'm back for our third game, against England at Lansdowne Road. We're trailing 13–12 approaching the hour-mark when Geordan Murphy comes up with a little bit of magic. He takes a pass from Strings, dummies Charlie Hodgson, and by the time Hodgson knows what's going on, Geordan has put me over in the corner.

Rog converts and the scoring ends there: 19–13, just like it was at Twickenham a year ago.

We're three from three. Two weeks later, France come to Dublin and overturn our early lead with two fast tries. It's late in the game and we're nine points down when I run hard at Freddie Michalak, hand him off and step Cedric Heymans before touching down under the posts: one of my favourite international tries. Rog converts. We've cut their lead to two and we've got eight minutes to keep our Grand Slam hopes alive.

With two minutes left, France extinguish them. Quick ruck ball, a pass to their flying machine Christophe Dominici and, like a bullet out of a gun, he's away. Game over.

We tell ourselves that another Triple Crown will do, but we don't even manage that much. Wales beat us 32–20 in the final game of the championship at the Millennium. They take the Grand Slam in front of their own delirious people and we end up with nothing.

*

Under Deccie at Leinster we've battered all comers in the Heineken Cup. We've put 92 points on Bourgoin at Lansdowne Road. For the first time we've won six out of six in the pool and we're comfortably seeded first for the quarter-final draw, which pits us against Leicester.

As the game draws near, a rumour goes around. It says Deccie has applied for the Munster job vacated by Alan Gaffney – and that he's going to get it.

Leicester course us around Lansdowne Road in front of 48,500 people. They kill us in all quarters and win with a 16-point margin that hardly does them justice. Then Deccie drops the bomb. He confirms he's leaving, for what he describes as personal reasons.

There's rancour in the squad. Deccie has just finished a round of contract negotiations and laid off some of the lads before jumping ship to our biggest rivals. He hasn't done it out of spite – he's not that sort of person – but it doesn't play well.

We're out of the Heineken Cup and nowhere in the Magners League. We're rudderless, again.

*

It's a foul day in Dublin when Clive Woodward phones. I'm at home in the Maples. He's calling from the beach in Barbados. He offers me the captaincy of the Lions.

It's an incredible moment of joy. The biggest honour of my career. I'm excited and nervous at the same time. The responsibilities of leadership are on a different level when players from four countries – mostly strangers – come together for a one-off tour against the best international side on the planet.

I think back to the 2001 tour when I had Rog with me in Australia. A pal of a similar age to hang around with. If he hadn't been there I might have been lost.

I think of Lawrence Dallaglio and whether people will think he should be captain instead of me. All that experience, all that knowledge, a proven and charismatic leader.

When Clive names his squad there are only six players in it who know what it's like to be part of a winning Lions tour – Graham Rowntree, Neil Back, Richard Hill, Will

Greenwood, Matt Dawson and Dallaglio, the survivors from South Africa 1997.

Only three of them started the key Tests – Hill, Dawson and Dallaglio.

Only one had been mentioned as a possible captain this time – Dallaglio.

It's nearly a year since Lawrence retired from international rugby but he has just captained Wasps to a third successive league title in England. He could easily have been asked to lead the Lions, and I can't help wondering if he thinks he should have been, but one thing's for certain: I need him by my side.

Three weeks later the Lions party meets at the Vale of Glamorgan Hotel in Cardiff. It's the biggest army of tourists in Lions history: forty-four players and twenty-six management. There's Clive and his main coaching staff – Andy Robinson, Eddie O'Sullivan, Ian McGeechan, Phil Larder, Gareth Jenkins, Mike Ford. There's a kicking coach, two fitness coaches, two video analysts, two doctors, three physios, three security guards, a chef, a tour manager, a team manager, a lawyer, a refereeing consultant and – in Alastair Campbell, Tony Blair's spin doctor – a media consultant, who ends up becoming a story himself.

Clive has the tour surrounded. He says he's effectively going to have two squads and two coaching set-ups. This has never been done before. Soon enough we'll find out why.

When I talk to the players I stress the importance of winning: the successful tours are the only ones that people remember. Nobody cares about 2001 any more. Nobody ever talks about it, because we lost. People remember 1997: Johnno, Woody, Dallaglio and the boys.

When we get to New Zealand we head for Rotorua.

Tattooed Maori warriors whip spears around my face at a welcoming party. I can hear giggling from the lads behind me, but this is their culture and I feel honour-bound to respect it. In our first match we grind out a 34–20 victory against Bay of Plenty. The catastrophe comes when Lawrence breaks his ankle twenty-two minutes in. He's out of the tour and we're down a warrior, the biggest one we have. I flick on my phone in the dressing room afterwards and there's a text from him, sent before the match: *Lead us well. Right behind you.*

Reading it makes it even harder to take that he has gone.

We beat Taranaki in New Plymouth but then lose to the New Zealand Maori in Hamilton. They set out their stall with a *haka* that comes from deep within and they out-battle us from the beginning, with Carlos Spencer pulling the strings at 10 and Marty Holah and Jono Gibbes supercharged in their pack.

It helps that they come out on the right side of Steve Walsh's blatant inconsistency in refereeing the breakdown. When I complain that he's letting them get away with murder and pinging us off the park, he treats me with preening contempt.

I get my first try of the tour but it's not enough to save us. It finishes 19–13, the first Lions defeat to a Maori side in touring history. They deserve their victory, but the inconsistencies of referees from different hemispheres are maddening.

Clive says the defeat will make us rather than break us, but a big part of the problem is that we haven't been given enough of a chance to come together as a squad.

It's in training that you develop a togetherness. Working hard as a squad – laughing, joking, bonding, all on the same

buzz. That's lost when you're split, and with everyone rooming alone the camaraderie never gets off the ground. In Denis
and Shaggy I've got two of my best friends in rugby on tour
with me, but in seven weeks away I get to train with Den only
once.

Rotorua, New Plymouth, Hamilton, Dunedin – there's
not a lot going on and the tour is not a barrel of laughs. I end
up killing time in the team room, allowing the captaincy to
consume me, feeling suffocated by the responsibility, unwilling or unable to cut myself a break and seek out some of the
enjoyment that comes from just being my normal self.

We get over the loss to the Maori by beating Wellington,
Otago and Southland. The Southland game is in Invercargill
at the bottom of the South Island, four days before the first
Test. It's one for the midweek side that we rarely train with, a
situation that does none of us any good because ultimately
any squad can only be as strong as the least motivated members in it.

Clive has spoken to a Maori elder and been given advice
on how best to face the *haka* before the first Test in Christchurch. We spread out in a half-moon shape, with me out
front as the leader and the youngest member, Dwayne Peel,
standing behind me. When the *haka* ends, I pull up some
grass and throw it at them, as if pulling the ground from
underneath their feet.

I like the symbolism.

You're laying down a challenge?

Fine, we accept.

Forty seconds into the Test I'm counter-rucking, pushing
against Jerry Collins, when their hooker, Keven Mealamu,
grabs my left leg and tries to uproot me.

He fails, at first.

Tana Umaga, my opposite number, comes from the other side.

I can guess what he's thinking because I've been in his shoes a thousand times.

If you're gonna come looking for ball in our ruck, you're gonna get smashed.

By the time Umaga wraps an arm around my right thigh and Mealamu grabs me again – lower down by my left knee – the ball has left the hands of their scrum-half, Justin Marshall, and Richie McCaw is gathering it ten metres away.

What happens next becomes excruciating in more ways than one.

First, the experience of being picked up, then dropped from a height, head first and helpless, my shoulder dislocated a split-second after I stretch out my right arm to break the fall, my tour over.

Then, and probably for ever, the sick feeling in my stomach whenever I'm asked to relive the incident, as if I'm being asked for the very first time, not the five-hundredth.

After they've given me a shot of morphine to dull the pain and yanked my shoulder back into its socket, after a Kiwi medic has asked me for the shirt off my back, after the All Blacks have dominated the game and won 21–3, the nightmare continues.

The TV footage that captures the incident best is seen as either incriminating or inconclusive, depending on who's watching it. It shows Mealamu and Umaga grabbing my legs from either side and lifting me off the ground, but there is no clear angle of me being turned upside-down and dropped.

The South African citing officer decides there's no case to answer.

When Clive complains, he's accused of trying to take the focus from our defeat, of burying bad news with a PR ruse.

The All Blacks and the New Zealand media finger Alastair Campbell as the spin doctor working overtime.

At an early-morning press conference I'm asked for my reaction and I've got no problem calling it as I see it.

I speak up because I'm a competitor, and if you take away – unfairly – my ability to compete, then I'm going to respond. I don't possess the equanimity to take a pounding like that and say nothing, to put it down as part of the game. Because it isn't.

I describe it as deliberate foul play, dangerous, a cheap shot.

I say I feel angry, cheated, disappointed with Tana – as a fellow captain – for not coming over as they stretchered me off.

Clive asks if I want to stay with the squad or go home for my operation.

As tour captain I feel I should see it out, not abandon ship. But the controversy over my injury is a story that keeps on giving, and for the next two weeks there is no escape. It keeps dominating the sports pages: picked apart, polarizing opinion, taking on a life of its own. Staying on is one of the biggest mistakes of my life.

I go out most evenings, trying to pass the time with friends who have travelled over, but mostly it makes me feel worse, not better. I'm a sitting duck and the locals want their say. Not much of it is sympathetic.

'Why are you making such a big deal out of it?'

'Couldn't you just have sucked it up?'

Like *I*'m the guilty party.

We lose the second Test by 30 points when Dan Carter

runs amok. Richard Hill and Tom Shanklin get injured and go home.

I stay, feeling increasingly useless. I turn up at training with my arm in a sling. Jonny Wilkinson kicks balls and I run after them, like a wounded dog, until he can't take it any more and tells me to stop.

Our final ignominy comes in the third Test at Eden Park, Auckland. The lads front up in brutally difficult circumstances but we're put away again by an awesome rugby team, beaten by double scores.

*

When I'm back at the Leinster training ground there's a videotape in my cubby-hole and a note that says, 'I think you might like to have this.'

It's from an Irish supporter, perfectly placed at Jade Stadium that night to capture the incident on his hand-held camcorder. A huge sense of relief comes over me when I watch it. After all the talking – all the accusations and denials – the film doesn't lie. It shows me being dropped from a height, upside-down and fully extended. It says more about the moment than the millions of words already written and spoken.

Better late than never, the International Rugby Board responds.

'We are determined that such tackles are removed from the game,' it says. 'They're totally unacceptable and have absolutely no place in rugby.'

The All Blacks coach, Graham Henry, is asked about the new footage.

He sighs. He hasn't seen it. 'I just think it's ridiculous, quite frankly,' he says.

He's disappointed that the question is being asked of him, four months on.

I agree with him on one thing, that it's time to draw a line – preferably for ever.

Wishful thinking.

The next time I see Tana it's 2009. He's coaching in Toulon, and Leinster are on a pre-season camp in Nice.

I spot him watching us from a distance and when I walk towards him I can hear Mal O'Kelly's voice behind me. 'Do him, Drico! Do him!'

I shake Tana's hand and ask him how he is. I don't carry grudges. Never have.

We talk about this and that. He doesn't mention 2005 and I don't have any interest in bringing up past history. What's done is done.

If only.

Like the hat-trick in Paris, it finds its way into the footage that defines my career. It follows me around like a dark cloud, growing more distant, it's true, but never quite fading away to nothing, forcing me to keep answering the same questions from which no good can ever come.

Can you remind us about what happened?

I'd rather not.

Do you think you were targeted, deliberately taken out?

No.

Do you think they meant to injure you?

No.

So it wasn't malicious?

No. It was two guys trying to put down a marker in the first minute. But it was incredibly careless.

Are you still bitter about it?

I'm not bitter, I'm just bored.

Bored and weary.

Bored of being asked about it.

Bored of repeating myself.

Bored of having to defend myself – as well as the two lads – when I did nothing wrong and the laws of the game were changed as a consequence of what happened that day.

Weary of having to bring it up again in these pages, even though I know I must.

Weary of leaving myself open again to the same old stuff . . .

Still whingeing after all these years!

Cry baby! Sook!

Can't he ever let it lie?

Wishing I could wipe it from the collective memory, so that when the Lions tour New Zealand in 2017, nobody will think of mentioning it.

But sometimes, in sport, you don't get to choose all of the things they remember you for.

5. Misery Loves Company

I come home and have my operation. I don't pine for the dressing room, or torture myself about the games I can't play. It's the first really long injury layoff of my career, but I bide my time and try to look on the bright side. If I have to miss half the season, then better the first half than the second.

My arm is in a sling for six weeks. I'm not second-guessing the physios and doctors but neither am I a sheep following their every instruction without asking what's going on. I want to have a proper understanding of my body and my recovery.

'Why am I doing this?'

'What's the rationale behind that?'

Four months pass before I start to run again. And it's murder. I pant my way through it, dead to the world. I tell myself that I should have been on the bike weeks ago, preparing myself for this, but the truth is that the bike could only have got me to a certain level of fitness. The running horror-show was unavoidable.

In early August I sit down with Leinster's new head coach, the Australian Michael Cheika. I know little about him, other than that his coaching background is with Padova in Italy and Randwick in Sydney, an underwhelming CV, just like Gary Ella's before him. He's not what you'd call a heavy hitter and the Leinster branch are taking another risk.

He offers me the captaincy and asks for my help in the

transition. It's a real show of faith, given that I won't be kicking a ball for him until the end of the year.

I'm grateful, flattered.

I take it on and let him know how I see things.

I tell him Leinster have been a shambles for two years, that we've got no meaningful future unless something drastic happens. We're learning nothing. He's our fourth coach in four years and mentally we're in a bad place.

There's one other thing, I say.

My contract is up next summer. I'm coming up to twenty-seven years old and I can't afford to hang around much longer. I need to win silverware – or at least threaten to. So I tell Cheiks straight up that I'm giving it a year. If there's real progress, then good. If not, it'll be goodbye.

He doesn't try to talk me into a new deal. He doesn't bullshit me. He just says, 'Fine. Let's go. We've got a lot of work to do.'

*

The final year of a player's contract can turn into a drawn-out game of poker, and you need to bring some decent cards to the negotiating table. By 2005 it's been years since an Ireland international was tempted abroad by a better deal. Not since Rog gave legs to the somewhat dubious story that he was on the brink of accepting a $12 million offer from H. Wayne Huizenga, owner of the Miami Dolphins, has anyone even picked up a gun, still less put it to the IRFU's head.

I'm not planning on any drastic action and I'm far from sure that leaving the country would be the right move, but I owe it to myself to see what might be out there. All the better if word gets back to the Union that I'm looking at options and they come to the conclusion that I won't necessarily be accepting whatever number they push across the table.

In France there are agents more than keen to hook you up with a deal, go-betweens who set up meetings with any club in the market for new blood. For years Dad has been looking after my professional interests to good effect. He talks to one of the agents and the word comes back that Biarritz and Toulouse would like to sound me out.

Subtlety is paramount. The last thing I want to do is ram it down the IRFU's throat. The plan is that I go to France and sit in the stand at Stade Aguiléra when Biarritz host Stade Français. If somebody takes a photograph, all well and good. The word will get around. Speculation will follow. The Union will get the message that I wasn't there for the good of my health without me having to spell it out in capital letters.

The plan blows up in my face. I visit Toulouse and they are models of discretion, but over by the Bay of Biscay the welcome isn't exactly subtle. Three months on from winning the French championship, Biarritz are still in party mode and their president, Marcel Martin, is the life and soul of the celebrations. He invites me to a pre-match corporate lunch at the stadium where the champions' shield, the Bouclier de Brennus, is on display.

So far, so good. I sit back and take it all in. There's a lot to like about the thought of a new life in the south of France with a team that wins trophies, a coming force in European rugby. Then Marcel loses the run of himself.

He interrupts his own speech and points me out. *'Je souhaite la bienvenue à Brian O'Driscoll!'* He calls me up to pose for a picture with the Bouclier.

About two hundred people turn and look at me.

I stay in my chair, embarrassed.

Marcel persists: he's not exactly a shrinking violet.

Up I go. The Bouclier is resting on the table and I stand alongside it. Cameras flash all around me.

Marcel isn't done yet. 'Will you do us the honour of kicking off the game?' he asks.

At this moment I need the French agent by my side, reminding Marcel that I'm there to talk, not to make an exhibition of myself. But I'm on my own and it seems rude to say no in a roomful of Biarritz supporters when joining the club is a genuine possibility.

Next, he asks me to do the kick-off while wearing a Biarritz T-shirt. Now things are getting out of hand. I draw the line – but I've already allowed myself to cross it.

I'm announced to the crowd and out I walk to loud cheers, as if I've just signed a four-year contract. The word comes back afterwards that some of the Biarritz players on the pitch think I've actually joined.

The game is live on French television and news of my little foray reaches the lads back home in no time. The slagging starts. The IRFU take a dim view.

So much for the cunning plan. As subtle as a shout from a rooftop.

But years later, when the Union is slow in coming to the table with certain players, I hear them mulling openly about their options.

'Maybe I need to take a trip down to Biarritz . . .'

*

Michael Cheika has David Knox as his backs coach, a pal from his Randwick days, capped thirteen times for Australia at fly-half. Knoxy is nuts and together they're the oddest double act going, but what they have works. They reinvigorate a tired set-up.

In training, the squad stands in a circle listening to Cheiks, while Knoxy's over the far side of the field, trying to drop balls right into the middle of the huddle. We see these bombs descending on us and cover our heads.

'Don't mind the idiot over there,' Cheiks says. 'Listen to what I'm saying!'

When I return to full training the difference in the mood of the squad is striking. The fun is back. We have new voices, new ideas and a level of coaching that I haven't had at Leinster for a couple of years. They've brought Felipe Contepomi – rarely Declan's idea of a first-team starter – back into the team at 10.

Cheiks says that he's got a plan: win the league in year two and the Heineken Cup in year three. I buy into what he's telling me. I put to bed – for a while at least – the notion of leaving Ireland and sign a new deal in December, a couple of weeks before making my comeback. The contract extension runs until the end of the 2007 World Cup, less than two years away. It's not quite an emphatic message that my long-term future lies with Leinster, but it's a start.

The return to action amounts to an uneventful half an hour against Ulster at Ravenhill in a Celtic League match on 26 December, the highlight of which is the lovely and much appreciated ovation I get when taking to the pitch as a replacement. On New Year's Eve I'm in from the start against Munster in a 35–23 win at the RDS. Two nice victories but something's wrong. I'm protecting my shoulder in the tackle, worried about getting a bang. Instead of extending my right arm and committing to a full-blooded hit, I'm tucking it into the sling position and trying to shove people over.

I'm missing tackles. I feel vulnerable in contact. There's doubt in me that hasn't been there since my early days at Blackrock.

Shane Jennings, flying it with his new club, Leicester, has been through a dislocated shoulder himself. He tells me there's going to be a moment when I make a tackle and get a clunk that tests the strength of it. It's then and only then that I'll start trusting it, he says.

My third game back is away to Llanelli in the first week of January 2006 and the uncertainty remains. In the penultimate round of the Heineken Cup group stage, I score two tries against Glasgow, but I'm still off the pace defensively, still wondering if the shoulder will ever feel 100 per cent again.

Eight days after Glasgow, we travel to Bath for a game we have to win to stay in the Heineken Cup. They've already beaten us in Dublin. They've won five from five and conceded just four tries along the way.

This is the day when the clunk comes. I make an early tackle and the shoulder holds up fine. In that moment my confidence sky-rockets, just like Jenno said it would. It's a big turning point on one of the most exhilarating days of my career.

In the first twenty minutes we rip Bath apart and score three quality tries. Slick and imaginative rugby. Everything done at pace and with accuracy. Everyone on song.

Den puts in a great diagonal cross-kick to Shaggy for the first, Felipe is as sharp as a tack and intercepts for the second, and I cut a nice line and snake past three tacklers to help create the third, with Darce running a support line and Will Green touching down.

I put Shaggy over for a fourth try, then score the fifth myself after another great move from deep that Bath can't do anything to stop. With eight minutes left we're 35–9 ahead and flying. Not even the concession of two late tries can wipe the smiles off our faces at the end.

You have days when you're hot and everything falls into place.

Paris 2000.

Brisbane 2001.

Bath 2006.

We qualify for the quarter-finals as eighth seed. Our reward is a trip down to the reigning champions, Toulouse.

*

Life in the Maples with Barry has been carefree and fun. But life moves on. A year has passed since I bought a new house two minutes away in Goatstown and started having it renovated. Now the house is ready and it's time to go.

Barry isn't joining me. We've agreed that I'm moving in on my own for a trial period, but we both know there'll be no going back. I need to experience something new, maybe grow up a little. It's the next phase of my life.

I go into the 2006 Six Nations confident about our chances. We have players on form and two teams in the quarter-finals of the Heineken Cup, Munster having topped their pool.

Some of the wind goes from our sails in a sloppy opening-day win against Italy and then the ship capsizes in the first forty-seven minutes in Paris. We're almost drowned, France scoring six tries and 43 points to our three.

Then Rog comes up with a try to take some of the ugliness off the scoreline.

Then Darce goes over.

Donncha O'Callaghan smashes his way in from close range.

Andrew Trimble adds a fourth.

Twenty-eight unanswered points in twelve minutes: from 43–3 to 43–31.

It's no longer a face-saving exercise. It's now about game-saving, about trying to complete one of the most unlikely comebacks of all time in the ten minutes we have left.

France are like a fighter clinging to the ropes and waiting for the bell. They're gone. Mentally and physically spent. We own the ball, create the chances but don't execute. Ten more minutes and it could have been one of our greatest days. Instead it's just one of our strangest.

We beat Wales and Scotland and go back to Twickenham looking for a second Triple Crown.

We're trailing 24–21 with two minutes left. Strings gets the ball away from the back of a scrum on our own 22. Rog chips over the defence and I'm about two yards ahead of him when the ball leaves his boot. Nobody notices. It bounces beautifully for me, up and into my hands without having to break stride. I get over the halfway line and ship it out to Shaggy on the right touchline. He pins his ears back and goes for it but Lewis Moody brings him down. We recycle once and go infield, recycle again and go back to Shaggy. He takes the hit from Moody, stretches out his telescopic right arm and bangs the ball down. I can't think of another player who could have put the chance away.

Rog lashes over the conversion from the touchline – a monumental strike that puts us four points clear. A penalty or a drop goal is no good to them now. They need a try and they don't have time to get it: Simon Easterby's brilliant retake from the kick-off sees to that.

Another Triple Crown. Just in case anybody thought our win at Twickenham in 2004 was a bit lucky, we've done them again.

*

The early months of 2006 are making up for a horrible 2005. I go back to Leinster to prepare for the quarter-final against Toulouse.

Knoxy's skills sessions with the backs are brilliantly bonkers. For too long our drills have been routine, over-familiar. His approach is anything but.

He sets up four sets of cones on the training pitch, each with different colour combinations. He shouts an instruction and you have to get to the right cone, then pass. But he doesn't shout a colour. Too easy.

'Newcastle Knights!' he bellows.

The Newcastle Knights rugby league team play in blue and red. Sprint to that cone and pass, until the next man up gets the shout.

'Russell Crowe!'

Instant confusion. Laughter.

Knoxy just keeps calling out the name. It's his game and we can bail if we want, but nobody wants to.

'Russell Crowe!'

I'm a rugby league fan so I work it out. Russell Crowe's team is the South Sydney Rabbitohs. Red and green stripes. Head for that cone then and pass. Bang!

Everyone agrees that Knoxy's off his head but he knows exactly what he's doing. He's making us think and react and he's making it a laugh, something we look forward to every day.

Toulouse, with my old team-mate Trevor Brennan in the second row, haven't lost a European match in their own city for five and a half years and they're not expected to surrender that record to us. Thirty-eight thousand people are packed into the Stadium Municipal and another ten thousand watching a big screen seven kilometres away at their regular ground, Stade Ernest-Wallon.

They see one of the great games. Toulouse go well but we play some savage rugby. Shaggy busts them open midway through the first half, and when Felipe gets on his shoulder I'm tracking him from way out on the left. He pops it up to me one-handed and I bolt between the posts.

We go 16–6 ahead, but Toulouse start forcing penalties and pull it back to 19–18. Just as it seems to be moving away from us, we hit them with three second-half tries in eleven minutes. Freddie Michalak panics under pressure from Keith Gleeson, and Cameron Jowitt, our blindside flanker, gallops on to score. Then we go at them from within our own 22, spinning it wide to Den, who disappears down the left touchline, linking with Darce, then taking the return pass to score in the corner.

Shaggy surges through them for our fourth and we lead 41–21 against the champions in their own backyard. Toulouse come on a late charge but we're too far ahead. We win, 41–35.

When it's over, the applause we get from their supporters really means something.

Respect.

*

Munster get past Perpignan in an arm-wrestle a couple of hours later, so the all-Irish semi-final is set for 23 April at

Lansdowne Road. We're into uncharted territory and the country goes ballistic in the three-week build-up.

On the back of our performances in Bath and Toulouse, and a total of thirty-two tries in seven games, we're installed as favourites. Trying to guess what Munster have in mind for us isn't rocket science, especially when you know the mindset of some of the big players in their pack – Paulie, Jerry Flannery, Donners.

We can almost hear them from 120 miles away.

'Workrate, workrate, workrate – we'll out-work them!'

They feel they're fitter than us. I don't think they work any harder than we do, but they see it differently and it's a big part of their armoury.

On the morning of the game I send Rog a text: *Let's go hard.*

He sends me one back: *Not too fucking hard.*

My heart starts to sink as our coach makes its way to Lansdowne Road. The ticket distribution is supposed to be 50–50 but there are red jerseys on the streets, outside the pubs, everywhere the eye can see. When we go onto the pitch for a warm-up it's already filling up and it's 75 per cent red.

We cling to the faint hope that our fans are like the cavalry, having one more pint before they appear on the horizon in massive numbers, but when we go back out it's an even greater sea of red.

Once the whistle blows it's every bit as one-sided on the pitch. Denis Leamy scores off a rolling maul after nine minutes. Whenever we threaten to get up a head of steam their defence smashes us back.

A lot of our tries in Europe have come from lineout ball taken at the back, but Munster have that sussed, and when we're forced to throw to the front, Felipe is under instant pressure when the pass comes his way.

Any time I question anything with Joël Jutge, he's flustered by their fans kicking up a racket as I'm making my way across from the centre. We might as well be in Thomond Park. He won't talk, he won't even meet my eye. He backs off from me with body language that says, 'Go away – I don't need this crowd on my back.'

It's a painful reminder of a few things I've come to feel about captaincy.

You're at a massive disadvantage doing it from the centre, because numbers 1 to 9 are the only players in the right position to fight a team's corner with the ref in the moments when the big calls are being made. The demands are different during the week, but on the field a captain needs to be at the coalface – on the scene when the fast decisions are needed, coming up from the scrum and getting in the ref's head straight away when he can go either way. Running across from thirty metres away to have a word just pisses people off.

But all this I keep to myself, because I don't want to do myself out of a job.

Time after time, Munster deny us the breathing space we need to create and they finish us off with two late tries. Rog hands off Mal, runs in under the posts and then hurdles the advertising boards in celebration. Trevor Halstead bolts downfield and scores off an intercept.

It ends 30–6. Certain scorelines flatter the winning team, but this isn't one of them.

It's a horrible experience. We are hurt, embarrassed, humiliated.

Den and Shaggy are with me on the way home. We stop at an off-licence to pick up a bottle of gin and some tonic to drown our sorrows.

Later on we head for town. Misery loves company. We figure we might as well see out a bad day together.

By the time the night is over I've broken up with Glenda.

*

A week after Munster become Heineken Cup champions, beating Biarritz in Cardiff, we play our last game of the Celtic League season in Edinburgh. If we win and Ulster lose or draw away to the Ospreys then we're champions and Cheiks has ticked off his first target a year ahead of schedule.

We beat Edinburgh handily. With two minutes left in Swansea, Ulster are losing 17–16. Then David Humphreys launches a drop-goal attempt from miles out that cannons off both uprights before falling over the crossbar. They take the title by a point.

It's another kick in the guts, but when we look back at our season as a whole – and remember the rocky place it started from – the truth is we have overachieved. The team is better. The coaching is better. The whole structure has improved out of all recognition. The days of changing out of the back of our cars have gone for good.

Through the fog of defeat, we can see hope.

*

My return to New Zealand comes in June. We play two Tests, in Hamilton and Auckland. Tana Umaga has retired from international rugby but Keven Mealamu is still on the scene and it's daunting going back there. Tough enough playing them in normal circumstances, but against a backdrop of what happened on and since the Lions tour, it's doubly hard.

The first Test in Hamilton starts horrifically. After thirty-five seconds they launch a breakaway from inside their own

22 and Doug Howlett scores in the corner. But ten minutes later I cut inside Joe Rokocoko and Ma'a Nonu and touch down for a try that Rog converts. With twenty-two minutes left we're eight points ahead. I know from bitter experience that eight points can be eaten up very quickly when you're playing New Zealand. And so it proves again. They score 19 unanswered points and snuff us out.

A week later they get off to an even faster start. After half an hour we're getting hockeyed 17–0. Then, Paulie and Jerry Flannery blast their way over before half-time and suddenly we're alive again. When Rog lands a penalty early in the second half we're just three points behind and they've given us a sniff.

Into the last ten minutes we're still asking questions, but history repeats. Luke McAlister smashes down our defence and goes in under the posts. Same old story.

The following day a gang of us have a night out in Auck-land. Joey Johns is in our group. He's the ultimate rugby-league legend, a god of the Newcastle Knights in New South Wales. He has played a National Rugby League match against the New Zealand Warriors earlier in the day and he's up for a laugh in an Irish bar.

A touch worse for wear, I climb up on Joey's shoulders. I'm unfazed by the punter with the camera who captures the moment and promptly emails it to a tabloid back home.

Skiddy texts the next day. I'm on the front page of the paper, looking like I'm demob happy, six days before we take on Australia in Perth.

I call Karl Richardson, our media guy, and ask him to break it to Eddie.

Eddie gets his debrief but says nothing. He doesn't even send somebody to have a word with me. Usually my cousin

Gary, our team doctor, does the job. The lads call Gaz the Consigliere – he's Tom Hagen to Eddie's Vito Corleone, the special representative of the boss bringing messages from on high.

I get on very well with Eddie. Always have done. It's a relationship built on mutual respect. I know he's not impressed with my front-page appearance, but he cuts me some slack. We carry on to Australia without a word spoken about it. We lose, 37–15.

There's a certain consolation from the brand of rugby we produced against the All Blacks. There is progress in the shift of attitude among us, the inner belief that we are good enough to win Test matches in the southern hemisphere. But at the end of another tour the bare stats have a disappointingly familiar look: played three, lost three.

Back at home, the economy is still roaring ahead. People are losing the run of themselves, parting with hard-earned cash on essentials like the hot tub.

I'm afflicted by the madness. I'm not normally one for splurging but I hand over an obscene amount of money for a tub so big it has to be craned over the roof of my new house and into the back garden.

As the summer moves on, there are Saturday nights when I come home and find friends I haven't even been out with sitting up in the hot tub.

'What are you doing here?'

'I heard you were coming back.'

'Who told you?'

'I met so-and-so. He said you were coming back.'

'Ah, right. Fair enough!'

I get one good summer out of the tub.

Years later, when the online auction sites are groaning

with unwanted Irish hot tubs, somebody tells me I might get two grand for mine, on a good day.

I think about the two grand and I think about the embarrassment of having it craned back over the house. I decide it could work as a paddling pool one day, but until then the insects are welcome to it.

6. Hope and History

When Leinster training resumes after the summer, it's the first time we've started a new season with the same head coach since Matt Williams's last stand way back in 2002–3.

I like the look of what we're building and I like the shift in our attitude. Munster's Heineken Cup win has raised the bar and changed the game, for us as well as for them. For the first time it feels like we need our careers to be defined by what we've won.

Cheiks has fought our corner at every turn. He has demanded and delivered better facilities and higher standards in everything we do. Along with Knoxy, he has improved us on the training ground. He has put his faith in Felipe at 10 and been rewarded with brilliance at times. And he has brought through some rising stars: Jamie Heaslip, Rob Kearney, Luke Fitzgerald and more.

Twelve months have passed since I told Cheiks I was giving it a year to see where he could take us, and after hedging my bets the previous season, I'm ready to commit long term. Four more years. Let's get it done. And let's see how far we can go.

I get over Munster's line for a couple of tries in my second run-out of the season and the headlines are all about our revenge, but it's not a word that has any rugby currency in early October. A month later, South Africa are first up in the autumn internationals, and with a gale blowing behind us we go in at half-time 22–3 up in a game beautifully controlled by

Rog. We see it out without too much trouble, 32–15. We're a coming team: everyone says it. Ten months away from the World Cup and we've never had so much respect.

The following day I'm home alone, crashed out on the couch, flicking through the channels. I'm watching a repeat of the chat show *Tubridy Tonight* when the host announces that his next guests are stars of a television series I've never seen.

'Please welcome – from the hit TV drama *The Clinic* – Amy Huberman and Leigh Arnold, ladies and gentlemen!' says Ryan Tubridy.

There's something about Amy once she starts telling stories. She's smart, outgoing, genuine, fun. The audience loves her. I sit up and think . . .

She's gorgeous.

Even though she's from south Dublin, a couple of miles from my house, I've never seen her around. I start wondering if she has a boyfriend. Tubridy doesn't go there and I can think of only one person on the planet who's likely to be in the know.

Joanne Byrne is more than a top-class PR agent, she's a good friend. I give her a call. I don't want to come straight out with Amy's name, like some kind of stalker, so I take the scenic route.

'You know loads of people,' I suggest.

'Yes,' she agrees.

'There was this girl on with Ryan Tubridy the other night . . . blonde, really good laugh, great way about her.'

'Amy Huberman. From *The Clinic.*'

'You know her?'

'I do. She's been working in London.'

'Well, actually, I was wondering . . .'

'Leave it with me,' says Joanne.

*

Two weeks later, I'm in my car on Fitzwilliam Square, look-ing at my Nokia and waiting for a text from Joanne. She's in the Merrion Hotel, just around the corner, alone but expect-ing company.

She has promised to deliver Amy, suspecting nothing, to the hotel's elegant lounge. Amy will arrive with Joanne's co-conspirator Norma Sheehan, another actress from *The Clinic*, whom I've met before. The three of them will order coffee.

From there, the scene will play out like this.

I will walk in and look around expectantly for my two wingmen, Barry and his buddy Kieron O'Boyle, who answers to Fruity. I won't find them because they won't be there. Instead, as my eyes scan the lounge, I will recognize Joanne. We will greet one another warmly. I'll also salute Norma, even though we've only met the once. The conversation will proceed along the following lines.

'Brian! Good to see you! What brings you here?'

'Hi, Joanne! How are *you*? I'm just meeting up with a few of the lads . . . They don't seem to be here yet.'

'Oh, right! Why don't you join us until they arrive? I don't know if you've met —'

'I haven't.'

'Amy . . . Amy Huberman.'

Approximately ten minutes later, after impressing Amy no end, I will glance across as Barry and Fruity make their entrance.

'Here are the lads,' I'll say. 'I'd better go. Listen, lovely to have met you. Hopefully see you again soon!'

I'm in position fifteen minutes ahead of Amy's ETA when the first hitch in this foolproof plan emerges, via a text to Joanne from Norma.

They're running late, half an hour late, maybe more.

Barry and Fruity are ensconced in a pub nearby, waiting for their walk-on parts. If they come in too early it'll completely mess up the plan, so I fire Barry a text: *Not yet. Have another pint.*

With time to kill I start getting nervous. I consider the Merrion's well-heeled clientele, the grown-up surrounds of its Georgian drawing rooms, and worry that Amy will judge me.

'Twenty-seven years old and he meets his mates for drinks at the Merrion! How wanky is that?'

I start fretting that she'll think I'm creepy if my cover is blown and she finds out about the plan.

Finally, Joanne texts through the signal, but she's too quick on the draw. I'm halfway there when I see Amy and Norma bearing down on the hotel from the opposite direction. I double back to the car and a voice in my head tells me to put the key in the ignition and leave them to it.

I text Joanne: *Maybe this isn't for me.*

Her reply is instant: *Are you a man or a mouse?*

In a twenty-second phone call, she makes it clear that she's leaning strongly towards the latter. 'This could be the woman of your dreams!' she says.

I'm not wearing my glasses when I walk into the lounge – call it vanity or eagerness to impress. I wander straight past them – twice – before Joanne calls me over.

Amy's in the Ladies: a major departure from the script in the very first scene.

Joanne and Norma sit on armchairs, all smiles and knowing winks. Norma motions me to the empty couch with a look that says, 'Big enough for two.'

'I'm in on this too, by the way,' she clarifies.

Two young boys come over and ask for autographs as Amy returns, and we've barely been introduced when Barry and Fruity make their entrance, half-cut.

Barry surveys the scene and immediately dispenses with the game plan to pull me away from it. He doesn't even pull up a chair. He plants himself right between me and Amy on the couch, and Fruity squeezes in at the far end.

'Lovely to meet you, ladies – I'm Barry,' he says.

After the first hour of laughs and jokes – half of them told against me – I take him aside. 'Will you stop trying to be Mr Hilarity here? I'm looking bleedin' vanilla!'

But the girls end up liking him so much it somehow works in my favour. He starts trying out material for his upcoming stand-up comedy debut in Temple Bar and Joanne sees an opportunity. 'Let's make a pact now,' she says. 'Even if nobody else turns up, the six of us here will be there.'

She calls me on the way home: 'After this, you're on your own.'

Three days later we're in the audience at the Ha'penny Inn, cheering Barry on. The place is packed with his supporters. He's declared the night's comedy king.

Me and Amy, we talk over a couple of beers. One of her great qualities is that she gives an incredible amount to every conversation she's part of.

Joanne has an early start in the morning. She heads away but texts me twenty minutes later: *Just had to pay €80 to get my car unclamped. You'd better ask her out now!*

Even though we're getting along like a house on fire, I'm

nervous and stuttering when I find the bottle to ask Amy for her number.

She hands it over. Nice one!

After five or six weeks, I finally feel comfortable enough to fill her in on the set-up at the Merrion.

'By the way, I hope you don't think I'm an absolute loon-bag, but . . .'

After eight weeks, I know I want to marry her.

*

We enter the Six Nations campaign ranked third in the world, thanks to our big November, after backing up the South Africa win with a powerful performance against Australia – another decent scalp. Ireland haven't won a Grand Slam in fifty-nine years but we know it's within us this time. We like our chances and the bookies have us down as favourites.

With the bulldozers heading for Lansdowne Road, we've got France and England coming to our home for the next three years – Croke Park, sacred ground for the Gaelic Athletic Association and a phenomenal stadium with 82,000 seats. For us, it's a deep privilege. For our country, it's history in the making.

Me and Eddie fly to London for the Six Nations media launch at the Hurlingham Club in Fulham. There's a carpet of snow on the rolling lawns outside and a posse of photographers looking to make tomorrow's back pages. They line up the six national captains and give us our instructions. 'Can you all throw a snowball straight ahead?'

'Brian – you were a bit slow letting your one go.'

Fabien Pelous is told to stand in the middle, holding the Six Nations trophy.

'Can the rest of you throw a snowball at Fabien?'

It's the curtain-raiser in a four-hour endurance test. Inside the Georgian mansion, I'm put behind a small table with Eddie alongside me and peppered with questions.

To varying degrees I know most of the reporters gathered round me in a semi-circle, but when their notebooks are out and the red lights show on their Dictaphones, it's game on. Once you let your guard down in any kind of interview, once you fall into conversational mode, more than likely there'll be trouble round the bend.

You get hammered for being bland, but there's no percentage in playing to the gallery. You're never far away from making a serious error. And there's no benefit in throwing out headline remarks, unless you want the headlines.

So you switch into character, you become a slightly different person. You do your best to give the journalists something they can work with, but you stay in control – remembering that your fellow players will be reading what you're saying. And when you do it often enough, for long enough, that persona is what 99 per cent of people put you down as.

Careful. Safe. The stereotypical southside Dublin rugby jock.

In that press-conference environment, you start seeing the headline before they're even done asking the question.

Q: 'Brian, you've got a favourable draw, you're coming off the back of a great autumn. You must be feeling quietly confident?'

Ireland have look of champions says confident O'Driscoll

A: 'The favourites tag is just that – it's a tag. I guess someone has to be favourites. But we've been favourites before and not won, so I think you don't read too much into it.'

Q: 'After nearly sixty years, would you say it's now or never for an Irish Grand Slam?'

DRICO – IT'S NOW OR NEVER!

A: 'No, I wouldn't say that . . .'

A look of mild disgust shows briefly on the now-or-never questioner's face. But I'm not done yet: I hit him with the old chestnut.

'If you start looking beyond your first match you're going to slip up, particularly when you're playing against Wales . . .'

And so it goes on. You butter up the opposition, you spread it on thick. Because everyone reads the media and every opponent is looking for a reason to get the hump.

You give them nothing but bouquets.

You're not there to sell newspapers. You're there to say whatever needs to be said in the best interests of your team.

*

A few hours after I fly back to Dublin a photographer sees me on O'Connell Street, waiting for Amy outside the Savoy Cinema in my car.

It's four days since a Sunday tabloid made our new relationship public knowledge and he starts firing off frames. Amy and Norma get in and we make off across the other side of the city for some late food.

The photographer follows us all the way. I make it hard for him to get the two of us together by walking ahead once I've parked.

I know him. I've posed for him at events before, sometimes against my better judgement. Unlike in LA or London, most of the Dublin snappers are courteous, but he's just plain rude. No concern for anything other than his picture.

He's not getting it.

A couple of weeks later, we're on the way out of some small-time première in town when a load of cameras start flashing. It's like a scene from the TV news. We get into the back of a taxi and a few of them run up to the window on Amy's side and start shooting. I turn away and bring my phone up to my face.

It's an instinctive reaction, like an injured player covering his face when he's being stretchered off the pitch. It's total nervousness at being caught in an uncomfortable situation.

The tabloids have a different take on it.

Smitten Drico plays dodge-the-camera

Rugger bugger leaps into waiting cab – nearly forgets bewildered date

We're both shaken by the experience. For me it's not the first time, but neither is it normal.

No matter how many times it happens, it never feels normal.

*

I enter the 2007 Six Nations with my match weight at 97 kilos, seven more than I weighed in the summer of 2001 on the Lions tour. I'm playing pretty well but my try-scoring stats have taken a hit: only three in the last nineteen Tests. You could argue that carrying around an extra stone isn't doing much for my explosiveness, or you could say it's the extra ballast that gets me another yard through contact in a game that is becoming more and more attritional.

We're trailing in the first half against Wales at the Millennium Stadium when Geordan Murphy thumps up a garryowen from just inside their half, collects it himself thirty metres downfield, then pops the ball to Paulie, who busts them another four metres over the gain line with red jerseys hanging out of him. Strings takes it from the bottom of a pile of bodies and ships it right, to David Wallace, who spins off his man and rips back into the contact zone, legs pumping.

Stringer isn't far off the left-hand touchline when he fishes it out of another ruck and fires out a long pass. It takes 5.9 seconds and three pairs of fast hands for the ball to reach me, a foot from the opposite touchline and ten metres from the try line. I step inside their winger, Chris Czekaj, and momentum carries me past a second defender before a one-handed finish. As a team try, it's right up there – but it's a rare enough piece of precision in a game that's more about bludgeon.

'If we play like that next week, we'll lose,' Eddie says.

When the team runs out to face France at Croke Park, I'm watching from the stand, awed by the occasion but sick about not being on the field. It's down to a slight hamstring strain I picked up towards the end of the Wales match. Even though I could have played at a push, Eddie reckons we've got enough without me to get past France and I'm best held off for the England game – which sounds like a plan until Vincent Clerc scythes through our defence and wipes out our four-point lead, with Paulie hanging off his back and less than two minutes left.

It's heartbreaking, horrible, hard to take.

It makes the idea of losing to England – of being beaten in both of our first two games at Croke Park – completely unbearable and absolutely unthinkable.

For two weeks the whole country gets caught up in a bigger narrative about the meaning of 'God Save the Queen' being sung on the same field where the Black and Tans opened fire and killed fourteen Irish civilians on Bloody Sunday, 1920. Among the victims was Michael Hogan, fullback in the Tipperary football team playing that day, after whom one of the Croke Park grandstands was named. The sense of occasion inside our camp – the intensity and togetherness that we feel – only adds to all of that. All we know is that we cannot lose.

No matter what, we cannot lose.

The beauty of our sport, what sets it apart from so many others, is that often it comes down to who has the greater desire on the day, because at Test level there's often very little between two teams. At Croke Park on 24 February 2007, there are no circumstances under which it is possible for England to want it more.

Turn back the clock to the Grand Slam decider of 2003 – in which England battered us from beginning to end – and you could say the same about the level of our desire versus theirs. We didn't feel anything less than 100 per cent up for it, but for that England team there was more at stake than a Grand Slam. It went deeper. They were better than us to begin with, but they had also found themselves in a place where they could not allow themselves to lose.

You can bring in a coachload of sports psychologists, but none of them will ever take you to where we are mentally when the president of Ireland, Mary McAleese, walks down the line of our players. She doesn't just shake their hands, she fixes them in the eye and gives them a message from the Irish people.

'This is the day.'

In rugby, you see it in the reactions – and sometimes in the lack of them.

Twenty-one minutes in, we're three points ahead when Rog hoists one from our half. As it falls from the sky Olly Morgan stands near their 22, waiting to collect. He sees me shooting up to smack him and calls for a mark. He's inches off the ground and in possession of the ball when I hit him a split-second later with everything I have.

It's an illegal tackle, it's arguably dangerous. As Joël Jutge signals for a penalty Morgan is stretched out alongside me on the floor while Josh Lewsey is the only one to cry foul with any purpose. It's all set up for the arrival of their enforcers, raising hell about the early hit that has put their man down, but the whistle has barely blown when their scrum-half Harry Ellis takes a tap and hares upfield, bringing their entire pack with him, away from the scene of the crime.

Eleven minutes later, shortly after Girvan Dempsey has run in our first try, he leaves the ground to field a high kick from Jonny Wilkinson and gets taken out in the air by Ellis and their openside flanker, Magnus Lund.

Slow down the video. Compare and contrast.

Paulie, Strings, Rog and Darce already have their arms raised at the exact moment when Girvan's body hits the turf, still clinging to the ball. Alongside them, I'm already effing and blinding and John Hayes is arriving from the opposite side, just in case he's needed.

Five of us head straight for Ellis and Lund, bunched together like sprinters charging at a tape. I just about get there first and then Monsieur Jutge runs in and breaks it up. As he backs away the crowd are going mental and Lund knows he's in trouble. England already have Danny Grew-cock in the bin and he's desperate to stay on the field.

Jutge signals for me to come across and I stand alongside him with my hands on my hips as Lund takes his bollocking and repents.

'I'm sorry! I'm sorry!'

Then the ref turns around and sticks his whistle in my face. He's not happy about my little vigilante moment. He points out that he had the situation under control. 'I blow my whistle immediately!' he says. 'Don't come here!'

I grimace for a couple of seconds. He's not sure how I'm taking it.

'Are you agree with that?'

'Fair enough.'

'Thank you very much!'

He closes the book on it, he keeps his cards in his pocket. 'No more!'

He's walking away, it's over – but then Magnus Lund throws in one last act of contrition. He apologizes to me.

'Mate – I'm sorry!'

When you're up against England, you need all the edge you can get. In our sport, there's a time and a place for niceties. This isn't the time and it definitely isn't the place.

I'm still giving him some chat as we walk back to our respective teams. The score at Croke Park is Ireland 16, England 3, and the best is yet to come.

On sixty-four minutes it arrives, a thing of absolute beauty. Denis Leamy rumbles into contact and trucks it up three metres short, left of the posts. Stringer zips it back to Rog, and if I live to be a hundred I will never tire of watching what happens next. Rog faces the opposite corner flag and floats the most beautifully weighted pass across the field. Shaggy jumps and plucks it out of the air, like a high-class Gaelic footballer rising to claim a goalkeeper's kickout. He's got Josh Lewsey upsides him but he's way off the ground and over the try line. Rog bangs the conversion straight through the middle from a metre off the touchline.

By the end, there's 30 points between us. Call it a perfect day.

*

A one-point win in Edinburgh gives us another Triple Crown, but in the dressing room it feels more like a Slam has slipped between our fingers. England's win over France means the three of us are level on points with a match to go; France are first on points difference, four ahead of us.

On the final Saturday, our match in Rome is first up. We win 51–24, which means France need to beat the Scots by at least 24 points to deny us the title.

There's a small television showing it in the lobby of our Rome hotel, but after a while I can't bear to watch and I walk away. When I come back the clock is in red and France are 20 points ahead – four short of what they need for the championship – and camped on the Scottish line.

Elvis Vermeulen picks the ball from the bottom of a ruck and disappears from sight under a pile of bodies. He comes up claiming a try.

The TV commentary is in French.

'*Arbitrage video!*' the guy says.

They show it from different angles and in every one the ball looks like it's been held up. The commentator can't see it grounded. Nobody can. They keep showing it – six, seven, eight times.

'*Où est le ballon?*'

'*C'est difficile!*'

After two torturous minutes, the decision is handed down to Craig Joubert by an Irish TMO, no less. Joubert lifts his arm.

It's St Patrick's Day in the Eternal City, we've scored 50 in the sunshine, and we feel sick to our stomachs.

A hamstring injury picked up late against Italy puts me out of Leinster's Heineken Cup quarter-final against Wasps. At Adams Park on the last day in March, we go down by 22 points. The Cheika project is still a work in progress: we're too inconsistent and we're short a couple of big-game players.

With a World Cup around the corner, I'm not risked for the rest of the season. I spend the last few weeks bulking up in the gym, lifting heavy upper-body weights, three or four big sessions a week.

I am twenty-eight years old, I've been a full-time rugby player almost nine seasons, and I've got one winner's medal to show for it: the Celtic League of 2001–2.

*

On holiday down in Florida with Shaggy, Denis and Victor, I discover the meatball and Parmesan sandwich. It's so beautiful that one is never enough. We fly to New York for part two of the trip and spend some time hanging out at a bar, Brass Monkey in the Meatpacking District, owned by my friend Sean Cunningham. It's four years since we ran into Sean and his mate Joe Carbonari and struck up a conversation out of the blue. Sometimes you just hit it off with people. And when you know Sean, you get to know the best of New York.

I'm on my holidays, so I'm tipping away at a nice few beers, grateful for the anonymity. I get chatting to one of the Brass Monkey's security guys about the World Cup, three months away. At the end of a heavy night, I spill out onto the sidewalk. Across the street, I hear a thick New York accent. I look over and it's the same bouncer.

'Hey *Bri*-an!' he says, grinning. 'What's going on, man? What about the world *champ*-ionships in France?'

The third leg of the holiday is Los Angeles. For this trip it's just me and my old pal from Clontarf, Damien O'Donohue, the playboy of the Western world. Damo's a trained solicitor who works with the music promoters MCD. I would have known him locally from living in the same parish and even though he's two years younger than me he was never stuck for something to say. Fifteen years later he still isn't – once you're born round you don't die square.

LA is pricey so we share a room at a hotel in Santa Monica and put down a couple of days getting on each other's nerves.

We meet nobody. We know nobody. Well, strictly speaking we're on speaking terms with two people in all of Los Angeles County.

1. Rory 'Roo' Kellett.
2. Rory's mate, Colin Farrell.

I'm fast coming to the conclusion that I don't like LA. It's my second trip, and the first – a few years earlier – was equally brutal. Then Damo puts in a call to Rory, which sounds promising, judging by his end of the conversation.

'Tomorrow? Yeah, cool.'

I've bumped into Colin Farrell a couple of times. Along with the rest of the Ireland squad, I've even been out drinking with him, in South Africa a couple of years before. I could think of worse things to do than hang out at his house in the Hollywood Hills of a Wednesday afternoon.

The following day we're lying out on sun-loungers, when Colin throws out a 'What are you guys doing on Friday night?'

It doesn't seem like the right moment to tell him I'm planning on attending the ten-year reunion of the Blackrock College Class of 1997 and I'll be five thousand miles away from LA. In any case, I don't get the chance.

'No plans yet,' Damo says. 'Why?'

'It's my birthday,' says Colin. 'Why don't we go out for the night?'

He suggests dinner somewhere smart, then on to a couple of bars he knows. Just the four of us.

'Sounds good,' says Damo.

He's not flying back until after the weekend, so I'm the only problem. A couple of hours later, as we're heading through the gates, I tell him I can't miss my reunion.

'Listen,' he says, 'the only people who go to ten-year class reunions are the ones who want everyone to know how successful they are. You don't really need to say it, Briano.'

I cave and change my flight.

We figure if we're on a night out with Colin Farrell, Hollywood movie star, we'd better not let the side down, so we buy some new clothes.

We decide we can't arrive with our hands hanging on his birthday, so we find some piss-take balloons as his gift.

We're getting ready for the restaurant when Damo's phone rings as he's about to take a shower. I see the number coming up.

It's Roo.

'Howrya, man?' says Damo, when I hand him the phone.

I can sense what's coming even before Damo starts giving it away.

'Okay . . . Don't worry about it . . . Fully understand.'

He hangs up. He looks gutted. I know what's just happened but I still ask the question.

'Did he just cancel?'

'There's paparazzi outside the house. He says they can't leave. He was really apologetic . . .'

I let him have it. 'I should never have listened to you!'

'Come on! We can still have a good night. You and me.'

'You can go on your own. I'm not going out!'

I figure I'm well within my rights to throw a strop, but

when Damo's all dressed up with somewhere to go he doesn't take no for an answer. He calls Roo back and asks if we can still take the restaurant reservation.

No problem, says Roo.

Over at Koi, a trendy Japanese place on La Cienega Boulevard, where they're expecting Colin Farrell plus three, they move things around.

Table for two nobodies.

Two hours later, after sushi and a couple of shots, we climb into a taxi and head north for 7000 Hollywood Boulevard. Three miles up ahead, we see a sign in pink neon on the roof of a building in the distance. 'Roosevelt Hotel', it reads.

On our Hollywood-with-Colin-Farrell night, the hotel's Tropicana poolside bar was pencilled in as the second stop.

We hear the head of security before we can see him, standing in front of a two-hundred-strong line. 'Residents only! If you're not a resident, you're not getting in!'

Unless, perhaps, your name is Colin Farrell. Or a couple of ordinary Joes carried along in his slipstream.

Me: 'I'm not doing this queue. Let's get out of here.'

Damo: 'No, no, no. We're not doing the queue. Just follow me.'

Me: 'Don't embarrass me.'

Damo: 'Don't flatter yourself! Nobody here has ever heard of you.'

Ouch.

I'm on his shoulder as he marches straight up the line and keeps going. He only checks his stride when one of the bouncers takes a step towards him.

'How're you doing, man?' he says. 'We're here to meet Colin Farrell. He's following us in five minutes.'

'You're here to meet Colin?' says the guy. 'Absolutely no problem, sir!'

There is no part of him that does not believe Damo 100 per cent. I hear the people at the top of the queue reacting as he lets us through and clips the red rope back into place behind us. Instead of the huffing and puffing that would have poured forth in Dublin, there is complete respect.

'Can't argue with that! They're here to see Colin Farrell!'

As I follow Damo towards the palm trees and the giant swimming-pool, I'm thinking this is a great country for Irishmen born with brass necks.

Does nobody bullshit around here?

The place is rocking and nobody pays us a blind bit of attention. We wander like a couple of total gate-crashers, until Damo starts a conversation with some girls by the pool. He's just about holding their attention and I have yet to open my mouth when he shoots off to the bar and tells me to keep them talking.

I've no interest, my chat is toxic, and it's getting embarrassing when I see him talking to a guy at the bar and pointing straight at me.

He comes back with the drinks and the guy from the bar in tow.

'Are you Brian?' the guy says.

I don't even get a chance to confirm it.

'Hey, man, your friend just told me! That's incredible news!'

'Yeah?'

'You're gonna be kicker for the Cowboys! No way! That's awesome! I love the Cowboys!'

Next, he starts looking me up on his phone.

'So you're a rugby star? You're gonna be the first ever Irish guy to play football? Oh man! Can I get a photo?'

He disappears and comes back with bottles of champagne on ice. He puts a hand on my arm as more strangers start arriving to toast my big news.

'Man, we've got a table right over here,' he says. 'Promise me you'll come and have a drink with us.'

'No problem, buddy,' Damo says.

One of the girls quaffing our champagne says we must be going to the show. Before I can say, 'What show?' Damo is off again.

'Absolutely! It's going to be brilliant!' He pulls over a waitress: 'Where's this show on tonight?'

'It's in Teddy's, sir,' she says. 'Right over there.'

'How do you get into that?'

'You don't get into it.'

'What d'you mean?'

'It's a private show.'

God loves a trier. Damo pulls out a fifty and slips it to a bouncer standing on a corner, hoping he'll step aside and slip us in.

The guy pockets the cash and doesn't budge.

'Hey!' Damo says. 'Don't take my coin and not be able to do anything!'

Up ahead, there are more bouncers standing in front of some fancy curtains. Damo ignores the queue again but this looks big-time, a whole other level. The security guys are larger than the ones outside. They're also sharper.

'Not tonight, sir,' says the main guy.

If Kobe Bryant or Dennis Rodman walk up, they're not going to have a problem. But the new kicker on the Dallas Cowboys' roster isn't getting in.

Damo tries another tack. 'Listen, I'm the head of Sony BMG Records. I've got a big party in here next week. This is mortifying. I'm here with three very important guests. Let me in the door.'

The guy shakes his head. He's not much of a conversationalist. 'Sir, not a chance.'

'I'm telling you, you're making a mistake here. This is very embarrassing for me and my company.'

'Not tonight, sir.'

At this precise moment – I swear – Kanye West arrives with a bunch of his cronies. There's a surge of electricity in the queue as he heads for the curtains. He's halfway there when Damo walks straight into his path. 'Kanye, my boy!' he says. 'What's up?'

As Damo low-fives one of his security guards, Kanye West appears momentarily confused.

Then Damo gives him to understand that they have a professional relationship of considerable standing. 'We had you in Dublin and you rocked the place! Great to see you again, man!'

A flicker of recognition crosses Kanye West's face at the mention of the word 'Dublin'. 'All right!' he says. 'Good to see you too, man!'

Kanye continues on his way and we walk up behind the entourage. As they are ushered through, the head of security has a word in Damo's ear. 'Hey, buddy, I'm sorry about that! You're with Kanye?'

'Yeah,' says Damo. 'It's me and three.'

'Right this way, sir.'

We find ourselves in a nightclub with high ceilings, low lights, leather chairs and crystal chandeliers. There's a small stage but nobody on it. There are no more than a hundred people there and we start recognizing a bunch of them.

Jamie Foxx. Mark Wahlberg. Sacha Baron Cohen.

Somebody brings us right up beside Kanye and pulls back some chairs.

'Is this table okay for you?'

'Yeah, this table's cool,' Damo says.

We bolt for the bar as soon as Kanye's crew start eyeing us up with a look that says, *Who the fuck are these two guys?*

When the live music starts there's a little guy front of stage with a band. It's Prince.

After he opens up with a couple of songs we've never heard of, Jamie Foxx calls for 'Purple Rain'.

'Shut up, Foxxy,' says Prince. 'This is my gig, not yours. I'll play what I want.'

An hour later Damo's still on fire at the club and I'm in the back of a taxi headed for Santa Monica. The cab driver is Lebanese. 'You have a good night?' he says.

'I had a *great* night,' I tell him.

Further up Hollywood Boulevard I see the golden arches of a drive-thru McDonald's.

'Can you pull in here?' I ask. 'I'm starving.'

*

When I step on the scales back home the following week, the needle zooms up to 102.5 – nearly six kilos over my match weight and the heaviest I've ever been.

A couple of weeks before I'm even back with Leinster I'm hearing that the word is already out on the training ground. I've been spotted around the town.

'Holy Jesus! You'd want to see the size of Brian O'Driscoll after his holidays!'

Before I get a chance to run off a few pounds, a good crew of us head up to Mike McGurn's wedding in Enniskillen. I'm chatting to Den at the hotel afterwards when he tells me he's just heard a good one. 'It's sort of a Paul Wallace story,' he says.

'Brilliant! I love an old Wally story.'

'You won't love this one.'

'No?'

'No. I was sitting beside Reggie at the church. He looks across at you, but he can only see you from behind. He goes, "I never knew Paul Wallace was invited to this wedding."'

Den finds it highly amusing that I've just been mistaken for a prop forward who is five years retired. He knows I can take a joke at my own expense, most of the time. I try to laugh, but I'm crying on the inside.

Three days later, one of Amy's friends drops off a Sunday tabloid with instructions to look at page 3. When Amy opens it she nearly chokes. She points to a big picture of herself and me walking into the church for Mike's wedding. 'Oh my God!' she says. 'Look at that!'

The photographer has caught her dress blowing up in the breeze. Just to make sure nobody misses this moment of immodesty, the newspaper has drawn a big circle on the picture.

But I don't see the circle. I barely clock that Amy is even in the picture. All I see is the fat guy in the shades by her side. I look enormous. I grab the paper off her. 'OH MY GOD!'

'I know!' Amy says. 'That's just not nice!'

'Not nice? It's horrific!'

At this point, I find out later, Amy is touched that I seem so hot and bothered about her public embarrassment. Meanwhile, I'm still in complete shock over my monstrosity of a head. 'That's not acceptable!'

'I know! It's really not.'

'Look at the size of my head!'

Amy grabs the paper back. 'I thought we were talking about my knickers,' she says, half laughing.

*

A week later, I take off my top at the Ireland training camp in Spala, Poland. Suffice to say I'm not cut.

Dr Liam Hennessy, our director of fitness, gives me the once-over and shakes his head at the block of white meat before him. 'Jesus, there's a lot of work in that,' he says.

I'm still shuddering from the sight of my jowls in the paper. For a professional athlete, I'm carrying too much body fat. I've never felt like I was dragging the weight around the pitch but the wedding picture is a slap across the face. I need to be in better shape and I'm not the only one who knows it.

It's a turning point.

For Leinster pre-season, Michael Cheika takes us hill-running in Killiney. Running for the sake of running. Up and down, over and over. Climb the biggest hill, wait for your heart-rate to come down, then go again. Some guys are built to run all day – Shaggy, Mal O'Kelly – but for some of us there's no enjoyment, nothing to get our minds off the fact that our lungs are heaving.

It's not about enjoyment, it's about pushing out our pain threshold. It's also about matching other teams' fitness levels and making sure we have the same mental toughness from 1 to 22.

On the hardest day, Shaggy is the first man finished. There is nobody within the squad who wants success for Leinster more, and nobody who's prepared to push himself further to achieve it. He looks up and sees one of our academy players struggling on the second hill. When he goes over to support him, the guy says he's spent, he's got a stitch, he can't go on.

Shaggy has already finished, but he offers to go again for another lap. 'Come on,' he says. 'One more. I'll do it with you.'

His offer is declined.

Shaggy tells me about it later and mentally cuts the guy loose: 'He's done with us.'

*

The All Blacks are virtually unbackable for the World Cup, but we're fourth on the bookmakers' list, behind South Africa and France but ahead of Australia and the defending champions, England. After our demolition job on the English at Croke Park, confidence is coursing through us. I consciously change tack when the media ask about our chances. I see no reason to play them down, so I do the exact opposite. I like the prospect of this new-found confidence projecting us all the way.

'We have to be one of the top four or five sides who can actually win it,' I say.

For Eddie, the prospect of coaching the 2009 Lions is very real. Two years out, nobody has better credentials. He knows no Irish team has been remotely as well equipped to do damage on a World Cup stage and, along with the rest of the coaching staff and the strength-and-conditioning guys, he works long and hard to get us there fighting fit.

For the five weeks of pre-season we barely touch a ball. There's a finely calibrated training plan in place and it's executed to the letter all summer. Straight off the back of a fortnight of tough conditioning with Leinster, there's another hard week in Spala with Ireland, then a month of training split between club and country. It's been designed as a low-risk strategy. It's about getting us in peak condition, then wrapping us in cotton wool until the team bus pulls up at Stade Chaban-Delmas in Bordeaux on 9 September, after which we'll start moving up the gears against Namibia before hitting something close to full throttle against Georgia the following week. Then full speed ahead to Paris for a crack at the French.

Except.

By the time we run out against Scotland on the second weekend in August, with a team that's nothing like first-choice, twenty-two weeks have passed since I played a game of rugby. Collectively, we're miles off the pace and the Scots put us away with little bother.

We fly to the south of France for warm-weather training and a run-out against Bayonne. We've got the national team in our pool and there's a small part of us that wonders if it's a good idea taking on a French club side, but as players we can only put our faith in those who have planned it and our trust in the referee.

Bayonne come out with guns blazing and fists flying. They're more interested in kicking the shit out of us than putting points on the scoreboard.

The ref is Wayne Barnes. Soon to be a name in the game, but as yet virtually unknown.

I'm in his ear all the time about what's going on off the ball: he doesn't want to hear me.

I start losing my cool as the cynical stuff continues: he warns Paulie to keep me in check.

An hour into it, I've had more than enough. I tell him my players are getting gouged, and if he doesn't do something about it, I'm taking them off the pitch.

Then it really kicks off.

I'm trying to break up a bit of argy-bargy when one of

their subs smacks me bang on the cheekbone with a cheap shot from a swinging right arm I don't even see until it puts me on the deck. Two yards away and a split-second later Marcus Horan also hits the floor and another scrap breaks out all around him as our medics burst onto the pitch, like scalded cats. When I take back my hand from the spot where I've been smacked there's blood running down it.

Not for the first time, or the last, I'm seriously lucky to have my cousin Gaz in my corner and he does an unbelievable job stitching me up. Once the diagnosis is in – a fractured sinus – there's media talk of me missing the World Cup opener. But there's no way I'm not starting that match. I desperately need to build up some match fitness for the bigger challenges that lie beyond.

In my absence, Paulie captains a strong-looking team in a friendly against Italy in Ravenhill the following week, but our victory at the death is nothing less than an act of grand larceny that warrants a note of apology pushed under the door of the Italian dressing room.

Eddie looks shaken when the team troops back in and he's too much of a straight shooter to hide his disappointment from the media.

'That might have been the wake-up call we needed tonight,' he says, but even before we pull out of Ravenhill the alarms are going off and people aren't just thinking it, they're saying it.

We're not ready. We're miles away.

We tell ourselves there's still time to find our skill levels and our sharpness, that we can be one of those teams that produce form out of nowhere. But we're not showing enough on the training ground to say it with any conviction.

Four weeks later, we stink the place out against Namibia in Bordeaux and from there it gets worse. We hang on for dear life to get past Georgia. We're so bad we shock ourselves. There are shedloads of journalists looking for stories, and some of them are just as happy to run with rumours and falsehoods.

The proximity of this World Cup, an hour's flight from Ireland, has brought the social columnists into the press room alongside the rugby correspondents and everyone wants to know why it's all going horribly wrong.

Can't find the answers on the pitch? Then look elsewhere. Put the latest rumour in print, then stand back while half the country wonders if there's something behind it.

We have a carriage to ourselves on the TGV from Bordeaux to Paris. Our girlfriends and wives travel with us, but it's a quiet journey all the way up. For us, the moment of truth is a few short days away and the huge pressure we are feeling hangs in the air. The expectation of the nation, a positive force back in March when England came to Croke Park, weighs more heavily on us now.

We know from our own families and friends just how big the tournament is back in Ireland, beamed into more homes than ever before. We have a good enough idea of the level of support already mobilizing for us ahead of the France game, the thousands making their way to Paris, their tickets bought a long time ago and their hopes raised high by what they saw in the Six Nations.

We made a good fist at almost losing the Georgia game but there are no freebies from here on in, no more chances to find our A game.

So we sit there, quietly, hoping against hope that things will change for the better but fearing deep down that we aren't ready for what's coming at the Stade de France.

In Paris, I try to remind everyone of the potency that's in

us, just waiting to come out. I get Mervyn Murphy, our highly respected performance analyst, to compile some footage of our best moments and I press Play at the captain's meeting the night before.

'Right, this is what we're capable of. Remember this?'

Up on the screen we see a team playing with precision and verve, busting gain lines and taking chances at will. Six short months ago.

We're fired up when the moment comes but the French – beaten by Argentina in the tournament opener – have a point to prove of their own. They blow us off the park.

We're left needing a bonus point win against Argentina to get out of the pool but we still can't muster any form and they see us off without a bother.

It's like we've spent the best part of four years preparing to be tested at the highest level, then some impostors have gone in and sat the examinations. Through it all we remain pretty united as a team, but it just doesn't happen on the pitch. After four sub-standard performances the report card has a seriously ugly look to it.

Namibia – F
Georgia – F
France – E
Argentina – D

For Den, it's particularly gutting. Before the tournament, he told us he was retiring once Ireland's involvement was over. A 15-point defeat by Argentina in the pool stages wasn't what he deserved for a send-off.

Thirty-one years old and walking away from rugby after a stellar career. In leaving the stage he reminds some of us that we're far closer to the end than the beginning.

Walking through the arrivals hall at Dublin airport, back out of our bubble and knowing that we've failed big-time, is a brutal feeling. For three or four years people have been jumping on our bandwagon and now they're throwing themselves off it in droves.

The inquest goes on for ever.

There is much talk of terrible food at a soulless hotel in some godforsaken industrial park on the far side of Bordeaux.

True, in spades.

There are rumours about trouble and strife in the camp.

False.

The tale of woe gets dragged out endlessly in the media and becomes an official report, then a chapter in people's books. Between them all, the details don't differ too much and nobody comes up with anything new, because there's really nothing there, other than the story of an undercooked squad underperforming on a huge scale.

For this slow-motion car crash, Eddie gets fingered as the man behind the wheel. He holds up his hand and accepts we weren't match-hardy when it mattered, that there was a balance to be struck and he put us on the wrong side of it.

For almost six years he has been one of the best and most successful coaches in world rugby. He has raised standards and expectations, won three Triple Crowns. He's got a freshly signed four-year contract and a lot of credit in the bank, all of it fully earned. He just needs another good Six Nations to put the wheels back on.

But sometimes when you hit a downward spiral it's hard to break the fall.

*

Eight months after our first encounter at the Merrion Hotel, I ask Amy to move in with me. I've never lived with a girl-friend before. Never asked the question. I've been saving it for the woman I hope will never move back out.

I've always wanted a relationship in which I could just be myself, 100 per cent, and with Amy everything feels natural and easy.

Living together is a massive step, for both of us. But we both have a strong idea of where we're headed.

She says no.

Well, actually, she says wait. Let's wait until December, when we're a year together.

She's always been her own woman, earning her own living. And even though my success as a rugby player makes her happy, she doesn't want anyone saying she's changed just because a well-known sportsman with a nice house has asked her to share it.

I tell her nobody will say it, or even think it, but she holds out for the extra four months.

Across the bed, on the morning after she moves her stuff in, I'm woken by the sound of an alarm clock going off. She reaches out and silences it, but four minutes later it rings again, and the same thing happens after another four minutes.

'Whoa!' I say. 'What's happening there?'

'Just hitting snooze,' she answers, still half asleep.

I've never used a snooze button in my life. I don't give myself the option of deciding if I'm too tired to get up. Twenty seconds after the alarm goes off, I'm under a power shower and wide awake.

So I give Amy a nudge and spell out my non-snoozing position.

'Snoozing should be allowed,' I argue, 'when whoever's up first has already gone – not when the person getting out of bed first is just *contemplating* getting up.'

'Whoa!' she says. 'I've always been of the opinion that if you don't snooze, you lose.'

*

The following weekend, ten days before Christmas, Leinster go to Edinburgh for round four of the Heineken Cup and we're soundly beaten. We've already been blitzed by Toulouse and the final nail is banged down by Leicester in January. On a personal level I'm not exactly leading by example. I'm struggling with form and confidence. I go through the entire season without scoring one try.

As usual, Munster make the quarter-finals. We can talk the talk about emulating them all we like, but two seasons on from the Lansdowne Road semi-final we're still nowhere close to backing it up on the pitch.

With Eddie's job on the line, Ireland lose three out of five in the Six Nations off the back of a terrible World Cup. Not many coaches are going to survive that, even when they've got a four-year deal in their back pocket. Maybe the one that hurts Eddie the most is Wales dancing around Croke Park with the Triple Crown trophy, as their new coach looks on like the cat that got the cream.

In the moment of victory, in the city where he was sacked by Ireland back in the day, Warren Gatland is not at his most humble. For him, it's personal. For Eddie, it's curtains after Twickenham the following Saturday.

After all he has done for us, I'm still thinking he's the man to lead us out of the morass, but he calls me on the following Wednesday night and tells me he's resigning.

I feel sorry it's all gone wrong for him, grateful for how far he has taken us. Like I did with Gats five years before, I write him a letter of thanks. But after the news sinks in I'm like everyone else, wondering if the next man in can take us to another level.

In early May, after Leinster batter the Dragons at the RDS, they erect a stage on the pitch and we line up under the banner overhead.

MAGNERS LEAGUE CHAMPIONS 2007/08

I raise the trophy above my head. We shake up some bottles of the sponsor's brew and pour them over the heads of the departing Keith Gleeson and Ollie le Roux, major contributors to our cause.

We're delighted with the win.

We fall over ourselves in trying to sound enthusiastic about our achievement.

I call it 'a very worthy competition'.

Felipe bigs it up as the truest test of consistency.

But within four days people are already beginning to forget who won the 2008 Magners League title and the rugby writers have bigger fish to fry.

As expected by all and sundry, Declan Kidney is unveiled as the new coach of Ireland.

All that remains is for him to leave Munster in triumph, by beating Toulouse in Cardiff and claiming a second Heineken Cup in three years.

*

For years, the question has been asked in practically every interview I've given, phrased in different ways but always looking for the same response.

'You must be really envious about Munster's success?'

'You must crave their consistency in the Heineken Cup?'

'You have to admire their ability to deliver when the chips are down?'

Yes, yes and yes again, through gritted teeth.

We will give them maximum respect, but don't ask us to applaud, because we won't expect it from them if and when the tables are turned. Guys like Paulie, Rog, Hayes and a few others, I'm happy for them as individuals. But that's where it ends.

Through all the years of their Heineken Cup romance, God knows how many people born and reared in Leinster have declared for Munster. How many of them came to Lansdowne Road wearing red when they broke us in the semi-final? Were any of these Lunster fans among the 17,260 at the RDS who saw us finally lift a trophy after all these years?

Or were they holding out for a bigger day, a better reason to remember where they come from?

In the little black book I keep in my head I have noted down some of these people – TV personalities and assorted celebs. And from time to time I have told Shaggy that I'm waiting for the day when they finally cough up for a blue jersey, because elephants don't forget.

But now, with our season over, we can't turn on a radio or open a newspaper without being hit with the latest on Munster's build-up to the final. We have to sit at home and suck it up.

Early in the week, Barry rings me.

He's got himself a new gig. He is now Barry Twomey, radio personality – the Saturday morning voice of sport for East Coast FM.

'It's about the show,' he says. 'I was just wondering . . .'

'No, Barry.'

'Just ten minutes over the phone!'

'Ten minutes about what? About how Munster are definitely going to win? About how great they are?'

He leans on me hard, says he won't even ask about the Heineken Cup final. There's loads more going on. We can talk about Leinster's season, about Ireland's chances in New Zealand.

And because it's him, I agree.

I'm barely out of bed when the call comes through, just after eleven. We chat about this and that, we discuss my itinerary for the following week: a flight to England in the morning, a game against the Barbarians at Gloucester before the trip down to Wellington. He studiously avoids all mention of Munster, but right at the end his co-presenter pitches in a soft question and asks me for a quick prediction.

I say Munster will shade it in a one-score game, that I fancy their smarts to come good. When the game kicks off I'm on my way over to see Skiddy at his in-laws' place in Mount Merrion.

He has his newborn son, Paddy, in his arms when I arrive. He's telling me what it feels like to be a dad when his father-in-law comes into the conservatory and sees us chatting away.

'Why aren't you lads watching the match?' he asks, incredulous.

He tells us Munster have just gone three points up and runs back to his television.

Me and Skiddy, we carry on talking.

7. Dark Days

On a Sunday afternoon at the Queen's Hotel in the centre of Cheltenham, it's raining hard outside when my phone rings. It's Barry's dad, Cormac, a.k.a. Slim. There is concern in his voice.

He wonders if Barry is with me. He hasn't called, he's not on his phone, it's just not like him.

I tell him not to worry, that he probably had a late night somewhere.

I tell him I was only talking to Barry yesterday afternoon – that he called me after the radio interview to say thanks for the dig-out.

Not long after, there's a phone call from Barry's fiancée, Barbara, wondering if I've heard from him, but even at the back of my head there's no alarm bell going off, until Monday morning comes and he's not at home, not at work.

Even then, there's no part of me that really believes anything bad could have happened.

I speak with Barbara again. Only two months have passed since he went down on one knee in Central Park, New York, and proposed. More than anyone, I know how much he adores her.

'I'm sure there's an explanation for it.'

And I *am* sure, but I just can't figure out what it is.

I talk to Shaggy. He can't fathom it either, can't understand why Barry's phone is off, because it's never off. Barry's always on.

I confide in Gaz, not because he's the Ireland team doctor and we've a game the following night, but because he's a good friend. Other than Shaggy, he's the only guy with the squad I feel the need to tell.

Maybe Gaz sees the situation more clearly. He says he'd better say something to Michael Bradley, our stand-in coach until Deccie starts officially.

Just in case, he says. I'm captain, after all.

'Yeah – whatever, Gaz. If you think so. Grand.'

Monday night comes and there's still no word. For the first time, a morbid thought flashes through my head . . .

I hope to God he hasn't done anything stupid.

It doesn't stay there long, because it doesn't seem remotely plausible.

There's no way.

Not Barry. Not possible.

He'll turn up soon.

He must have fallen or something.

There has to be an explanation for this.

Even when I'm getting texts and calls from Fruity and Skiddy on Tuesday morning, even when I know the gardaí are out looking for him, with sniffer dogs, I can't bring myself to contemplate the worst outcome. The finality of that.

In a hotel room in the south-west of England, I feel a million miles away from what's going on back home, helpless as the information drips through on my mobile.

He might be in Glendalough.

Somebody spotted his car in Enniskerry.

They've tracked his phone.

They've found his car.

The Wicklow Mountains.

There's a search party going out there.

In mid-afternoon, I'm down in the team room looking for company, trying to keep my mind off it, when Shaggy walks in.

He's on his phone. He looks serious. He finishes the call.

Now I notice that his face is white as a sheet. He asks me if I've heard anything.

'No. You?'

There's barely anyone else in the room, but he takes me outside, down some steps, down a corridor, just the two of us.

For some reason there's no sense of dread. I don't see it coming. Not even close.

He says the phone call was from John Kelly, a close friend of the Twomey family.

He says Barry's gone. They've found his body. In the woods, near Enniskerry.

The shock hits straight away, like nothing I've ever known. The legs go from underneath me. For the first time in my life I completely break down and lose all control of my emotions. Shaggy tries to carry me to my room, but I'm in a hysterical state, crawling back up the stairs.

The rest of the day passes in a blur. Somebody books me on a Ryanair flight home from Bristol airport and our logistics man, Ger Carmody, comes with me. There isn't much said between us, but I can't think of anything worse than having to travel back alone.

Trying to avoid the late-afternoon traffic, the taxi driver gets lost. Inside me, the shock gives way to stress.

You don't understand! I've got to get this flight!

They hold the check-in time for us. We're the last two to reach the gate.

In Dublin, somebody looks for an autograph as we're

walking to the arrivals hall. I never refuse when people are polite, but I've never felt like this.

'Sorry. Not now.'

Amy, her brother Mark, and Damo are waiting. None of us can begin to understand it. Nobody can. There are no answers. There never will be.

None of it seems real, until the moment I see him laid out at home in Stillorgan, with the top button of his shirt done up.

Oh Jesus, Barry!

It comes into my head that they should have put a tie on him. But then I think that wouldn't have been Barry.

He wasn't a tie person.

*

At the funeral in Foxrock, in the Church of Our Lady of Perpetual Succour, there are photographers waiting as Amy and I arrive, and reporters in the pews. It distresses me that my rugby career is responsible for such an intrusion on what should be private grief.

Four of us speak: Barry's brother, Cormac, Barbara, Fruity and me. Mostly I talk about memories of the laughter we shared living like some married couple in Bird Avenue; funny stories about the Barry I knew and loved, the Barry who was such easy company, who loved his family and his friends and who deeply loved Barbara.

The Ireland squad fly to New Zealand without me on the day of the funeral. I'm given the option to travel down after them or pull out of the tour. I feel like I should go, throw myself back into rugby, because the pitch is the only place you can switch off from whatever's going on in your life, but I need to hear from Barry's family that it's okay for me to feel that way.

I don't even have to ask the question. Barry's dad recognizes my confusion – maybe it's guilt. He tells me I should tour, that Barry would have wanted me to go. It's a relief to hear him say it, to leave with his blessing.

At the team hotel in Wellington, Rog doesn't really say anything when I arrive. He just gives me a hug.

And a hug is what I need, because my head is still spinning, still full of questions for which there will never be answers.

Why? Why? Why?

*

Even for an emotional wreck, it's not hard to recognize the winds of change blowing through the Ireland set-up.

When the team to play New Zealand is named, it's nothing new to see seven Munster forwards out of eight in the pack, with more on the bench. What's new is they are now two-time Heineken Cup champions, the second trophy freshly lifted by their dominant personalities, Paulie and Rog, with a hand on either side.

What's new is that the man with both of those titles on his coaching CV is waiting just offstage, with a watching brief on the summer tour.

Outside the camp, people are already asking if Declan Kidney will take the captaincy off me and give it to Paulie. And within a day of joining the squad I'm wondering if the writing's on the wall after a year of underachievement.

The confidence in the Munster guys is unmissable. They've got the winning formula, they know what they're at. They have huge belief in their ways, and with Eddie gone, maybe they're expecting Ireland to play more like Munster.

At the Westpac Stadium there are moments in the match

when Barry comes into my head, but not nearly as often as he does during the days I spend sitting in my hotel room.

Apart from the freezing-cold conditions, the Test is like the 2006 tour all over again – we're competitive for the first sixty but unable to see it out.

Afterwards, a text message arrives from Eddie, who has watched the game from the other side of the world: *It looks like Paulie's assuming the role of captain.*

It's not intended as a criticism of Paulie, more an observation about my own body language, or lack of. The thing about Paulie, he's an incredibly competitive animal. It's just innately in his character to be a leader. I've never wanted him to suppress that quality, just because I'm the one wearing the armband. I've never felt threatened by him.

But now there's a question mark in my messed-up head.

Is he thinking about the captaincy?

On the way into the post-match function, the All Black wing Anthony Tuitavake – a guy I have never spoken to – comes my way.

'I was really sorry to hear about your friend,' he says.

After five days with barely a mention of Barry, I am deeply moved by his kindness.

*

In Melbourne, I score my first try in twenty games, running a support line for Tommy Bowe, but we're beaten by a score.

Paulie talks in the changing room afterwards, which is nothing new, and there's a part of me that's grateful someone else is taking the responsibility after I've spent two weeks going through the motions when it comes to leadership. But there's another part of me that feels vulnerable.

Later on, over a drink, I try to talk to Rog about it, but he sees where I'm going and he won't even let me get the words out.

He says Paulie's sole motivation is trying to better the team. Conversation closed.

And, of course, he's right. But after a lonely, miserable tour, insecurity has taken hold and that's not how it feels.

It feels like the captaincy is slipping away from me.

I decide that I won't let Deccie make the decision for me – I'll make it myself.

Once the tour is over, the first time I see him, I'll just come out with it. I'll make it easy for him.

But first I need to go home, get away from here, get my head straight.

Back in Dublin, I honour a commitment to accept an award for Dubliner of the Year, mostly because I want to dedicate it to Barry.

Barbara's there, deeply distressed. It's three weeks on and nobody close to him has even begun to take it in.

*

It's our second summer as a couple and the second year Amy and I can't go on holiday together. When I get back from the tour she's shooting season six of *The Clinic*, pretty much all day every day.

Plan B is a holiday with the lads, New York and then Florida. I'm not really in the form for it, but I feel better when Fruity says he'll come for the first weekend: there's something comforting about spending time with one of Barry's oldest friends.

A couple of days later, five of us board a plane to New York. There's me, Damo and Fruity, plus Damien Duff and his pal Ciaran Ryan.

Shaggy, Denis and Victor are already in New York and we meet them for food at the Spotted Pig on West 14th Street. Then we take a cab ride uptown to Madison Square Garden, where Damo divvies up the tickets to see REM. He's with Fruity, me and his friend Brian Whelan in a hospitality suite. Shaggy, Den and Victor are in seats on the other side of the arena.

I can take or leave REM. Mostly I can leave them. In the box, me and Fruity tip away at a few beers, talking about Barry, until the concert's over and we start making our way down to street level.

The escalator is broken so the lift fills up quickly, but we squeeze ourselves in and there are more after us before the doors close. A guy standing a few bodies back starts shouting aggressively. He's in his early forties, dressed in jeans and a shirt. Respectable-looking guy, apart from his mouth. And absolutely stocious.

'Stop pushing on me! Stop pushing on me, motherfuckers!'

Someone tells him that nobody's pushing, because nobody can move, but he's not having it.

'Get outta the elevator! It's too packed! Get the fuck out!'

He's still mouthing off as the lift starts descending. He sees that Fruity is wearing a pink shirt, starts unloading on him. 'Hey – fucking gay guy! Get the fuck outta the elevator!'

The doors open at mezzanine level, and as everyone gets out, the drunk guy stumbles and falls. He starts effing and blinding again. He's so plastered there's not much point talking to him.

I have a word anyway. 'What's your problem, pal? There's no need for that sort of chat!'

Damo comes over and tells me this gobshite isn't even worth speaking to. 'C'mon, Briano. Let's get out of here,' he says.

We turn and Damo leads the way towards the escalator.

Suddenly this maniac charges across the foyer in our direction. As I watch him running at us, something tells me he's not coming for me: he has Damo in his sights. Just ahead of me, Damo clocks the same thing and has just enough time to brace himself and shout at the guy, 'Don't fucking do this! I'm warning you!'

He's not listening. He's still running. He winds up a dig and launches it at Damo.

Damo throws out an arm to protect himself. The guy runs straight into it and drops, like a newborn lamb.

He's picking himself up off the floor when his friends arrive on the scene. There's three of them, a couple and another guy, all screaming blue murder.

'Security! Security!'

It's self-defence, no question, but I figure Damo would be best advised making himself scarce.

'I think you'd better get out of here,' I tell him.

The exit is at the bottom of the escalators. He merges into the crowd and just as he walks out one door two security guards arrive through another. They're like ships passing in the night. I watch Damo disappear and I think it's all over, but it's not over.

*

In the concourse, near the exits, I review the situation with Fruity and Brian.

'Listen, lads, we'll just walk out.'

We go left and pretty soon we've got company. One of the guy's friends follows us up the street. We hear him talking on his phone, like he's on to the NYPD.

'They're on Penn Plaza! . . . They're heading west!'

It's a weird, unsettling situation, but we've got no reason to panic.

'Listen,' I tell the lads, 'he can't follow all three of us. Let's split up.'

We head in different directions and he's forced to choose. He chooses me. I start walking faster – he steps up his pace. I duck behind a van and double back but I can't shake him. It suddenly strikes me that I'm acting like I'm guilty, running from the truth.

What the hell am I doing?

Just up ahead, on the corner of Pennsylvania Plaza and West 33rd Street, is the bar we've agreed to meet up in after the gig. Den sees me through the window, looking around. He steps outside to let me know he's there with Shaggy and Victor.

I tell him there's been some hassle, that the police have been called.

He looks concerned, but completely calm. 'Tell me exactly what happened.'

I tell him.

'You've done nothing wrong,' he says, when I've finished. 'The stupid thing to do here would be to act like you have. Just stay here with us.'

We head inside for a beer. The guy following me waits by the window, with the phone to his ear.

'Fuck you!' he says, as we walk in. 'You're going down!'

Next, Damo calls me.

'What's going on?'

'They're after calling the cops.'

'Where are you? I'll come down and set them straight.'

'Don't come anywhere near the place.'

Pretty soon my stalker friend has reinforcements – the couple he was with in the arena. Then a police car pulls up and two officers step out. The guy with the phone points me out and they make for our table.

'Excuse me, sir – could you come outside, please?'

I do as I'm told. The boys walk out with me.

'Stand over there, please, sir.'

'I haven't done anything.'

'Excuse me, sir – quiet for the moment.'

'Fine.'

I'm in the bold corner, up against the wall. I'm waiting for my opening, waiting to say my piece, but the woman in the group gets in ahead me.

'Yeah, he's the guy!' she says. 'He's definitely the guy!'

'Excuse me?'

She jabs a finger at Shaggy.

'He was there as well!'

At this precise moment, before Shaggy can point out that he was on the other side of the arena, Emmet Byrne walks around the corner with his mind on a couple of beers.

It's news to me that he's even in the country. It's two years since we last played together for Leinster, but it turns out Den heard he was in New York and got him to come along.

'What's this?' asks Emmet Byrne.

'He was there too!' the woman says, pointing straight at him. 'Yeah! He was one of them!'

'Hang on a minute!' Den shouts. 'He's just come around the corner! He wasn't even *at* the concert!'

The cops have heard enough. One of them comes up to me.

'Sir, will you turn around and put your hands behind your back?'

'Why?'

'Please just turn around and put your hands behind your back.'

He pulls the handcuffs off his belt.

'What's happening here? Am I being arrested?'

'We're taking you down to the precinct for assault.'

'Hang on a second! Are you not going to listen to me? Do I not get my say? No?'

Victor and Den try to reason with the cops.

'Why are you arresting him?' Den asks.

'A complaint has been made, sir. This woman here has identified him. We're taking him in.'

'Well, I'm saying he didn't do anything! Why do you believe her and not me?'

'We're taking him in, sir.'

I'm about to be put in the back of an NYPD patrol car. As the cop leads me to the door, I clutch at the last straw.

'Check my hand! Does it look like I've just hit someone?'

They have no interest in examining the condition of my knuckles. They put me in the back seat and I lower my head. The handcuffs are tight against my wrists.

Victor sticks his head in the window. 'Where are you taking him? What precinct?'

'Midtown South.'

The car pulls away. It's half past eleven in the city that never sleeps.

*

After two blocks they turn left into West 35th Street and park up. The lads follow in a cab and Den is allowed to give me his American mobile number.

I'm asked to hand over my wallet, watch, phone, passport. They give me back a few dollars for the vending machine.

I tell the cop taking my stuff that nobody has told me anything. 'I don't know what's actually happening here.'

'You're being booked for assault.'

I don't know if it's the done thing or not but I buy a muffin and a bottle of water. They lead me down a corridor lined with cells and put me in one. Three-quarters of an hour passes. My head races, wondering about the process, how long it's going to take, what's coming next. But I keep coming back to the same thing: *I haven't done anything! At some point someone has to listen to my story!*

I'm taken away for fingerprinting. The guy doing it is friendly enough.

'What did ya get brought in for? Fightin'?'

It comes into my head that there's no point in defending myself to him, but I do it anyway.

'Yes, but it was a misunderstanding.'

'Yeah?'

'It was nothing to do with me.'

'Right.'

'What's happening after this?'

'It's got to be processed. Then there's a court hearing. You'll be moved.'

'Moved? When?'

'I don't know what time. Could be any time.'

'Moved to where?'

'Central Booking. Lower Manhattan.'

So now I know: I'm being locked up for the night and there's nothing anybody can do.

I try to help him with the fingerprinting, rolling with him as he brings my hand across.

'Sir, you don't need to help me. I've got this.'

Next he takes down my name and address.

'Occupation?'

'Rugby player.'

'Rugby! Okay . . . Are you good?'

'I'm all right.'

'Who do you play for?'

'I play for the national team.'

'Oh, right! I'm sure you'll get it all sorted out.'

But in the meantime, it's back to your cell, sir.

Some time after 1 a.m., New York time, twenty-four hours since I last slept, there's a rap on my bars.

'Stand up! Wait at the front of your cell!'

Six or seven of us are brought out and handcuffed to each other. I look down and notice that the homeless-looking guy in raggedy clothes cuffed to me has only one shoe.

They load us into a van, and ten minutes later we're led onto a pavement outside the Manhattan Detention Complex on White Street, Tribeca.

It's more than a holding facility, it's a municipal jail, a concrete monstrosity.

They call it The Tombs.

We wait for the massive steel door to rise up, and we're led through corridors, un-handcuffed and processed again. More fingerprints and then the killer.

'Stand there. Face the camera . . . Hold that . . . Now turn, side on . . . Okay, back in line.'

*

We're led down a winding staircase to the basement and I'm put in a bullpen with around thirty other prisoners. I'm the only white guy. There's another big cell to the right and two more across the corridor. All pretty full.

There are steel benches to sleep on but they're all taken. There's barely room on the floor.

The only spot I can find is right next to the most wasted-looking guy in the cell. He's shaking from the DTs, dribbling and moaning, twitching and farting.

'Man, you need some liquor or what?' someone asks him, just for badness.

He barely opens his eyes, but there's nothing wrong with his ears.

'Yeah!'

'Got some right here.'

'Huh?'

Nobody talks to me. Nobody makes eye contact. So I shut my mouth while the loudest guys big themselves up. Drugs, women, money, respect: once they get out of here it's all coming their way.

After a couple of hours, a skinny guy picks up the telephone in the opposite cell and calls his missus. He talks to her like they're alone in the sitting room at home. He doesn't care that everyone's listening and jeering. We can hear only one side of the conversation but some key facts emerge.

1. It's two months since she had his kid.
2. She won't be coming down to bail him out.
3. She doesn't love him any more.

He asks where she is right now and we don't hear the answer but we guess the news isn't good.

'You are fucking kidding me!'

His voice gets even louder to drown out the cheers and the jeers coming from all four cells. He can't believe what she's telling him.

'You are fucking kidding me!'

He pumps her with more questions.

She gives him her big news, a stiletto through his heart.

She loves the other guy.

There is a massive eruption, a full-on roar.

'YOU ARE FUCKING KIDDING ME!'

She's not kidding. She hangs up.

While everyone's listening to this, a guy makes for the toilet in the corner of my cell, shuts the door and lights up. Smoke rises overhead and the smell is like nothing I've ever known. It drifts into the nostrils of the nearest cops and they come running.

'Hey! What's goin' on here? Who was that?'

They look around our cell. The guys who aren't already unconscious keep their heads down.

For six or seven hours I don't speak one word. I listen to them talk about how long they've been stuck down here waiting — two, three, four days. Waiting to be bailed out or brought to court or whatever happens after this place.

Around eight o'clock, a couple of officers come down holding blue sheets of paper.

'When I say your name, step out and give me your birthdate.'

Please, God, call my name.

They start reeling them off in threes and fours. But not mine.

We hear their footsteps approaching again and they call out some more names.

I must be next. I'm definitely next.

Still not me.

It's Friday morning and the judge doesn't do weekends. If you don't hear your name, you're here until Monday.

I'm done with watching and waiting. I need to know. I

walk up to the bars, trying to catch an officer's attention, when a Hispanic guy comes over from across the cell.

'You in for fightin'?'

'Yeah.' I don't want to go into it. I just show him Den's number. 'Listen, what's the story with calling this?'

'You need to put in a one there.'

Den answers first time. He tells me Victor's pal Chris Durnan is doing all he can with the people he knows to have things moved along as quickly as possible. He knows I'm stuck here for the weekend otherwise. I'm shaking after the call. Just hearing Den's voice has put a lump in my throat.

At least I'm not on my own.

Another couple of hours. More footsteps, more names, more disappointment.

Breakfast is served, or maybe it's brunch: a cheese sandwich.

'Want some milk?'

'Nah, I'm okay.'

Around twelve o'clock they call my name. As I walk out of there someone objects to my big moment.

'Fuck, man! You must know some peoples! You're right down the list – you should be in for the weekend!'

He's only the second guy behind bars to speak to me in eleven hours, but I'm not mad keen on having a chat right now.

*

Up at ground level, they put me in a holding cell with about a dozen other inmates. There's more space and less weird activity. It's practically comfortable by comparison.

A guy with short dreadlocks, a sideways cap and a super-sized T-shirt gives me the lowdown on his latest bust. He's proper ghetto, in for drugs. I understand about 20 per cent of what he says, but I get that it's his sixteenth time in The Tombs.

'You?'

'First time.'

I'm called through, across a connecting bridge and down to the New York City Criminal Court. Some kind of clerk meets me outside.

'Have you got representation?'

'No.'

He points at a guy in a suit. 'Okay, he's going to represent you.'

My new defence counsel goes, 'What happened?'

I tell him the story. He's listening, but he's not taking it in. It's like he's heard it a thousand times.

'Yeah . . . Okay . . . Right . . . I'll say that . . . Are you pleading guilty?'

'No! I'm not! I just told you – I didn't do anything!'

'Okay.'

They bring me in and Shaggy and Victor are there. They've been waiting for hours, taking turns with Den to make sure someone's there for me when I get out. I'm so, so happy to see people I know.

'My client says he wasn't involved,' says the lawyer. 'He pleads not guilty to assault.'

The judge says he'll see us back here in ten days.

Victor heads off to give the rest of the lads the news. Me and Shaggy walk out onto Centre Street, a couple of blocks off Broadway. It's two in the afternoon.

Shaggy says we could do with a stiff drink.

*

Later, back at the hotel, Damo's feeling really bad about what happened and I don't feel like facing reality. I call my parents and Amy. I play it down, give them the positives.

'Look, I'm out now. It'll get sorted.'

Then we all hit the town and for the next two nights everything is put on hold. Time enough to think when I sober up.

I fly down to Victor's place in Florida with Shaggy and Den, stressed but still in escape mode.

Damo's due back at work. He heads for home. He's gutted about what I'm facing and he says he'll do whatever he can to get me off, but the prospect of having to go back to New York on my own fills me with dread.

Once we're out of the big city, everything slows down and the air is easier to breathe. But not for long.

At a bar in Fort Myers, a couple of hours after we land, I feel it rising up inside me.

First, the sense of panic, the worry about what's coming next.

And then, out of nowhere, Barry.

I haven't grieved for him, not really. After the shock of being told, and the distress of the funeral, there was only numbness and confusion.

And now, four weeks on, when I've never needed to hear his voice more, it hits me like a tidal wave.

I can't call him: he's gone.

I walk outside because I can feel the tears coming and I don't want to be around anyone.

I'm still sobbing my eyes out when they come outside to comfort me. Victor says it took him weeks and weeks to properly grieve for his father and that makes me want to call home and talk to Amy, Mum and Dad. I make the calls, still in bits.

Then I call Barbara, because I need to tell her, more than anyone, all the things I'll miss about Barry and what he meant to me as a friend.

She listens as the emotion pours out of me, more than I knew was there. She cries some tears of her own.

When I put down the phone I just want to go home on the next flight out.

*

The rest of the week is a nightmare, the furthest thing possible from a holiday. I spend so much time on my phone, the next bill is for four and a half grand.

Back in New York, my friend Sean Cunningham is unbelievably supportive. Through her friend Liv Morgan, Amy puts me in touch with an Irish lawyer called John Gardiner. He has a connection to Liv's brother-in-law, Niall Fitzgibbon, and he can't do enough for me. He understands the justice system in the States and he gets my head around what's coming next. At a time of real angst, people are really turning up for me.

My head nearly bursts with all the questions.

If I stick with my not-guilty plea, does that drag it all out until there's some kind of trial?

If there's a trial, will they believe me?

If it gets out back home, what's that going to do to me?

Some of the advice I'm getting from other quarters is to plead guilty and accept a misdemeanour. They say I'll get away with community service. It'll be so far below the radar nobody will find out.

I'm still emotionally shredded over Barry, but even in my fragile state there's nothing about this scenario that I like.

'No. No! I'm not pleading guilty! That's nuts! I'm not

admitting to something I haven't done, just to make life easier!'

A friend of a friend says I should lawyer-up big-time. 'I've got this really high-end guy,' he says. 'It might cost you ten or fifteen grand but we'll blow this thing out of the water.'

'Whoa! Whoa! Hold on! First of all, what do I need a high-end lawyer for? I'm innocent here! I just need someone to represent me and to listen to me.'

Which is what the laid-back Phyllis Mingione does the following Monday, after Sean makes the introductions.

'We're challenging this,' she tells the judge. 'This is *not* how it went down.'

It's over in seconds. Case adjourned.

8. A Different Kind of Player

Phyllis M. Mingione, attorney-at-law, goes about getting the charge against me thrown out.

She says it's an open-and-shut case of mistaken identity, but they won't let it go.

She tells the district attorney's office that Damo will come forward, but they suspect his motives: taking a bullet for his buddy, the well-known Irish sports guy.

Even after Damo files a sworn affidavit, absolving me of any responsibility and stating that he acted in self-defence, it drags on through the summer.

When Phyllis looks for the CCTV footage from Madison Square Garden, it turns out the camera we need was broken on the night.

All the while, I keep thinking the story is going to break on the front page of some newspaper and I keep worrying about the consequences, but somehow it stays under the radar.

Back in Dublin, there are triggers that bring Barry into my head, little things that only he would have got, sometimes a note in his handwriting that I kept for some unknown reason, or letters forwarded from Bird Avenue with his name on them, or when I see a red Mini, the car he drove. The more I think of him, the more I'm thrown off kilter.

It takes the kindness of close friends to bring some perspective. A beautifully written card arrives from Den, reminding me of the good times with Barry, of how he kept my life real at a time when things were changing so fast and bordering on the surreal.

But still it's tough. As the new season arrives I'm in a negative space – questioning things, including my rugby. It's more than a year and a half since I scored for Leinster. I'm a glass-half-full kind of person and I've never let a run of try-less games bother me before, but now it feels like an age since I played well and I start wondering if there's a good reason.

Am I just on the way down now?

Amy does her best to shake me out of it – 'You're being too hard on yourself! Nobody's career is always up!' – but I find it hard to reignite myself for the new season.

In August, I meet up with Declan Kidney. He has assembled a new coaching team with impressive credentials. Gert Smal, forwards coach for South Africa when they won the 2007 World Cup, is over the pack. Les Kiss, a former rugby league pro in Australia, is our new defence coach. With David Knox heading home to Australia, Alan Gaffney is returning as Leinster backs coach six years after taking the head coach job with Munster and he's double-jobbing with Ireland. Our performance analyst, Mervyn Murphy, who served under both Eddie and Gats, is still on board, as is Mark Tainton, brought in by Eddie as kicking coach back in the day.

Four years on from his unhappy spell with Leinster, Deccie strikes me as far more formidable and more sure of his strengths. Man management is probably his strongest suit. He operates on the basis that the guys he's working with are people first and players second. When I tell him how hard Barry's death has hit me, he responds with compassion.

When I trust him with the details of the New York episode, he's not worried about the story breaking. He sees the situation for what it is: a distraction that needs to be put to bed and out of my head.

When I say I'm unhappy with my form – that I've been stuttering since the World Cup – he is reassuring but also practical. He suggests giving up the Leinster captaincy.

'Do your own pre-season – don't worry about the other fellas,' he says. 'Just see if you can enjoy it.'

We both know he has a decision to make on the Ireland captaincy, but I keep my powder dry and he keeps his cards close to his chest: 'We don't have to make a decision on that until November.'

Cheiks is all for the idea of me stepping down from the job at Leinster, probably because he needs me to start stepping up as a game-changer. Telling a coach that you're low in confidence can be a dangerous place to go – you're reminding them how well you're *not* playing. But he has some massive signings on board and he's going hell for leather to win a Heineken Cup. In the back row, Rocky Elsom has joined us on a one-year deal from Australia, we've got a seasoned Springbok prop in C. J. van der Linde and an absolute genius in Isa Nacewa, signed from Auckland and equipped to play almost anywhere in the backline.

We might be tired of being written off as a soft touch when the chips are down, but it's going to take more than a Magners League to change people's perceptions. 'The only way we can shove it down their throats is to win the Heineken Cup,' Cheiks tells us. He tells me it won't feel any less sweet if we win it and I'm not captain after leading the team for three years, and I buy into that.

Leo takes the armband, an excellent choice. We start the season looking pretty good. We put 50 points and six tries on Edinburgh in game two, three from Luke Fitzgerald – already a star on the day before his twenty-first birthday. With Kearns on the other wing and Shaggy on the bench, the backline has never been harder to get into. Johnny Sexton is pushing hard for the number 10 jersey but Felipe's the incumbent and we've got another option in Isa.

In the pack, some serious players are coming through, home-grown in our academy. With the Edinburgh game won, Sean O'Brien and Cian Healy come off the bench. The following week, Rocky Elsom flies in and he's named at number 6 in our fourth game of the season and the one that will show us where we're really at: Munster at home.

It's sold out three days before kick-off and there's a massive buzz in the RDS.

We're more than up for it, but we don't even scratch them.

Leinster 0, Munster 18.

*

Two weeks later, we beat Edinburgh in the first pool match of the 2008–9 Heineken Cup, and I do something I haven't done in a Leinster jersey for one year, eight months and twenty-three days: I score a try. Felipe busts them on the halfway line and once I get on his shoulder it's a straightforward run-in from thirty metres, but it gives me pleasure because I've seen it early, and if I'd been lazy I wouldn't have picked it up. Rocky barrels through them for a try of his own and it's blindingly obvious that after a couple of weeks he is already giving us something different.

The following Saturday we're 30 points better than Wasps and I put two more tries on the board. The second is all about instinct – a chip over Eoin Reddan's head two metres in from the touchline, then a fly-hack into the sky from practically out of Jeremy Staunton's hands. By the time it comes back down and into my arms I'm three metres short, with Tom Voyce on my back, but there's no way I'm not finishing it from there and he falls over the line with me.

When the autumn internationals come around and Deccie offers me the captaincy, I gratefully accept. I'm still not fully happy with my form, but I'm hoping to play my way back and at least I've finally starting scoring again.

It's been eighteen months since we played well, but there's no doubting the quality in the Ireland squad. The idea of being captain for six years and then losing it just as we're doing something special kills me. It's never offered for more than a single stretch of games, but it always feels like too great an honour to turn down.

The ritual is always the same. We talk for twenty minutes, maybe half an hour, about nothing until finally he puts it out there.

'How do you feel about the captaincy?'

'Well . . . are you offering it to me?'

'Would you like to take it again?'

'Of course.'

'Grand, so.'

Deccie picks eleven Munster players in the twenty-two to play New Zealand at Croke Park. I'm one of six from Leinster. It's the fiftieth time I've captained my country. With the new coaching team on board there's a fair bit of optimism about us finally beating the All Blacks, but we never get going.

*

Quite a few media blades have been sharpened up for Leinster, and the double-header with Castres in December brings them down on top of us. We batter them 33–3 at home but pass poorly, drop balls, squander chances and leave the bonus point behind us.

Up to this point I've resisted sports psychology, partly because I've always thought it gimmicky, but mostly because I've never felt the need. The few brief experiences I have had, I found them trying to get you to answer *their* questions, rather than your own.

Cheiks is a believer. Or, at least, he believes in Enda McNulty, an All-Ireland-winning Gaelic footballer from Armagh building a career as a sports psychologist and helping a few of the Leinster players with the mental side of their game. So when he suggests a sit-down with Enda, I figure there's nothing to be lost.

On a wet Monday night two days after the Castres game, Enda is already *in situ* when I walk into Cheiks's poky office at Riverview. He's lean, fit-looking, barely thirty. I've seen him around but we've never really spoken.

Cheiks pulls down the blind on the only window and sets up the conversation.

'Brian hasn't been at his best for a while,' he says. 'He needs something to get him going again . . .'

Then he leaves.

I sit back with my arms folded, feet crossed, and I like Enda from minute one. He talks to me like a peer. He's got my immediate respect because he knows what it takes to win. He's easy-going and he hasn't got me on a clock, but he hasn't come to make small-talk either.

When somebody is underperforming, he says, there's usually more than one reason why. 'So – where are you at, Brian?'

'I'm not enjoying it as much,' I say. 'I'm doubting my ability at the moment.'

Hanging on the wall behind him there are framed pictures

of the different Leinster squads coached by Cheiks since 2005. Den is in the front row with me in all of them. We're sitting up with big smiles, not a care in the world.

I nod at the photograph taken last summer. 'I've got some good friends who aren't here any more. It's not the same as it was.'

He says he can understand that, up to a point. But: 'Is there not something to be enjoyed about the new kids coming on the scene?'

When I tell him I'm thinking of giving up the Ireland captaincy he drills down for the reasoning.

'My captaincy is about leading by example,' I tell him. 'I don't think I've been doing that for a bit.'

For every negative thought I come out with, he throws two or three positives back at me.

'Can you not develop as a leader?'

'Do you not think you'd feel more confident as captain with a run of form behind you?'

'Do you think Michael Jordan never had a performance slump?'

There's something manufactured about the process – X leads to Y leads to Z – but I find myself buying in to the man.

'Physically, how do you feel?'

'I'm in decent condition.'

'How about your nutrition?'

'Considerably better than it used to be.'

'How would you score it, percentage wise, the last two weeks?'

'Seventy?'

'Can you make it eighty-five or ninety?'

His questions keep coming, but he has one essential point behind them.

'It doesn't sound like a lot is different. What's changed about you?'

'I'm just not as confident. I always thought I'd be able to change a game until the day I quit playing. I don't feel that at the minute.'

'You're twenty-nine, Brian. You're not thirty-nine. What's your self-talk like, out on the pitch?'

'Not very good. I'm annoyed about the negative thoughts I'm having.'

'What are you thinking?'

'I'm thinking that I don't feel I have the capability of beating guys, the way I used to.'

He asks me to compare the attributes I had as a young player back in 1998, the year before my Ireland debut, to those of the player I am now. He gets me to rate myself, percentage-wise, for both years and writes down the numbers.

Self-confidence in 1998 vs 2008: 90 per cent vs
   50 per cent
Self-talk: 90 per cent vs 30 per cent
Ability to change a game: 90 per cent vs 70 per cent
Ability to play off the cuff: 100 per cent vs 40 per cent

'We need to halt that negative self-talk,' he says. He tells me he was in the crowd when I scored the two tries against Wasps. He pulls out a notebook and starts hitting me with more positives – the good things I did in that game. 'You were absolutely blitzing guys.'

Not quite true, but the second try was all about instinct and it's nice to be reminded of one of the better days.

Whatever guard I had up at the start is well down after an hour, so I start talking about how I'm still down over Barry, about how the New York thing is still hanging over my head, stressing me out. Six months on, I still don't know how it's going to pan out for me.

I tell him there are mornings when I don't have the same motivation as before to go training, evenings when Amy is working and I'm lying on the couch for most of the night, thinking about what was in Barry's head.

He says that what I'm feeling is natural, normal, that all the pieces are interconnected: 'It's not what happens in life – it's how you choose to react to it.'

He says he's finding it hard to see how I'm not the same player I was during the 2007 Six Nations, the last time I played really well.

He asks me to think about my best tries, tackles, passes, poaches. He says I need to watch them on YouTube, to remind myself of the ability I have.

When we finish up he says the conversation is worthless unless there's a call to action at the end of it. He asks me where I want to get to in 2009, and I tell him I want to be nominated for IRB world player of the year – and Lions captain in South Africa.

We walk back to our cars and he gives me his number.

'We need to have a bit of a plan here,' he says. 'You really need to reflect on whether this can add value. If it doesn't I won't waste your time.'

I text him a couple of days later and tell him I'm in.

The following Friday night in Castres we put up our worst performance in a long time. We can't string anything together. We can feel it slipping but we can't produce anything to stop it. We need somebody to step up and nobody does.

The three-point defeat puts us on the back foot in the pool from a position of full control.

A former Ireland international – not exactly noted as a

warhorse in the trenches during his playing days – knocks himself out in the *Sunday Tribune*.

Disgraceful. Gutless. Leaderless. Spineless. Ladyboys. Now out of the Heineken Cup.

Cheiks circles the wagons. We're hurting, but there's a togetherness in our squad that's not going to be broken.

*

On the Monday evening after the Castres defeat, I arrive in Enfield, County Meath, for a three-day international camp knowing I'm going to need to do something if I'm to hold on to the captaincy – like be a real leader when we split into smaller groups to talk about where we're going. Things have been too negative in the camp and a change of tack is needed.

There are journalists calling for the captaincy to be taken off me and given to Paulie for the Six Nations. I know I still have the Leinster guys with me, but Munster outnumber us two to one.

So, the way I see it, it comes down to Rog.

If he still thinks I'm the right man, I'll have other Munster players on board.

If he doesn't, I'm in trouble.

We've got on really well since he first came into the squad, but his admiration for Paulie is at an all-time high. Straight after Munster's second Heineken Cup win, he was comparing him to Martin Johnson and heading up his campaign to lead the Lions in South Africa.

'You have to be looking at this fella,' he said. 'Paul is an exceptional captain.'

As soon as I saw the quote in the paper I texted him: *Don't you worry about your old buddy – the guy who was captain on the last Lions tour!*

I said it jokingly – and nobody could have doubted Paulie's credentials – but many's the true word spoken in jest. Rog was in his Munster zone then and there's no better man to get emotional about the red jersey. Five months later, in the week of the New Zealand game, he sat alongside me and Deccie at an Ireland press conference and threw out a hand grenade of a soundbite.

'I don't believe our problems are with the opposition,' he said. 'We just need to start buying into the Irish jersey a little more.'

Now, behind closed doors in Enfield, Rob Kearney puts another cat among the pigeons by questioning if the Munster players bring the same passion to the green jersey that they show when wearing red. It's a ballsy point for a young guy to make and it doesn't make a difference if there's something in it or not, because a team underperforming for sixteen months needs all the honesty it can get.

Marcus Horan speaks from the heart and rebuts the point, but putting it out there in the first place for it to be shot down is a big thing to do and Kearns soars in everyone's estimation, none more than in my own. Even if the Munster players don't believe it, they definitely think about it. Just having the discussion brings us closer together as a squad.

Once we break for coffee I make for Rog and lay some honesty of my own on him.

We haven't really spoken properly since the summer tour, so I'm not sure where I stand with him. It's the first time I've ever had to ask the question, but I need to know the answer.

'Do you still believe in me as captain of this team?'

He could kick for touch. He could give me a watered-down 'Yes'.

But that wouldn't be Rog.

'Yeah. I do,' he says. Then he qualifies it. 'But I think you could be a bit fitter.'

'Okay . . . Fair enough.'

It's not the kind of comment you like to hear from a team-mate but it's also undeniable that one of Munster's strengths in winning Heineken Cups has been a high level of fitness. So I take it on board and make my mind up once and for all about the captaincy.

I'm not giving it up.

At least, not willingly.

When the camp breaks up, the squad is in a much better place ahead of the Six Nations.

As players we've been brutally honest with one another. We've got a simplified game plan with an emphasis on aggression.

There's no reason we can't give the championship a good rattle.

*

Early in the new year, I meet Enda McNulty again and we talk for an hour and a half at my kitchen table. Sometimes you just need to be reminded of your strengths, the attributes that got you this far, things you've known all along but lost sight of, for whatever reason.

Slowly but surely, I feel my confidence coming back and reports of our Heineken Cup elimination turn out to be exaggerated. Felipe kicks four penalties and we dig in to take a losing bonus point off Wasps in a dogfight at Twickenham, which puts us back in control of the group. He knocks over four more the following week against Edinburgh, and the win is enough to put us in the quarter-finals, drawn away to Harlequins.

The following week, at the Strand Hotel in Limerick, I'm two steps behind Deccie as we walk into a room of journalists and photographers ten days before the start of the 2009 Six Nations.

Deccie flashes them a smile, maybe because he knows I'm not the guy some of them were hoping to see on his shoulder.

If Paulie is disappointed he doesn't show it. My friendship with him isn't as close as the one I have with Rog, but we talk on the phone from time to time to give one another a steer on something or other. Away from the Ireland camp we're healthy rivals but I very much enjoy his company off the field and I couldn't have any more respect for him on it.

It's been a while since we talked properly and it's a measure of the man that he comes to my room to make sure there's no problem between us.

Typical Paulie, he cuts to the chase.

He says he's not looking for the captaincy, not unless I don't want to do it any more.

He says he heard a few whispers after the summer tour about his intentions. 'Where do you stand on it?' he asks. 'Do you think I was looking for the job?'

I tell him it came into my head in New Zealand, but that I was all over the place about Barry at the time.

'Well, I'm quite happy in my role,' he says. 'Just so you know.'

By the time we're through talking any unspoken tension between us has gone, and it's mostly down to Paulie for taking the bull by the horns.

A big man in more ways than one.

The opening game of the Six Nations is a week and a half

away. As if on cue, the word comes through from Phyllis in New York.

The case against me isn't going anywhere. The district attorney has had enough.

He throws it out and drops the charges.

*

It might be a cliché but it's 100 per cent true: the Six Nations is a tournament of momentum. Lose the first game and you're looking at mid-table. Win it – particularly against a big beast like France – and all things seem possible.

We run out feeling confident, in a good place, determined to front up and force a confrontation. People ask about fear on the rugby pitch, but once you cross the white line it's not really about safety because, other than a neck injury, everything else is pretty much repairable. If somebody hits you with a good shot, you can worry about another coming your way or you can pick yourself up and think, Right, that's one–nil. Let's see if we can make it one–all.

The fear that you feel before you run onto the field is different. It's a fear of not delivering, of not living up to your own expectations. Sometimes it can smother you, but when your preparation is right, it's not a bad feeling to have.

No doubt about it, we owe France one. We haven't beaten them in seven years. They're not lacking in ambition either. They want to play, to keep the ball alive, to come at us hard and fast, and they do.

At half-time we're ahead 13–10, thanks to a seriously good team try finished off spectacularly by Jamie Heaslip. Our movement is sharp, we're building phases, punching holes, choking them in the tackle zone.

I'm becoming a different kind of player: less dangerous as

a broken-field runner, more effective in the defensive line and around the rucks. If aspects of your game are waning, you have to enhance others and be grateful for the parts that don't have a best-before date, like the ability to see things that maybe others don't, or see them a split-second earlier. A particular pass, a possible gap, a defender who can be taken out with one step.

But I'm not quite pensioned off yet as a strike runner.

Two minutes into the second half, Paulie takes another perfect dart from Jerry Flannery high above his head and delivers it fast to Tomás O'Leary. When it comes to me from Rog I'm thirty metres out, with zero thought of making their try line. I'm just looking to give us some go-forward, but once I get through Lionel Beauxis and Yannick Jauzion it all opens up, and Julien Malzieu is coming across so hard from the far wing that any step inside is going to do him. Try.

Beauxis recovers impressively. He sets up Maxime Médard for a try. Then he kicks a drop goal to bring them back to two points down: 20–18.

On comes Darce, a year to the week since breaking his arm in five places, back among us after the rumours that his race was run. He's only a few minutes on the pitch when the pack drive us forward again – sucking in defenders, getting us closer, a few metres short. When it's shipped to the backline Darce is the first receiver. I'm on his outside, waiting for the pass. He runs at them from seven or eight metres. He has defenders left, right and dead in front of him. He has no right to score, but he gets a yard on Thierry Dusautoir with a brilliant step, and even when one of the most lethal tacklers in world rugby has two arms wrapped around his waist – and two more defenders between him and the try line – Darce twists and turns and finds a way through. I'm right up close as he comes up with the ball still tucked under his arm and the biggest smile in the world on his face. He is mobbed by half a dozen of us – team-mates and friends, thrilled to have him back.

We see it out, 30–21. The official end of the World Cup hangover.

In Rome we hammer away at Italy, only a score ahead at half-time, but we kick on from there and open up near the end.

Confidence in Test-match rugby is about backing yourself, about anticipation. Without it, you don't see the same opportunities, or you see them too late.

Once you hesitate, they vanish.

React early and the rewards will come.

And sometimes it's like a game of chess.

With three minutes left at the Stadio Flaminio, the Italian full-back, Andrea Masi, comes onto the ball ten metres short of our 22. He has three men outside him and they're still chasing the game. Masi is trying to make something happen and – in our defensive line – I'm trying to get into his head.

In his position, I wouldn't be throwing the simple pass to the guy next to me – that's not going to unlock a defence. I'm going to throw something with a bit of width, get it out there to a more vulnerable area of the pitch, where the space is, as quickly as I can.

He throws the miss pass. I'm out of the blocks as soon as it leaves his hands and under their posts ten seconds later.

We're two from two, but we're not getting carried away. Plenty of us have been here before. It's my tenth Six Nations, my ninetieth start for Ireland. For Luke Fitzgerald, scorer of two tries in Rome, the number of starts is now five. For

Tomás, it's four. Later on, over a few beers, our new scrum-half sees no reason to rein in his optimism.

'You fellas have been hammering away for years,' he says. 'You need some of us young lads to come in and win you a Slam.'

He doesn't mean it as a throwaway remark. He's having a laugh, but there's belief behind his point, just pure confidence coming out of him.

Grand Slam? No biggie.

And it plants a seed. We look at the three fixtures ahead – England in Croke Park, Scotland and Wales away – and we all start thinking the same way.

This is 100 per cent achievable.

Martin Johnson, England's boss for less than a year in his first coaching job, takes a strong team to Dublin two weeks later. We're never lacking in motivation when England come to town, but it says plenty about his stature in the game that the idea of beating them with him at the helm adds a touch to the incentive.

In the dressing room at Croke Park, after the captain's run the day before the game, I get chatting to Darce about the living legend who goes by the name of Rala.

Paddy O'Reilly – kit man, confidant, itinerary king, friend to one and all – has come up with a new wheeze. Every night he pushes the schedule for the following day under our doors and on every itinerary since we went into camp for this Six Nations there has been a piece of wisdom for us to mull on, listed under the heading 'Rala's Thought of the Day'.

Tuesday, 24 February 2009
Courage is not how a man stands or falls, but how he gets back up again.

Thursday, 26 February 2009
Love your work.

Friday, 27 February 2009
Knowledge is knowing that a tomato is a fruit. Wisdom is knowing not to put it in a fruit salad.

Darce is loving Rala's latest thought. My Friday-afternoon press conference is imminent. He bets me I can't get the line into one of my answers.

I laugh. I fancy my chances. 'I'll bet you I can.'

'No way.'

'Okay – if I get it in, you have to get a back, sack and crack wax.'

'You're on.'

The press conference is meandering along when I decide the moment has come. It doesn't matter what the next question is, the answer is going to be the same.

'Brian,' somebody says, 'you share a sponsor, or did share a sponsor . . .'

I smile, grimace, bite my lip, wait for him to finish, barely hearing a word.

'. . . with what's his name, that English bloke, Martin Johnson. Can you tell us something about him, what you thought of him?'

I avoid eye contact until the first part of it is out.

'I dunno, ahm, you know . . . knowledge is knowing that a tomato is a fruit . . .'

By the time I've delivered the pay-off line I'm in full control. I start nodding, as sagely as I can. The journalists laugh.

'Eric Cantona,' one of them says.

Deccie rubs his eye, as baffled as the rest of them.

My smile is partly for the assembled media, but mostly for Darce.

'I don't care how long it takes,' I tell him later, 'but I'll be seeing through that forfeit.'

England, well drilled in defence by our old coach Mike Ford, are incredibly difficult to break down. We force a couple of penalties but it's not Rog's best day with the boot. It's 3–3 at half-time, anyone's game. I put us ahead early in the second half with a free drop at goal after the referee has signalled for a penalty.

A few minutes later I fly out of the line and put a half-decent shot on Riki Flutey, which evidently doesn't go down well because within ten seconds he's body-checking me as I'm putting boot to ball. He hits me high and late, bang into the temple with a glancing blow from the side of his head. I stumble backwards and hit the floor. It takes me a while to get back up. I'm not seeing double, I haven't lost my balance – I've just got a banging headache.

Not much more than a minute later I'm back down, blocked by Delon Armitage after kicking ahead and cutting infield off the left-hand touchline, hit late again with a bang to the sternum.

I've still got a splitting pain in the head from the first incident as I jog back into position, expecting Rog to go for the posts with the penalty, but as I turn around the ball is already in the corner after a conflab between Paulie and Rog, and the part of my head that isn't pounding is thinking: *Fire away there, lads – don't worry about me!*

But sometimes you can only shake your head and smile at the relentless drive of these guys.

Our pack have the bit between their teeth. They're pounding away, sniffing the try, forcing England to compete illegally on the deck, which brings a yellow card for Phil Vickery and a five-metre scrum. We're camped on their line, but one after the other our big ball-carriers are stopped centimetres short.

Another ruck. I hover at the fringes, watching and waiting. My head still hurts but I'm in full control of my senses and I fancy my chances. I'm thinking, Just give me a shot.

Tomás pops it up to me. Two metres from the line, I take it in low and fast. They've got two big men defending the line – Nick Kennedy and Julian White. They're beaten by speed, unable to get down and under me in time.

Ireland 11, England 3.

They come back with a penalty, but with ten to go, indiscipline costs them again and the cameras pick up a moment of TV gold. Johnno slams down a fist as Danny Care is shown a yellow card – England's second – not long after coming onto the pitch.

Rog makes it a two-score game from the penalty, and we're more than grateful for the cushion when Armitage goes over in the corner a minute from time for a converted try.

It finishes 14–13. We are battered, shattered, but still on course.

Ahead of picking the team to face Scotland at Murrayfield a fortnight later, Deccie pulls me aside. I've already picked up a vibe from Rog that he's planning changes, but I'm not expecting four guys to fall out of an unbeaten team. Nobody is, particularly the four who are given the bad news – Fla, Jamie, Tomás and Paddy Wallace.

'I didn't want to wait until we lost before I made some changes,' he tells me.

I don't quite follow the logic but I don't have a say in selection.

'Some people aren't going to be happy,' I tell him.

In come Rory Best, Leams, Strings and Darce – all four proof positive of the depth in our squad.

We're average enough against the Scots, slow to get going, three points behind on the scoreboard with a minute left in the first half.

Thom Evans chips a ball over my head and follows his own kick, running hard at Rog and beating him without breaking stride after the ball bounces obligingly into his arms.

I'm slow to react, I'm dawdling. Their fly-half, Phil Godman, rockets past me and shows for the pass just as Tommy Bowe comes flying across and onto Evans. As Tommy swings off him I can see it all unfold: the offload to Godman, the score in the corner a couple of seconds before half-time – killer timing.

Sheer panic kicks in and I accelerate after Godman.

Tommy brings Evans down but he gets the pass away, two-handed and straight into Godman's path, two metres from the try line.

I'm on him as soon as the ball is in his hands and I bundle him in touch with a tackle that's more satisfying than any try.

We take the game to them in the second half. Strings busts them with a twenty-metre break and Jamie – on for the injured Leams – is on his shoulder when he looks for support.

We win by seven points.

Four down, one to go.

*

On the following Monday evening, at our hotel in Killiney, Deccie calls out the team.

Everyone is desperate to start. We know our families will all be there, our closest friends, travelling by boat and plane, willing us on, hoping for history – a first Irish Slam in sixty-one years.

For three of the boys left out against Scotland – Fla, Tomás, Jamie – there is massive relief. Darce keeps his place so Paddy Wallace doesn't make it back in, tough on him after a big tournament.

It's a 22 with a formidable look: Rob Kearney; Tommy Bowe, Brian O'Driscoll, Gordon D'Arcy, Luke Fitzgerald; Ronan O'Gara, Tomás O'Leary; Marcus Horan, Jerry Flannery, John Hayes; Donncha O'Callaghan, Paul O'Connell; Stephen Ferris, David Wallace, Jamie Heaslip. Replacements: Rory Best, Tom Court, Mick O'Driscoll, Denis Leamy, Peter Stringer, Paddy Wallace, Geordan Murphy.

Once the game draws near, my stress levels rise. I sleep badly, too caught up in what might be, wanting it so much, knowing what leaving it behind would do to us.

It's our second Grand Slam decider and we're certain of one thing: there's no way we'll be blown off the park, like we were by England in 2003. Wales are a good side, Slam winners last year, but we travel to Cardiff on the Friday morning believing in ourselves completely.

Once I start writing down my points for the captain's meeting, the stress leaves me. What I say when the lads are in front of me can be summed up in a word: believe.

On the night before a game there's nothing to beat a rub from the great Willie Bennett, the world's most positive man. Dave Revins, our other masseur, has the most talented pair of hands ever, but Willie brings a different dynamic.

He reckons every player on his massage bed before a game is 110 per cent ready to play. The guy could be falling apart, bothered by any amount of niggles, but in Willie's world you'd never know it.

'What sort of shape is he in, Willie?'

'He's in phenomenal nick!'

Even if a guy comes back from long-term injury, brutally conditioned and carrying a lot of weight, he puts the best possible spin on it.

'How's he looking, Willie?'

'Very good, yeah. Very *strong*.'

A little on the lean side after feeling unwell?

'Great, yeah. Very *fast*.'

It feels like I've been getting special treatment from Willie for the best part of a decade and now, hours before the biggest game of all our lives, he knows what we need to hear. We know it's coming, but it still feels brilliant when he comes out with it, especially when you've got more than a few miles on the clock.

'Jeez, you're in great shape! . . . Ten years of rugby and you're still in incredible condition!'

We wait for his pay-off line as we clamber off the massage bed and he never disappoints.

'You're flying it! Absolutely flying it!'

For us, the time-honoured tradition of a visit to Rala's room on the evening before an international is nothing short of sacred.

'Is this a social call,' he'll say to the lads, 'or do you have business?'

People drop in and out, sometimes looking for a stud or a lace, but mostly just to shoot the breeze and relax before the stresses that lie ahead.

We know that when the time comes to hang up the boots, this little ritual is one of the things we will miss the most. I like to arrive last, knowing there'll still be a jelly or two left from his stash and plenty of chat to round off the day.

There's something comforting and reassuring about cleaning my boots in his room as he makes sure all the gear we'll need for the game is ready to go, despite the best efforts of the boys to mess everything up on him. It can be a brutal business and coaches come and go, but they've all had the good sense to recognize what Rala brings to the squad.

For us, he is so much more than a kitman. It was Shaggy who coined the expression 'A happy Rala is a happy camp' and we players feed off his good form. There's nothing he won't do for the lads – so it's no surprise when he puts up little resistance as he is wrapped in a duvet, bound with masking tape, then gagged and bundled into the glass lift of the Hilton hotel. The lads send him straight down to the lobby and when the doors open and various guests step back in shock, we are laughing our heads off from the balcony overhead.

*

The Millennium is the greatest rugby stadium in the world. On the biggest days, the atmosphere is sensational. The place is already rocking ten minutes in when we lose Stephen Ferris with a hand injury. Cruel luck for a class player, a one-man wrecking ball. Leams comes on, a week after injuring his shoulder, in for a longer shift than anyone had imagined.

At half-time we're 6–0 down but not panicking, still believing.

We fly into them in the second half. It's like a mirror image of the pressure we put on England – forwards hammering away at them, phase after phase, close to their line.

First Leamy.

Then Marcus.

Donners.

Wally.

Paulie again, with Lukie latching onto him. A foot short.

I come up from behind, straining to see the ball, crouching to collect it once Paulie lets it go.

Their hooker, Matthew Rees, is guarding the line in front of me, fully alert and bending low, but I can see a patch of grass between his feet and my body trajectory is flat enough to get under him.

I think I'm still in control of the ball as it brushes the line, but I'm a long way from sure. When Wayne Barnes blows the whistle and goes upstairs to the TMO, there are 74,645 people in the stadium and only one who seems convinced that a try has been scored: Jerry Flannery. He nods vigorously. He assures me it's good, based on his view through a forest of legs from ten metres away.

It takes Romain Poite, the TMO, less than a minute to make up his mind.

'Wayne, I 'ave a decision for you . . . It's a try.'

Three minutes later we're 14–6 ahead, thanks to a planned move that's all about how Shane Williams reacts in their blitz defence. A lovely chip into space from Rog bounces up and catches Gavin Henson cold. Tommy Bowe has serious pace and he picks a line that puts him straight between the posts.

Now we should kick on and finish them off, but we let them back in.

Two penalties, both landed by Stephen Jones: 12–14.

Another from Henson on halfway: short.

On seventy-three minutes I see another intercept waiting to happen, the chance to make it a nine-point game. Stephen Jones, ten metres inside our half and moving right, shapes to throw a miss pass to Shane Williams. I've analysed their set-up for this particular play. No different from ourselves, they have staple moves. I just need to back myself. I read it but hesitate for a millisecond, caught between intercepting it and nailing Williams, and ending up doing neither.

The pressure comes on. We don't buckle but they get Jones in the pocket for a drop goal and he bangs it straight through the middle: 15–14.

From the kick-off we've got four minutes and forty seconds to save ourselves.

And we have Rog.

We catch a break when Stephen Jones kicks a ball out on the full seconds after the restart. From the moment that Paulie claims the lineout, there's only one play.

When it finally comes, the pass from Strings couldn't be sweeter. I'm right alongside Rog as he drops the ball on the 22-metre line. There's nobody in world rugby I'd rather have for what comes next. He is ice cool. He nails it.

Two minutes and fifteen seconds to go. We run back together. We've both been around too long to think that it's over.

With fifty seconds on the clock we see Paddy Wallace compete for the ball in a ruck just inside our half. We see Wayne Barnes signal a penalty advantage and then blow. And not one of us has any doubt that Stephen Jones will send the ball through our posts.

I'm ten metres from the goal line when the ball flies over my head, low enough to send hope shooting through me. I turn and see it falling into Geordan Murphy's hands. I watch Paulie charging off like a lunatic and Geordie running to the corner with the clock in red and the ball under his arm.

Mostly what runs through my head is a massive sense of relief.

We've got one, thank God. If I don't do anything else in my career, at least I've won a Grand Slam.

In those first seconds, when my fellow players are dancing around the pitch and the stadium is exploding with the happiness felt by tens of thousands of Irish supporters, my body is too stressed to react in the same way. Had the kick gone over, it wouldn't have changed the outcome of the championship – Wales needed a 13-point winning margin to take the title – but for us it would have changed everything. I would have had to lift the Six Nations trophy feeling like we had failed. Without the Slam, it would have been hollow and horrible.

As I stand near the posts trying to take it in, the complete agony of waiting for the kick – the certainty I'd felt that our best efforts were all for nothing, the *injustice* of that – is still too much of a shock to the system for me to suddenly switch to party mode.

But when the stress and the relief begin to subside, perhaps within ten or fifteen seconds, they are slowly replaced by a feeling of overwhelming, life-changing, unforgettable joy. Kearns comes to embrace me and we wrap our arms tight around each other, so grateful and so proud to have gotten over the line. Everywhere I look on the pitch I see grown men hugging – players, physios, support staff and then the coaches, down from their box after an emotional huddle.

The Field of Athenry rings out as they erect a presentation platform on the halfway line. Maybe I'm still catching up with the rest of the lads, but as President Mary McAleese stands alongside Prince William, waiting for us to be called forward, my level of happiness is off the chart.

I walk up when all the boys are on the platform, after Paulie has raised the Triple Crown shield.

Prince William puts a medal around my neck.

President McAleese looks just as excited as the rest of us. She lifts the trophy off the dais. She makes me wait, just a second or two, while my heart bursts out of my chest.

'I think I have something for you,' she says.

Finally, I get my hands on it.

And it means everything.

*

On the lap of honour, there are more memories that will never fade. The great Jack Kyle, out-half in the Ireland team that last won a Slam, way back in 1948, comes down from his seat in the stand and shakes my hand. Eighty-three years young, he is one of life's gentlemen and it's a thrill to see him so pleased.

'I'll gladly pass on the mantle,' he says. 'It's a weight off our shoulders.'

Further along, I meet Mum and Dad, more excited than I've ever seen them. One of the greatest things that high-level, high-pressure sport brings you is the expression on your parents' faces when everything works out. On the biggest days, it's a mental picture that stays with you forever.

I'm too blind to lay eyes on her but somewhere in the stands Amy is celebrating too, and Jules and Sue and so many more of the people who really matter to me. Dunny, my oldest friend, who's there with some of the Clontarf boys, calls out to me as we walk around the perimeter of the pitch, taking turns to parade the trophy. I could be wrong but it seems like the lads might already have had a few refreshments to help the day along. And they are beyond ecstatic.

For our new coaching team, it's a massive achievement in year one. But in his moment of triumph, Deccie has the class

Leinster had been underachieving for a number of years when Michael Cheika took over as our head coach in autumn 2005. Cheiks brought fun, ambition, frankness and – eventually – success (*Dan Sheridan/Inpho*)

With my old friend Damien O'Donohue and Colin Farrell in Los Angeles, summer 2007. A couple of nights later, we were going to go out with Colin to celebrate his birthday, but he had to cancel. That didn't stop Damo from blagging us into a private gig by Prince …

Arriving back at Dublin airport with Amy after the 2007 **World Cup** – earlier than expected. That World Cup was a disaster for us, with **four poor performances** in the group stage (*Morgan Treacy/Inpho*)

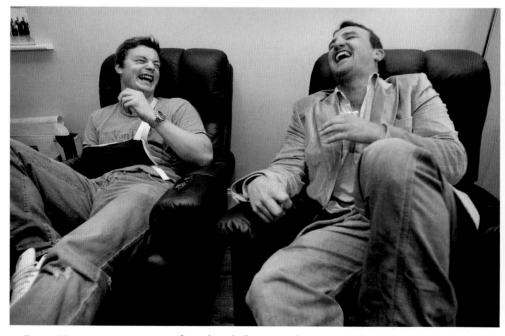

Barry Twomey was a great friend and, for several years, my house-mate. We were always laughing. His death in 2008 was **a terrible blow**

Burrowing through the English defence to score in our extremely tight 2009 Six Nations match. I'd taken two heavy knocks in the run-up to that score, and my head was hurting badly, but I was in full control of my senses (*Billy Stickland/Inpho*)

Lifting the Six Nations trophy, with Prince William and President McAleese looking on, after our narrow win over Wales. We'd have got the trophy even if Stephen Jones had landed his long-range penalty with the final kick of the game, but it would have felt hollow if we hadn't taken the Grand Slam (*Billy Stickland/Inpho*)

I got to meet Jack Kyle – captain of the last Ireland team to win a Grand Slam, in 1948 – in the run-up to the Wales match, and it was great to talk to him afterwards (*Morgan Treacy/Inpho*)

With my father – an Ireland international himself, but never officially capped – after winning the Grand Slam (*Morgan Treacy/Inpho*)

After a number of years of playing second fiddle to Munster, we turned the tables in the 2009 Heineken Cup semi-final at Croke Park. We already had the game well under control when I intercepted a pass by Ronan O'Gara and ran it in for a try *(Billy Stickland/Inpho)*

Celebrating at the final whistle of the 2009 Heineken Cup final, a hard-fought victory over Leicester and sweet redemption for a group of players who had taken a lot of stick over the years *(Billy Stickland/Inpho)*

In the ice bath with Jamie Roberts and Stephen Jones, on tour with the Lions in South Africa in 2009. Stephen is almost as pale as me – not an easy thing to achieve (*Dan Sheridan/Inpho*)

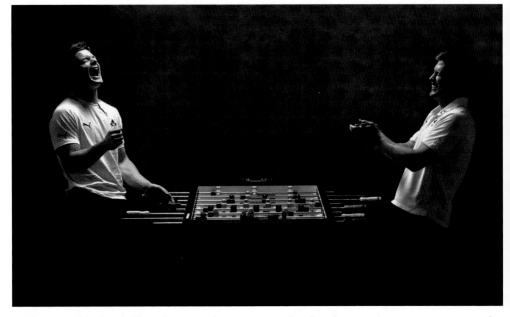

Playing table football with Rog – long-time Ireland and Lions teammate, provincial rival, and friend (*Billy Stickland/Inpho*)

With my three groomsmen on the morning of the wedding: Damo, Skiddy and – opening a bottle of vintage Dom Pérignon someone kindly gave me – Dunny (*John Ryan Photography*)

Amy and I – with Dunny and Amy's cousin Noleen – laughed our heads off at the wedding dinner (*John Ryan Photography*)

Running a support line behind Shaggy in the 2011 Heineken Cup final against Northampton. We were down 22–6 at half-time … (*Colm O'Neill/Inpho*)

… then stormed back to win 33–22, and celebrated accordingly (*Billy Stickland/Inpho*)

to remember Eddie and give him the credit he deserves, to acknowledge that, with a little more luck, it could have happened under his watch.

In the dressing room, for all of us, there is a feeling of incredible satisfaction.

*

With celebrating Irish fans everywhere, there's heavy security at the Hilton as we return from the Millennium, but I get Amy and my family in through the back door and up to my room on the fifth floor, where the trophy has pride of place and we take some treasured photos.

I'm so physically shattered and spent that I start to feel sick. I'm too unwell to attend the post-match dinner, so Paulie has to give the speech instead. It's a night when Cardiff belongs to the Irish and back home there are reports of the kind of nationwide party not seen since the glory days of Jack Charlton's Irish soccer team, but I'm tucked up in bed by 11 p.m., lights out and oblivious to it all.

I'm up at seven, full of life again, and I make my way to the hotel swimming-pool to kill a little time while the lads sleep on. But when I drop into the team room on my way back, I find the last of the night's revellers still going reasonably strong, with empty bottles of champagne close at hand.

'Morning, lads!'

'Drico! Have a drink?'

'I'll take a raincheck – thanks anyway!'

A homecoming reception is arranged for late afternoon outside the Mansion House in Dublin. On the plane home, we pass the trophy around again. Geordan Murphy, one of the partakers of champagne at dawn, is feeling a little peckish. He orders a ham sandwich and gets through half of it. The rest he drops into the Six Nations trophy, packet and all.

There's a sea of green when we arrive on Dawson Street, and it's brilliant to see what the Grand Slam means to the Irish people. It's only eighteen months since so many supporters travelled to Paris for the brutal disappointment of our non-existent World Cup. The economy has gone into meltdown in the meantime and it's nice to provide a brief distraction from all the doom and gloom.

Inside the Mansion House, after we show off our new acquisition, I go to fill the trophy with champagne one more time. I take the lid off and I'm about to pour away when I notice something resting at the bottom of the cup.

I take out the remains of Geordie's ham sandwich and empty the bottle.

The following morning, when I wake up alongside Amy at the Killiney Castle Hotel, the trophy is resting on the bed, maybe a little the worse for wear, but still real.

*

Me and Amy, we know our future is together. I want the moment I propose to her to be as memorable as I can make it, which calls for an element of surprise. So when she makes a point of commenting on other people's engagement rings . . .

'My God! That is stunning! Brian – isn't that beautiful?'

. . . I affect as much indifference as I can, having already stored the knowledge from a previous throwaway remark.

'Yeah, yeah, nice, whatever.'

I've got a very good idea of what she'd like but I need to make sure I get it right, so I take a close friend of hers into my confidence and get it custom-made. Then I come up with an elaborate plan to propose on her thirtieth birthday, which falls on the Saturday after we win the Slam.

There's no way on earth I'm doing it in front of an audience, so we have her birthday party at the house on the Friday. By the time she gets to bed it's six or seven in the morning after an epic night. To make sure she doesn't rumble my plan I book her an hour's massage in the house, and when she finally emerges in late afternoon, still in her dressing-gown and somewhat hung-over, I'm all set up. She has no idea.

The plan is to hit her with multiple birthday surprises, as in a treasure hunt around different parts of the house, leading to a crescendo in the back garden where she thinks the last present is waiting. Then – *ta-da!* – I produce the ring.

There's one flaw in this scenario, which is the unnecessarily large box for the ring. I'm worried she'll spot it in my pocket and guess, so I leave it in the garden. She has no inkling of what's coming when the big moment arrives, but when I pull the box out of its hiding place, I'm suddenly struck with nerves. I try to speak but there's a lump in my throat and for a few seconds I can't get the words out.

I compose myself. I start again.

She says yes.

Once she has the ring on her finger she gets curious.

'How long have you had this?'

'A couple of weeks.'

'What would have happened if you hadn't won last Saturday?'

I tell her our engagement has nothing to do with a game of rugby – win, lose or draw. 'This was happening one way or the other.'

I feel a real sense of happiness. Life is good.

9. Pokerface

Success is definitely a drug, but you need to win big to get properly addicted. If there's any part of Michael Cheika that worries about the Grand Slam sating the appetites of the Leinster players involved, then his concern is unnecessary.

When we get back to Riverview we couldn't be hungrier. If there was a tinge of regret for me on the day we won the Slam it was that some of the Leinster lads who soldiered with Ireland for years weren't on the pitch when it finally happened. I would have given a lot to share the moment with Den and Shaggy, in particular, and guys like Mal, Girv and Leo were a big part of the journey too.

Four of those five are in the squad when we run out at the Stoop in London on the second Sunday in April – our sixth Heineken Cup quarter-final in eight years.

Felipe kicks an early penalty and the rest of the first half is an arm-wrestle. With fifteen seconds left I chase my own kick and bolt for the line when the bounce takes out three of their defenders. I've got thirty metres to cover, and maybe the 2001 version would make it, but the one guy not beaten by the bounce turns out to be Ugo Monye, a winger with a 100-metres PB of 10.33 seconds. He gets a hand on my shoulder, and David Strettle arrives to stop me getting the ball down, but we still come away with three points when they're penalized in the ensuing ruck. Those points turn out to be precious.

With one minute and twenty seconds on the clock we lead

6–5 and they've got a lineout ten metres from our line. They've broken the law to get their All Black fly-half, Nick Evans, back on the pitch as a blood substitute, but we're oblivious to the circumstances.

We've never heard of blood capsules. We've seen their substitute Tom Williams walking off the pitch not long after coming onto it, looking like he's taken a left-right combination in the kisser from Mike Tyson, but we're too tired to ask questions. We've got our own shit going on. All we know is they've somehow got Evans back on to kick a drop goal and we need to stop him; any way, anyhow.

Put me up against a wall and ask for my biggest memories in a Leinster jersey and I'll go for tackles ahead of tries. And maybe, when all's said and done, I'll struggle to find a more satisfying moment than what comes next.

Nick Easter takes the lineout and gets it away to Danny Care in virtually one movement. Care fires it to one of their best strike-runners, Jordan Turner-Hall, as he's crossing the 22 with ten metres of open space in front of him. From here it's a straightforward drop-goal play: crash up and take the contact as close-in as possible, then wait for Care to come back around and ship the ball to Evans in the pocket.

Turner-Hall gets five or six metres over the gain line when Darce wraps himself around him – one of the all-time great defenders at his awesome best. He doesn't just soak him, he starts hauling him back to where he came from. I hit Turner-Hall from the opposite side and we double-team him until he's a metre short of the 22 and Evans – back-pedalling – is a lot closer to the halfway line than the posts. When he finally takes the pass from Care he's in hit-and-hope country and still carrying the knock that forced him off the field in the first place. The kick is short and left and it's game over.

Back in the changing room — and long before the word 'Bloodgate' enters the language and the Harlequins coach Dean Richards loses his job over it — Cheiks is in no doubt about the stunt they've tried to pull, faking Williams's blood injury.

In rugby sometimes, you get away with what you can, because it's a game of inches and fine margins. So you slow up their ball, try to kill their momentum and hope the referee doesn't reach for a card. Every so often you could argue that ten minutes in the bin is a price worth paying. You could look on it as cynical or you could make the case that it's about sacrificing yourself for the team.

But there's bending the rules and there's full-on cheating. And a world of difference in between.

*

The reward for beating Harlequins is a semi-final at Croke Park against Munster. They're coming off the back of maybe their most complete performance ever — an annihilation of the Ospreys in their home quarter-final — and they have eight players named in the Lions squad to our four: Kearns, Lukie, Jamie and me.

Paulie is captain. It was expected, but it's still a big enough disappointment when Ian McGeechan calls me with the news. I'm captain of the Grand Slam-winning team and the Lions feels like unfinished business, but on the plus side I'll be free of the endless responsibilities that come with the job.

I call Paulie to congratulate him, to tell him I'm looking forward to helping him any way I can. For both of us, the Lions experience can only get better.

The build-up to the Munster–Leinster semi-final feels even bigger than it did back in 2006. We're up against the defending European champions and we've lost to them twice already in the season. We've never been as nervous, but we're also sick of carrying the baggage of being losers when the chips are down, tired of the unflattering comparisons with Munster.

We want our own success, our own standards.

We have listened to guys with southside Dublin accents justify their allegiance to Munster on the basis of a mother born in Limerick, or a handful of childhood summers in Skibbereen.

On match days we have driven past pubs in our own city with Munster flags flying above them, unchallenged.

We have met, time after time, the people who feel the need to approach us for no particular reason other than to clarify their allegiance: 'We're Munster fans first – then Ireland.'

Even now, with 82,000 tickets sold in no time, a world-record crowd for a club game, we worry about running out to another sea of red in the heart of our own province.

More than anyone, Shaggy brings a siege mentality to the training ground as the game gets closer. He's at his best in these weeks.

For Cheiks, it's the moment of truth. He tells us we're more than good enough to win if we front up at the break-down, get our detail right and execute when the chances come. What we don't need, he says, is to get dragged into a war.

He comes up with a phrase for the attitude he wants from us – Pokerface.

He drives it home in training.

'Show them nothing!'

'No tells!'

'If they push you – don't react!'

'If they stand on you, if they cheap-shot you – don't react!'

'Stare back at them – give them nothing!'

'Pokerface – every fucking time!'

On the morning of the game I think back to the text I sent Rog three years ago: *Let's go hard!*

But it's different now. Friendly-friendly is out the window. My head is in a different place: *He's not getting one today – no way. We'll be going hard – he just won't know about it until it happens.*

The stadium looks close to fifty–fifty between blue and red when we run out. In three years our support base has grown and maybe we've turned a few of the Lunsters.

Felipe sets out our stall in the first minute. There's a line-out right on the halfway line and we pull out a training-ground play. Bernard Jackman hits Mal at the top of his jump and the ball comes down to Chris Whitaker in space. Whits throws a crisp pass to Felipe and we come up in support.

He shapes to move the ball right and Darce is bang in position to truck it up past the halfway line when all of a sudden Felipe straightens and carries on into the 10 channel, directly at Rog.

For him, it's personal. He and Rog, they've had their moments – verbals on the pitch for club and country, a rivalry with more than a little edge. And you don't need training in body language to work out what's in Felipe's head: *I don't care what the call is – I'm running at him!*

He crashes into Rog and knocks him back three metres and onto the turf.

We come up with a new play after that, named in his honour. We call it 'Phil'.

He puts us in front with a sweetly struck drop goal, but banjaxes his knee in contact ten minutes later, just as we're awarded a penalty in kickable range. Johnny Sexton comes off the bench and runs right into a test of character and nerve. He rifles the kick through the middle and a star is born.

We keep running hard at them.

We keeping forcing turnovers.

We hit them with two quality tries.

Isa runs a great line through the middle, and when I pop it up to him he shoots in between Lifeimi Mafi and Doug Howlett. He makes twenty metres and Darce finishes it on the left flank. As he slides over the line, Sexto comes running in and has a quick word with Rog. It's the beginning of a new rivalry.

Three minutes into the second half, Lukie takes a lightning-fast pass from Shaggy near the touchline and swerves back inside with an unbelievably good step. Sexto converts the try and we're ahead 18–6.

Twenty to go. We still lead by 12 points. Our forwards are immense – there's no way through them.

Rog takes a ball on our 22, moving right. He's got Donners and Paulie as his outside runners. We're fanned across the pitch, ready to come up and hit the receiver.

I know where it's going. It doesn't take a genius to read the evidence.

1. Paulie's the better ball-carrier.
2. Rog likes to go to him whenever it's on.

So it's just a matter of when he lets it go.

For more than ten years I've been watching Rog move a rugby ball. You get to know a player when you're around him that long.

He's got a little kick, a slight wind-up before he throws out a long pass, a pumping movement before it leaves his hands. Blink and you miss it.

Turn back the clock. We're in the Six Nations camp with Ireland and Rog is banging a drum for the benefit of his backline.

Line speed! Line speed! Up faster on the ball carrier!

It's been in my head ever since.

Once I see the little pump before he throws it, I'm gone. I'm accelerating as the ball comes across and I pick it out of the air just as Paulie is reaching for it.

Dougie Howlett is running forward just as I make the intercept – a seriously good break because there's no way I've got the gas to beat him without a head start. By the time he stops and turns I'm in the clear with only Rog anywhere near. I keep looking over my shoulder but he's not getting any closer.

Ten metres from the posts, I get a flashback to 2006. I see Rog crossing our line with the ball in hand and the game done and dusted, jabbing the air with his index finger and jumping the hoardings, into the embrace of the Munster fans just behind the in-goal area.

The Croke Park advertising boards are twenty metres up ahead. I've already run eighty at full throttle. And I'm thinking, *It'd be funny to jump that . . . but I could easily snot myself.*

I fall over the line, spent.

And even then, with a 21-point cushion – three converted tries just to draw level – I don't think it's done. Not against Munster.

One more score. One more and it's over.

Even when it's signed, sealed and delivered, their heads never drop. They keep pummelling our line and we keep defending as if one breach will cost us everything.

With a couple of minutes left, when they're still camped on our line, there's a short break in play and I'm allowed to talk to my team-mates.

'They get nothing!' I tell them, as loudly as I can, so that some of the Munster guys can hear me. Because it's no longer about this game, it's about putting down a marker for the hereafter.

There isn't much love coming my way from Rog after the game, and there's even less five days later when the Grand Slam squad get to meet the Queen at Hillsborough Castle.

It's blatantly obvious that he's off with me, so I seek him out.

'Are you and I not friends any more?'

'Ah, yeah,' he says, 'we are when it suits you!'

Nobody loves losing, but he's more upset with me for getting him in a headlock during the game, a couple of seconds after he'd done the same to Jamie.

There's a touch of the 'Old pals shouldn't be like that to one another' about his reaction, but not for the first time we agree to disagree and move on. We've got too important a friendship to let anything fester.

*

Leicester, the newly crowned champions of England, stand between us and our first Heineken Cup. With Felipe still crocked we've got Sexto at 10, but after his nerveless performance against Munster nobody has any doubt that he's now a man for a big occasion.

There's another certainty we're more than aware of: nobody will remember the Munster victory if we don't go on and finish the job.

Kearns is back in the mix after a bout of mumps and his

availability gives Cheiks a high-class selection problem, but he sticks with the back three that beat Munster, and having some game-breakers on a strong bench gives me a good feeling when he calls out the 22: Isa Nacewa; Shane Horgan, Brian O'Driscoll, Gordon D'Arcy, Luke Fitzgerald; Johnny Sexton, Chris Whitaker; Cian Healy, Bernard Jackman, Stan Wright; Leo Cullen, Malcolm O'Kelly; Rocky Elsom, Shane Jennings, Jamie Heaslip. Replacements: John Fogarty, Ronan McCormack, Devin Toner, Sean O'Brien, Simon Keogh, Rob Kearney, Girvan Dempsey.

Murrayfield isn't always the most atmospheric of grounds but the two sets of supporters make it a huge occasion and ours travel in unprecedented numbers, a sea of blue in a jam-packed stadium.

Coming into the game I'm struggling with my shoulder — short of power on my right side, unable to pass the ball more than a few metres. I've been carrying it since the Six Nations, feeling it get a little worse week by week, getting through the games but conscious that it's not going away.

For thirty minutes we're the better team. I kick a decent drop goal and Sexto lands a monster from the halfway line, but the most significant score of the half comes with ninety seconds left in it. We've got Stan Wright in the bin when their flanker, Ben Woods, barges his way over, and as we're walking off at half-time, 13–9 down, their Kiwi winger, Scott Hamilton, has plenty to say for himself as we head down the tunnel for our break, bigging his team up.

At half-time in your first Heineken Cup final, turning around a deficit against a side of Leicester's quality takes real mental strength. Without it, you can find negative thoughts at the back of your head. You can give yourself an out . . .

Ah, well, we played our final against Munster.

This is Leicester we're up against.
No shame in losing to them.

But there's none of that in our dressing room. We know we're good enough. They stretch their lead to seven points but then we get after them. Rocky is immense and his fellow back-rows force the breakthrough eight minutes into the new half. Off a ruck practically on their line, Jamie has Jenno pushing him forward with a massive leg drive, a phenomenal piece of support play. Blue flags go up all around the stadium and it's an even game: 16–16.

For twenty minutes there's no score and I'm forced out to the wing to recover after taking a bang on the shoulder. There's no way I'm coming off with the game in the balance, and when I take the ball into contact inside their half I'm at the bottom of a ruck when the whistle blows and they're penalized. From thirty-eight metres, Sexto puts us three points clear with what can only be described, in golfing parlance, as a draw bordering on a hook.

The last ten minutes are about resistance, hitting everything that moves, complete desire to get it done.

The clock is in red when they're penalized at a ruck. We know it's over but until the ball is off the pitch and we hear the long blow from Nigel Owens's whistle I can't allow myself to feel it.

I go in search of the ball. I'm dying to hack it into the stand.

Whits comes across. We're ten metres from the touchline but he doesn't trust my boot.

'We'll give it to Johnny,' he says.

Fair shout.

Sexto lines it up and hoofs it.

I'm embracing Darce when Shaggy comes across. I wrap

my left arm around him and bring him into the huddle. I'm happy for myself – beyond happy. But seeing what it means to Shaggy after he missed out on the Slam – seeing that out-pouring of raw emotion after ten years of effort – trumps everything.

Leo speaks brilliantly when he's asked to describe what it means to us. He talks about the tough times, the dis-appointing days and how sweeter the moment feels because of them.

Winning a Heineken Cup is hard. It takes years to get there and not everyone who is part of that journey can be with you when you finally arrive. When I'm interviewed I think of some of the guys watching it at home – Den, Victor, Reggie – and I wish they could be with us.

'Those guys deserve to be out here as well,' I say.

But knowing them, I feel certain that they all share the huge sense of joy.

I'm standing behind the trophy with a medal around my neck when Leo and Whits put a hand on either side of it.

They lift it high above their heads.

Good times.

*

Back in Dublin, the celebrations are building up a head of steam when I bail out a little earlier than some, mindful of the 9 a.m. flight to London and the longer haul to South Africa with the Lions later that night.

I pick up Kearns on the way to the airport and he hasn't slept. Good effort. I already have that T-shirt.

Four years on from New Zealand, the dynamic is differ-ent. For starters, there aren't as many bodies – seven fewer players, a tighter group sharing rooms and bonding well from the beginning. Lee Byrne of Wales is my first roomie and we get on great.

I've spoken to Gerald Davies, the Lions manager, and given him my tuppence-worth based on my two previous tours – what worked, what didn't. He's been on a couple of tours himself, including the legendary series win of 1971 in New Zealand, and, like Ian McGeechan, he commands maximum respect.

Aside from Geech and our scrum coach, Graham Rowntree, the rest of the coaching ticket is borrowed from Wales: Warren Gatland (forwards), Shaun Edwards (defence), Rob Howley (attack), Neil Jenkins (kicking coach). This time round, all the coaches are there to guide one group of players and everyone feels they have a crack at making the Test team.

Barry's first anniversary falls in the first week we're over there and I find myself getting emotional doing shoulder rehab in the gym. At the first training session, I can't throw passes right to left. I don't feel like making excuses for myself – shit happens and you have to suck it up – but I'm worrying about what's in Rob Howley's head as he's watching us . . .

Geech! Get over here! This guy can't pass the ball!

I'm starting to get stingers, starting to become aware there's a problem somewhere that needs looking at. But it can wait. Right now I just need a short-term fix and a physio who can get me back in a good place. Bob Stewart of Gloucester steps up and sorts me out.

I do my best to stay out of the way of the guys with the cameras. I don't want to be a show pony, a character in the latest Lions DVD – I'd rather just do my own thing. But there's no hiding place in the dressing room, and when Paulie is rested for my tour debut in game two, they film me effing and blinding when I'm giving the team talk.

It feels awesome to be back in the red jersey and my confidence is sky-high. I haven't been on a losing team since the middle of January. We put 74 points on the Golden Lions. When the first Test in Durban comes around we're six from six and feeling good about our chances.

South Africa are world champions and formidable pretty much everywhere, but we're clicking as a team ourselves and it helps hugely that we're having fun along the way. I've got Jamie Roberts alongside me in the centre and the partnership is working a treat.

Paulie fires us up in the dressing room and when their kick-off comes right at me I bang it fifty metres back down the pitch and into touch. Let's play.

We ship an early try and get hit with scrum penalties but respond with a well-worked score. I'm on Jamie's shoulder when he breaks a couple of tackles in midfield, and when I'm taken down five metres short, Tom Croft is right there for the offload.

Then it starts slipping away from us.

Bryce Lawrence keeps killing us with penalties. They keep taking advantage.

I'm coming up from the bottom of a ruck with a penalty already given against us when Bismarck du Plessis shoves me onto my back.

Once you let that kind of stuff go unchallenged, you might as well go home.

He's up on his feet when I take a swipe at him from the floor.

He pins me to the ground with his left boot and winds up a big right-hander.

As he brings his fist down slowly, then leaves it clenched above my face, there's an unbelievably good opportunity to take the piss.

I can blow him a kiss.

I can say, 'Mwah! Come on!'

But I think of it a split-second after he has pulled his arm back.

Five minutes into the second half we trail 26–7.

With five minutes to go it's 26–21.

They're a relieved team when they get the ball off the pitch at the end and we face into game two feeling like the momentum is shifting in our direction.

*

At Loftus Versfeld, Pretoria, there are less than thirty seconds on the clock when Lukie is blatantly gouged in a ruck by Schalk Burger. It's a red-card offence all day long, but he gets away with ten minutes in the bin. Bryce Lawrence completely bottles it from the touchline after getting a perfect view and the referee, Christophe Berdos, doesn't have the stomach to do the right thing in the first minute.

Kearns, brilliant off the bench in Durban, scorches in for an early try and even when J. P. Pietersen responds as soon as Burger is out of the bin we're playing the better rugby and a half-time lead of 16–8 doesn't overly flatter us.

All the way through it's incredibly physical, attritional, two bloody good teams going hammer and tongs at each other.

The injuries start mounting. Five minutes into the second half I'm collateral damage in a double hit on Bryan Habana, which leaves Gethin Jenkins with a broken cheekbone and me with a bang in the head.

Fifteen minutes later I'm seeing stars after a hit on their

replacement forward, Danie Rossouw. He's only on the field a few minutes when I see him coming up hard onto a pass from Fourie du Preez. I run straight at him and catch him right on the money. I'm trying to get a wraparound on him, but the jolt when we collide is so severe that both of us hit the deck before I can get my arm around.

The first thought hits me while we're both going backwards.

That's a good shot!

The second comes when we're down.

Fuck, that hurt!

The third thing to come into my head is that I need to get up and show him I'm not hurt. I don't see him staggering backwards and falling down, or being taken off the field. I get back in play but I'm down again when the ball goes dead.

Gaz runs on. He doesn't like the look of me. I carry on for a few more minutes but make a bad read when they attack us off a scrum on our 22 and leave a gap that Habana bolts through to score.

Gaz comes on again. My head is all over the shop. I'm a liability.

I come off and Jamie Roberts lasts only another three minutes. We're down both centres and both props and our lead has been cut to four points.

I watch it play out from the bench, dazed and barely taking it in.

The try in the corner by Jaque Fourie that puts them ahead.

The penalty from Stephen Jones to level it at 25–25.

Rog, on a sub, chasing his own kick and trying to win it in the last minute, eyes only on the ball, not seeing du Preez in the air until they collide.

I watch the penalty being struck by Morné Steyn from

inside his own half, and when it sails over I'm too out of it to feel anything like the same devastation as my team-mates. I'm barely taking it in . . .

Oh, we lost. Okay.

They take three of us to the hospital and I feel brutal lying on the bed. I sit on an exercise bike the following day and get a headache as soon as I turn the wheels. When they rule me out of the third Test, I've got no intention of repeating my mistake from the previous tour and sticking around, feeling useless. I fly home with Adam Jones. Gethin Jenkins is forced to stay on, not recovered enough to fly. Me and Adam miss his unique company on the plane home – for a moany bastard, he's a good lad. And for a guy who looks like he's got about fifteen minutes in his engine, he goes and goes and goes.

I get back disappointed with the outcome, ruing the small margins that cost us, but grateful for the experience; happy that I got the most of an enjoyable tour with some good friends made along the way.

The following Saturday I'm with Guy Easterby at the Fifty-One bar on Haddington Road, roaring at the TV as the lads win the third Test convincingly, thrilled to see what winning in the red jersey means to guys like Paulie, Kearns and the rest of my fellow 2009 Lions.

On holiday in San Francisco, me and Amy rent bikes and cycle across the Golden Gate Bridge over to Sausalito, me pushing her back all the way up the hill as she cycles. There's no way she'd make it through pre-season. Then we drive the Pacific Coast Highway down to Huntington Beach.

It's the perfect end to an almost perfect six months in my life.

10. High Definition

Scene one: Royal Dublin Golf Club on Bull Island. I swing hard on the first hole, a par four straight up ahead. The ball pings off the clubface and I turn my head to look for it in the air. I see . . . nothing, just a green blur under a cloudy sky. My ball could be in the middle of the fairway, in the bunker on the left or out of bounds on the right. I have no idea where to find it because I'm not wearing my glasses.

Scene two: I'm on the main street in Donnybrook. I hear my name being called from across the road. The voice seems friendly, a little familiar. I look over and see a blurred figure waving at me. 'How's it going?' he shouts.

Even though we are less than fifteen metres apart, I have no idea who it is. Rather than risk being thought rude, I answer: 'Howrya?'

I take a chance and cross the road, hoping that the person who hailed me will turn out to be a friend, or at least somebody I'll recognize. A few yards from the opposite pavement, I can see clearly enough to know: I have crossed the street to greet a complete stranger.

'Thanks for coming over. I wasn't expecting you to!'

'No problem.'

A brief and awkward conversation ensues. I walk away and think: *Jesus! You've got to get this thing sorted!*

As the 2009–10 season draws near – my eleventh as a professional – the record shows that I've played ninety-nine games of Test rugby for Ireland and the Lions. Never once have I been able to read a scoreboard. Without my glasses, I can't make out the number plate of the car directly in front of mine in bumper-to-bumper traffic. I can't read a newspaper headline if it's two feet away from me.

Unless I'm right up close, I can't tell the opposition players apart by looking at their faces. From the day I first picked up a ball at Willow Park, I have relied on body shapes to identify the defenders five or ten yards away. It's how I work out which of them might be easier to step, if there's half a gap to exploit. Sometimes it's the colour of their hair, or a call from one of my team-mates – '*Fatties!*' – alerting me that big, less-mobile forwards are defending in midfield.

Because of my astigmatism I can't wear the soft contact lenses that work for other short-sighted people. I tried the hard lenses but fumbled every time trying to get them in. Even when I managed it, they made my eyes sore after a while and they cost so much I couldn't risk losing them playing schools rugby.

When a new kind of soft lens came along, I tried them out before a training game with Ireland in 2004. After fifteen seconds, in the middle of a ruck, Tyrone Howe's hand flicked across my eye and knocked one of them clean out. I picked it off the ground, ran to the touchline and pulled the other out. I took it as a sign that they weren't for me. I didn't want to be that guy scrambling around looking for a lost lens in the grass while the physio runs on with a pocket mirror.

When laser treatment started getting popular, I checked it out, but my eyes weren't suitable for the surgery. So I just got on with it – wearing glasses around the house, going without in social situations because I'd never liked myself in them. In my teenage years, when girls came on the scene, the glasses stayed in my room whenever I tried to put myself in the marketplace. I was no David Gandy and they weren't going to improve me, not with their awful frames and lenses as thick as the bottom of a milk bottle. Once in a while, the lads in Clontarf got hold of them – they made out like they were tripping when they tried them on.

And so, on and off the rugby pitch, I learned to get by. It had its upside: no eye contact walking down Grafton Street with people you don't particularly want to talk to, and maybe vice versa. But before each new season I looked at the Leinster fixture list and came to dread a Friday-night game at Hughenden in Glasgow or Rodney Parade, Newport – places where the floodlights are low and the body shapes of the opposition players are harder to make out in the gloom.

I thought I'd see out my career without ever being able to read the time on a game clock, until I was referred to an eye surgeon, who looked me over and said laser treatment was now an option. The techniques had moved on, she said. My level of astigmatism was no longer a problem.

Then she talked about the professor who had pioneered laser surgery in Ireland back in the early nineties. 'He's the guy you need for this,' she said.

*

The first Wednesday in August 2009, Leinster are in pre-season training and I'm at the Mater Private Hospital with Michael O'Keefe, consultant ophthalmologist. It's a few months since I first met him, but I've delayed the surgery until now, conscious of the need for a decent break from the game after the physical demands of a Lions tour. He has insisted on doing one eye at a time. If everything goes okay with the first eye, he says, he'll do the other one next week. He doesn't talk a big game or promise instant miracles. He tells it like it is – a complex procedure with a high success rate, but no guaranteed outcome.

He tells me the only reason I've been able to cope on the rugby field is because I've had bad eyesight all my life – 50 per cent of the average person's unaided vision and a level of astigmatism that's way above the norm at six diopters, the unit of measurement.

'Your brain adapted to what your eyes *could* see,' he tells me.

He says if my preferred sport had been cricket or hurling – games played with a small ball – my eyesight would never have allowed me to play to a decent standard.

I brace myself on the operating table, unsure of what to expect. I'm unprepared for the smell of burning as the laser reshapes my cornea, eliminating nearly all of the astigmatism.

It's highly uncomfortable for three or four days, but it gets the all-clear, and a week later he does the second eye. A week after that, behind the wheel of my car, I find myself clocking the number plate of the vehicle in front as the traffic lights change to green. I move off slowly and allow the other driver to get further and further away, my lasered eyes glued to the plate.

Still seeing it . . . still seeing it . . . still seeing it . . . gone.

In normal life, it's a complete game-changer. In rugby, the balls kicked down to me look massively sharper in the air and the picture all around changes to high definition, but there's little or no difference in how I play the game.

*

Rocky Elsom always said he was in Europe for one year only and there's nothing Leinster can do to persuade him to change his mind. He returns home to play for the ACT Brumbies and leaves a big hole in the heart of our pack.

In one way, the gap is filled by Nathan Hines in the second row, one of my fellow Lions in South Africa. He plays in a different position from Rocky, and he's less of a ball-carrier, but he's another serious player – a go-to guy with massive physicality and the same kind of nuisance value that Leo brings to his game. When he arrives, we go for a coffee. I tell him I'm thinking of retiring after the 2011 World Cup and he's surprised, bordering on amazed. He's thirty-two years old to my thirty and says he has no intention of stopping any time soon.

'Why would you want to quit?' he asks. 'Keep playing as long as you possibly can!'

But I'm not sure I want to. I'm not even sure I'll be able to.

The stingers are causing me grief. I have pain in the right side of my neck that's transferring down into my shoulder. I go to the Santry Sports Clinic to see Jimmy Colville, the orthopaedic surgeon who did such a good job with my shoulder op back in 2005. Jimmy's a little concerned about my neck so he refers me to Ashley Poynton, a spinal surgeon at the Mater Private Hospital in the city centre.

I meet Ashley in early September. I need to know that I'm not in danger of doing lasting damage to myself by carrying on playing. He says I'm okay and tells me to stop my weights programme.

Then he fills me in on what might be needed if things get worse. There's a surgical procedure called a fusion where the disc giving trouble is removed and the vertebrae are biologically fused, with a metal cage holding everything in place. He says I don't need the fusion – or, at least, not yet.

I tell him that if I'm ever bad enough to need it I'll stop playing, there and then.

*

One month later I'm back on the field, starting my season in front of a full house at the RDS. Munster are in town looking for payback for the Heineken semi-final defeat, but we give them nothing, literally.

Kevin McLaughlin, Rocky's replacement at number 6, punches the first big hole. He drives hard up the middle and creates the space for myself and Shaggy to put Darce away. At half-time we're 13–0 ahead. Six minutes after the interval I get past their new signing, Jean de Villiers, and score our second, after some smart work from a recent acquisition of our own, Eoin Reddan – signed from Wasps and already clicking nicely with Sexto at 9.

Then Munster launch the heavy artillery from the bench: Paulie, David Wallace and Jerry Flannery all come on to try to salvage something. But almost as soon as they're on John Hayes is off, red-carded for a very uncharacteristic stamp on Cian Healy's head. Against fourteen men we turn the screw and win 30–0. It's Munster's biggest loss in a competitive match in more than five years and the first time in the professional era that they've been nilled.

It's another reminder of how far we've come under Michael Cheika, but all good things come to an end. Three days after the Munster game, Cheiks announces that he's leaving at the end of the season. He's won one Heineken Cup and he wants a second this season, but after that he wants a new challenge somewhere else. He has brought fresh ideas and success – he's been huge for us and I'm never bored listening to him – but five seasons is a decent stretch and he'll be leaving us in a far better place than he found us.

We flit from Leinster to Ireland in the blink of an eye, from Magners League to autumn internationals, Cheiks to Deccie. In my hundredth Test – number ninety-four in green – we draw 20–20 with the Wallabies at Croke Park. On his Ireland debut at loosehead prop, Cian Healy catches every eye in the stadium. We're trailing by seven a minute from time when Tomás O'Leary hits me with a peach of a pass off a training-ground play and I get in under the posts. We beat Fiji in the middle week and the last of our three Tests is against the Springboks.

Paulie prepares as only Paulie does. He sits down with Gert Smal, our South African forwards coach, and gets Gert to teach him Afrikaans – or at least the bits of it that could help him crack the Springboks' lineout. He spends endless hours in the video analysis room, trying to identify the calls from the guy who runs their lineout, Victor Matfield. That's Paulie in a nutshell – a level of professionalism that makes you smile, especially when we end up having a field day on their ball.

Sexto starts. So soon after the Slam, it's a tough one for Rog to swallow and Deccie tries to sugar-coat the pill. He says he already knows he has a world-class fly-half in Rog – now he needs to find out more about Sexto. It's a fair enough argument but you couldn't expect Rog to buy it. When the world champions come to town, everyone is desperate to play. Keith Earls, a fast-rising star with Munster and already a Lion, makes his first start on the wing.

On a day of swirling fog, Sexto's five penalties put us 15–10 ahead going into the final play, with the clock already in red.

They come at us hard and spin the ball out the line, left to right. They're six or seven metres inside our 22. Ruan Pienaar throws a miss pass to their full-back, Zane Kirchner, and I rush up and hit him with everything I've got. I've made up my mind that he's getting hit, ball or not. A nanosecond after

he gathers it, I catch him flush and it's like a tennis ball getting hit out of the middle of a racquet – a sweet connection
that sends him backwards and has me seeing stars.

In a pouch on my jersey, between my shoulder-blades,
there's a GPS unit tracking the data on our performance –
metres covered, high-speed metres, the impact of collisions.
These hits are measured in G-force units from accelerom-
eter data. There's a scaling system, so that 6–7 g counts as
moderate-to-heavy impact and 8–10 g is very heavy impact,
such as in a scrum engagement. Later I learn that the hit on
Kirchner clocked in at 14 g.

Once he hits the floor I roll away, spaced, as a ruck forms.
A second later Nigel Owens blows for a penalty to us and the
game is effectively over, but my senses are a bit scrambled
and the celebrations start without me. Our record for the
year is ten wins and a draw from eleven games.

Straight after the game, I'm fully alert for the announcement of the 2009 International Rugby Board player of the
year. There's a shortlist of seven – Richie McCaw, Fourie
du Preez, François Steyn, Matt Giteau, Tom Croft, Jamie
Heaslip and me.

Just being in the frame was the target I set myself after my
chats with Enda McNulty, when I was feeling low last December. But after the biggest year of my career – a Grand Slam
and a Heineken Cup, top try scorer in both tournaments –
I've raised my hopes higher. It's the one time in my life when
I really want an individual award.

I hear the winner's name: Richie McCaw.

I manage to hide my deep disappointment from most
people, but Dad sees it a mile off at the post-match function.

The following week, he writes me a four-page letter, some
of which will always remain between the two of us. He

knows me inside out and he knows what to say to pick me back up.

Dear Brian

I want you to keep this letter to remind yourself that 2009 was the year of Brian, to quote one of my patients [...]

When you came into the reception after the win against SA, I could sense that all was not right with you. You were devastated after the IRB announcement had been made. Mum and I were terribly disappointed for you, but your dignity in the face of such an insult was incredible. Let's be honest, the world and his wife knew that you deserved to be the IRB player of the year.

[...] Irish people are very fair. They love loads of sport and this year the country's fourth favourite sport after Gaelic football, hurling and soccer came out on top. More importantly, though, the other sports acknowledged it totally.

[...] Sometimes I say to Mum that it's probably just as well that we drift along not knowing what the country thinks of you. We try to keep a balance but in all honesty any accolade that you receive is totally deserved. Nothing will convince me that you were not deserving of this particular honour too, but we have never needed you to win trophies and awards to be proud of you.

Love to Amy.
Dad

A little biased, perhaps, but from the heart.

*

Spring dawns and the defence of our Six Nations title begins. After eighteen months, there's no longer a novelty factor about Deccie and his way of doing things. He's cautious and

measured, inclusive but also a little distant. He consults me
more than Eddie used to do, looking for the odd steer – 'Have
you got anything for me from the lads?' he'll ask – but the
conversation doesn't always flow between us. We're quite different, I suppose. In life, you connect with some people and
with others there's never going to be the same kind of bond.

He doesn't pretend to be a coach with cutting-edge ideas
for the training ground – he's an overseer, a taker of the temperature in a squad. He has enough self-confidence and
common sense to empower the talented coaches around
him, but there's always a trade-off because the buck stops
with the guy who picks the team. One way or another, his
rugby philosophy is always going to be the single biggest
influence on a squad.

We start with a scratchy win in a poor game against Italy at
Croke Park. I sit alongside Deccie at the press conference
and we make the usual noises . . .

'Plenty to improve on.'

'Take the positives and move on.'

We travel to Paris with twelve of the team that started the
Slam decider in Cardiff. Donners and Lukie are injured, and
Cian Healy has established himself in the front row at loosehead, but we're otherwise unchanged. We are hammered,
33–10. The sharpness of last season isn't there.

After a lot of success with my line speed in 2009 – especially
on the Lions tour – I'm gunning for more good reads. Get it
right and you'll smash your man or make an intercept. Get it
wrong and you'll look like a chump. And even if your read is
on the money, enough speed in a pass will beat any man. I
make a couple of bad decisions when France have the ball,
shooting out of the defensive line and ending up in no man's
land, with a hole behind me.

Two weeks later we play England and I know I need a performance, but I contract a virus almost as soon as the plane hits the tarmac. I skip the captain's run and go to bed with no food in me: I'm zapped.

I shouldn't play but I don't want to miss England at Twickenham. After fifteen minutes I'm feeling awful: I've no tank, no energy to get going in a fast-tempo game.

Then it rains. The frantic pace slows and it gives me some respite. I live off the positivity of a tackle on Riki Flutey. I know he likes to come off his left foot. As he steps I stay inside and he runs straight into the hit. My confidence grows. It's what you need to do: shelve any mistake and keep yourself going on the back of the last good thing you did. Then try to put another positive on top of it.

It's 13–13 just after an hour when Jonny Wilkinson chips over the top of our defence and I go scrambling back to gather it, with Flutey alongside me. I take a tumble, then Paulie comes thundering through and accidentally catches me with a knee to the side of my head. I get up, my legs buckle and down I go. I try again and the same thing happens. On another day I might wait for the spinning to stop, then carry on, but the doc convinces me to call it a day. I watch the rest of it in the medical room. Tommy Bowe cuts a brilliant line off Tomás O'Leary and slices his way through to score the winning try. I go and clap the lads in. Later, in my hotel room at Moran's in Chiswick, I'm sweating buckets but there's no way I'm missing the dinner because it's John Hayes's hundredth cap.

Ordinarily, myself and Hayes wouldn't have a connection. He's a farmer and I'm a city boy, we're different people, but I'm very fond of him – he's got a great personality that not many get to see. When he's around people he knows, he's a laugh. He has no interest in doing media or turning up for functions. Even the Grand Slam celebrations he saw as hassle. He likes winning and he likes going home – either farming or spending time with his family. That's how it is. He's the first Irishman to earn a century of caps – a great accolade, truly deserved.

A fortnight later I join Hayes in the 100 Club and we beat Wales in our second-last game at Croke Park.

The swansong is against Scotland and we want to bow out with a Triple Crown, but their out-half Dan Parks chokes the life out of us. We lose 23–20. It's brutal, but the Six Nations never owes you anything.

Kicking on from the Grand Slam was always going to be tough because the most challenging thing in sport is backing up one big win with another. You need to keep bringing something new to your game – a freshness, an element of surprise, a relentless focus on standards, driven from the top.

And maybe we had more of those things the year before.

*

Friday night lights at the RDS in early April. Joe Schmidt, the Leinster head coach in waiting, is in town with Clermont Auvergne for a Heineken Cup quarter-final. Back around Christmas time, Joe signed a three-year contract to succeed Cheiks. It was Isa who pointed us in the direction of a fellow Kiwi, his backs coach at Auckland Blues for a couple of seasons. I wasn't around when Leo and Sexto met him, but we spoke on the phone and I liked what I heard. Now he's alongside Vern Cotter in the Clermont coaches' box and there's a part of us that likes the idea of showing him he'll be taking over a decent team.

As senior players, with a Heineken Cup win behind us after a five-season journey with Cheiks that challenged and changed us, we feel like we're ready to drive the ship ourselves. We need a certain amount of direction, sure – and after all he's done for the team, Cheiks is going to be a tough act to follow – but we're in a good place, with an extremely talented and experienced squad.

Once we drew Clermont in the quarters, a month after Joe signed his deal, Cheiks put the kibosh on any familiarization trips he might have had in mind. Fair enough.

Now, at the RDS, Clermont hit the ground running. We go 10–0 down – they're dominant, ferocious. Twenty-two minutes in, I get a step on Brock James, and when Aurélien Rougerie comes in to take me, Jamie's on my shoulder. He makes the line like a runaway train and we're back in the game.

It ebbs and flows. Brock James, normally ultra-reliable with the boot, misses a few from well within his range. It's anyone's until the last kick. We're 29–28 ahead with the clock in red when the ball comes back to James, standing in the pocket for a drop goal from thirty metres. Three of us fling ourselves at him but he gets the kick away. When we turn the ball is sailing well wide of the right-hand upright.

In the semi-final we're drawn away to Toulouse. We prepare ourselves for the hard ground of the south of France under a scorching sun. We wear sweatsuits in the gym and bin-liners under our T-shirts in training. When we arrive in Toulouse it's pissing down, almost to the point of flooding. They win it by 10 points and it's not even that close. We have no complaints.

There's one more chance to send Cheiks off with some silverware. But against the Ospreys in the Magners League final at the RDS we start terribly and never catch up. It leaves us feeling sick: we've worked hard all season for a home final and ended up with nothing to show for a year's worth of effort. And the more advanced you are in your career, the tougher the big defeats are to take because you know the games are running out.

After five transformative seasons, the curtain comes down on Cheiks's time and it's not the glorious goodbye we were looking for. The same goes for Mal O'Kelly and Girvan Dempsey, leaving us after stellar careers. Rugby doesn't give out many happy endings.

On the summer tour with Ireland, the only highlight after a heavy defeat to New Zealand and a closer game with Australia is that I come out physically unscathed.

Sitting in the dressing room in Brisbane, I console myself with the fact that at least I won't be hobbling into the church on crutches – or sporting a nice big black eye – when I marry Amy a week later.

*

The night before the wedding, at a holiday cottage on the Lough Rynn estate in County Leitrim, I hand over a gift to the lads in my wedding party. Just for the laugh I give them monogrammed robes to match the one Amy bought me. Mine says 'The O'Drisc' – which is what Cheiks used to call me. Amy has four bridesmaids, but I leave it at three alongside me because I like to think that Barry's with us in spirit, beside Dunny ('The Don'), Damo ('Furious D') and Skiddy ('Skiddy Kiddy').

We hang out in the cottage wearing the robes, and after breakfast the following morning Dunny pops the cork on a bottle of vintage Dom Pérignon someone kindly gave me, because if you don't share it with good friends on the day of your wedding, when are you ever going to break it open?

Waiting for Amy at the altar in St Joseph's Church, Aughavas, I don't glance behind me much because I could do without people wondering if I'm nervous. I am, a little, but once Amy comes up the aisle, looking incredible on her dad Harold's arm, I settle down and enjoy it. The priest who pronounces us married is Fr Vincent Twomey, Barry's uncle.

On the road back to the reception in Lough Rynn Castle, we're blown away by the good wishes of local people. There are banners wishing us luck, scoreboards on GAA pitches with our names on them, dogs dressed up in Ireland jerseys. The people of Mohill have the place looking spotless. It feels nuts, but in a nice way. Once our car drives through the gates, I feel at ease because we wanted it totally private and it absolutely is – just ourselves and the people closest to us. I shrugged it off when we got kudos for not selling our pictures to a magazine, because I couldn't comprehend the idea of doing that – it would have felt alien. Early on in our relationship, when the media in Ireland were focusing attention on us as a couple, we decided we weren't going to go down that road. We had our own careers and we supported each other absolutely but we were going to keep our own autonomy. Keep our relationship as private as we could.

Dunny and Damo are joint best man – Dunny gives the best-man speech and Damo's the MC. They both speak about our friendship and what we've all been through together. Then Damo veers off in a new direction.

'People just see the Brian O'Driscoll that goes on TV and gives nothing away,' he says. 'They have no idea what you're really like.'

I'm not sure I like where he's going. Then I see TV screens

descending from the ceiling all around the function room and I like it even less.

Damo carries on, deadly serious: 'This morning,' he says, 'we got a complaint about your behaviour last night. I had to review the CCTV footage with the management . . .'

I have no idea what's coming next. I look around at the uncles and aunts in the room and I'm in dread of what's about to be put up on the screens.

With a showman's flourish, Damo tees it up.

'I think, ladies and gentlemen, you'll all have to look at this and judge for yourselves about the *real* Brian O'Driscoll.'

The screens jump to life. Lying in bed, with his back to the camera, is a man wearing a green number 13 jersey. He yawns and stretches himself awake. I have no idea who this person is, but at least I know it's not me – my pride in putting on the green jersey doesn't extend to wearing it in bed. As he turns I see it's the comedy actor, Risteárd Cooper.

He picks up the teddy bear sitting on his chest and starts talking to it. 'Today is a big day,' he says. On the bed is a copy of the *Irish Independent*. There's a big picture of me next to the front-page headline:

HUBERMAN STRIKES GOLD

Actress tackles Ireland's sexiest man

Our hero picks it up and nods approvingly. 'So true,' he says. 'So true.'

The film casts me in the role of a self-admiring, ranting muppet and it brings the house down. Damo's the executive producer and he, Dunny and Skiddy appear alongside some interesting co-stars. There's Louis Walsh, the pop mogul, and two of his protégés, Jedward. There's Louis Copeland, who made my wedding suit, and Shay Dempsey, who cuts my hair. It's brilliantly done. In every scene I come across like an absolute gobshite and the guests can't get enough of it.

The fun never stops all night. The hotel staff join in. Shaggy even does his Bruce Springsteen impression – and he rocks the place. It's a truly great day. Me and Amy, we don't want it to end. So many people stay around the next day and the fun kicks off again. The Coronas join us – a favourite band for both Amy and me.

We honeymoon in Tanzania and Zanzibar and it's the holiday of our lives.

11. Our Best Stuff

I blink and I'm back in pre-season for Leinster, re-energized and ready to go. We're playing a variation on tip rugby on Joe Schmidt's first day in charge and friendships are out the window. Shaggy runs a blocking move and I tell him if he tries it on again I'm going to take his head off.

So he tries it again and the red mist comes down. I charge at him and there's a digging match. We're pulled apart before either of us lands a major blow, but it's not like we haven't tried.

I'm blowing hard when I look across and catch his eye. A couple of seconds later we're both laughing at the absurdity of two friends trying to beat the shit out of one another during a game of tip. But it sets a tone for the new season ahead. Shaggy says he looked at the faces of the younger lads after we were separated. If there was a thought bubble coming out of their heads it would have said, 'If these guys are doing this to each other . . . ?'

It's a good message to send out. Give it everything, all of the time. And when it's over, whatever's happened stays on the pitch.

The media critics come for Joe in the first weeks of the season. We're beaten in a few friendlies, then lose three out of the first four in the Magners League. In the papers they start doing their comparisons of Joe's record and those of his predecessors, the subtext being that this guy's a joke, a mistake, and he won't last.

Results equal acceptance and players need to be winning games before they fully buy into a coach's methods, but I know the tide will turn. And it does.

We beat Munster in our first game at the new Aviva stadium in early October, in front of more than fifty thousand. Then the Heineken Cup begins and we take care of Racing Metro and Saracens in the first two rounds. We go to France to play Joe's old team Clermont in round three. In the build-up he talks in nicknames, like an affectionate uncle. He goes on about the threat that Ro-Ro will pose.

We look at each other. *Who's Ro-Ro?*

Sure enough, Aurélien Rougerie helps set up one of the tries that take Clermont over the winning line, but we get a losing bonus point, then do a job on them a week later at the Aviva. It's the winning of the pool. Joe's would-be critics know they can start putting away their knives now.

I've never seen a coach show such massive attention to detail, or one with such a smart rugby brain. Joe works so hard and prepares so well that he makes you feel he's always right. He can be Mr Nice Guy, but he can be ruthlessly honest when he needs to be. He rarely shouts, but his words can be lethal. He can cut you down in an instant and the pitch of his voice doesn't need to rise or fall.

He's a player's coach, because he notices what you do. If you're a workhorse, doing your best stuff unseen by almost everyone, *he* knows you've done the work. If you do something seven phases before a try is scored that no one is giving you credit for, *he* gives you credit. And he stores it. He mightn't necessarily say it to you, but it's there – a green tick in the box by your name for the next game. A reason that you belong in his team.

If I challenge him, I know I need excellent back-up for my argument. But my trust in him is enormous. He has a freshness about him that's exciting, a way of talking that commands respect. Sometimes it's tiny things but they make a difference. Sometimes it's criticism and you hang your hat on that, too.

He expects high standards, all the time – complete understanding of the game plan and what it means for every player, whether you're on the ball or twenty metres away.

New ideas, new plays, subtleties that demand absolute attention to detail.

'What's *your* role in this?'

'What *exactly* are you doing and why are you doing it?'

He makes little tweaks in a backline play and all of a sudden an opposition defence opens up in front of you. And you look over at him and he's smiling.

*

Kevin Maggs was my midfield partner when I made my Ireland debut in Australia. He won seventy caps and I played in the same team for more than forty of them. He was a big part of my early life as a professional – a very fine player and a good friend.

On the first Friday in January 2011, I fly to Bristol with Amy and the Leinster manager, Guy Easterby, to attend the unbearably sad funeral of Maggsy's five-year-old daughter, Jessica. For nearly three years, he and his wife, Jayne, watched Jess bravely fight leukaemia to the last.

After the funeral, Amy takes the train to London for an audition and I travel back to Dublin for a league game against Ospreys that night. I go directly from the airport to the RDS.

I think I'll be okay to play, but I'm not. Normally, out on the pitch, you forget about whatever else is going on in life for a couple of hours, but not this time. I can't begin to understand the grief Maggsy and Jayne are experiencing, and I can't stop thinking about the sadness of the day.

When the game ends, I drive out to collect Amy off the last flight. We're through the Port Tunnel and heading for the East Wall Road when a guy in a battered car breaks the lights by a couple of seconds and shoots around the corner in front of us.

I flash him and he sticks his hazards on: fair enough, honest mistake.

When we reach the East Link toll bridge, he's at the barrier. I drive up to the lane alongside him but my tag isn't working. I try to get the attention of the staff member in the cash booth where the guy has just paid.

As I shout out, he hits the brakes. He thinks the call has come from the guy in the booth. He puts his car in reverse but the barrier has gone back down and he drives straight into it – absolutely clobbers it.

'Are you all right, bud?' I shout.

He's in his early fifties and he looks mangled. He mumbles something in reply.

'Hey, are you drunk?'

More mumbles. He's not just drunk, he's completely smashed. Now I'm angry.

'You're a fucking moron! Getting behind the wheel of a car in that state!'

I ask him where he's going. Sandymount, he says.

'Where in Sandymount?'

The answer is so slurred I can't hear it. I'm not sure I need to be getting involved in this but the thought of waking up and hearing somebody has been killed by a drunk driver on the road to Sandymount makes my mind up. I pull out in front of him.

'Right, follow me – okay? Stay right behind.'

I'm going super-slow but he's still all over the road behind me. At Sandymount Strand I motion for him to pull in. I get out of the car and give him another mouthful. 'Get into the passenger seat, you prick!'

'Are you a policeman?' he asks.

'No, I'm not a policeman – but if I was you'd be locked up by now.'

'No, I wouldn't,' he says. 'I know some people.'

He's drunk *and* he's lippy. He hasn't had six or seven drinks – more like sixteen or seventeen. I get into the driver's seat of his car. 'I'm doing you a major favour here,' I tell him. 'I'm trying to get you home without you killing yourself or anybody else.'

He directs me to his place and Amy follows behind in our car. He tells me he's a separated father of three. I slow down when I see a parking space near the house and he goes, 'No, no – I never park here.'

I pull in anyway. '*Are you for real?* You could have killed someone and you're worried about a parking space?'

He staggers up to the front door of his house. Through the glass I see him talking to an oldish man in the front room, then going upstairs. I ring the doorbell and gesture for the other guy to come out.

'Just so you know,' I tell him. 'Your friend is an asshole. He's lucky he's not in a cell tonight. You'd better tell him that in the morning.'

'Oh, all right,' he goes, casual as you like. He's got a few on board as well and I'm thinking: *Christ Jesus! Has anyone around here NOT had a drink?*

He moves to close the door. I hammer home my point: 'Make sure you do – because he's not going to remember a thing.'

'Okay, okay,' he says. 'Thanks, Brian.'

I get back in the car with Amy and we head for home. A surreal end to a dreadful day.

*

We have nine Test matches before the start of the World Cup in New Zealand, and the beginning of the Six Nations doesn't exactly mark us out as serious contenders. We beat Italy by two points in Rome when Rog comes off the bench to land a trademark drop goal in the seventy-eighth minute. Then we lose 25–22 to France, despite outscoring them three tries to one. At Murrayfield we get three tries to Scotland's nil but end up hanging on for a three-point win.

It's a strange and unsatisfying rhythm.

During the gap week before our trip to the Millennium Stadium I spend a day in London doing a TV advert for Gillette. You've got to be ultra-careful with ads because you'll get dog's abuse from the lads if they're any way corny. But the way I see it, nothing I will ever do could possibly compare for sheer awfulness with the worst TV advert of all time – the one where Denis Hickie advertises Wavin pipes and tries to persuade the people of Ireland that there is a legitimate connection between playing rugby and piping a house.

The Gillette script has me and Jonny Wilkinson bursting out of two cubicles in a gents' toilet full of hidden cameras. We thrust a couple of razors in the face of some unsuspecting chap washing his hands and I'm given the killer line, to be delivered as he's still reeling from shock: 'Are you ready to take the Pro-Glide Challenge?' The hope is that whoever comes in will recognize us as rugby players and look suitably stunned – rather than wonder who the hell we are, or run screaming from the jacks.

It's a bit of fun, and afterwards the sponsors ask me and Jonny to say nice things about one another while the camera rolls.

'What sort of player is Jonny?' the interviewer asks.

I could big him up by talking about his prodigious ability to kick goals under pressure, but I prefer to highlight a different part of his game. 'To be honest,' I say, with complete sincerity, 'the hardest tackle I've ever been on the receiving end of was Jonny's.'

I notice a couple of smirks but I think nothing of them and carry on.

'Yeah, I tried to go down Jonny's channel once and he caught me so hard that I couldn't walk for a fortnight.'

Jonny erupts when they call 'cut'. He's practically on the floor, he's laughing so much.

'That can't be played!' he says.

I'm none the wiser until my words are called back to me.

On the way back from London, Amy phones and says a letter has arrived from Buckingham Palace addressed to Brian O'Driscoll Esquire. She has read somewhere that the invites to the royal wedding of William and Kate have gone out. I got on pretty well with William when I met him on the 2005 Lions tour. When we won the Slam in Cardiff, he came into our dressing room and was good fun. Amy's as giddy as a schoolgirl and I figure I can knock some fun out of the situation.

'Can I open it?' she asks.

'No way! It's addressed to me.'

'Come on! Please …'

'Nope.'

When I walk through the door she has the envelope in her hand. I tell her I'm wrecked, in need of a lie-down. I'm not the worst actor ever – I get a little practice helping Amy learn her scripts. But she's not having it.

'Open it!'

I break the royal seal and pop out the gold-embossed card revealing that the Lord Chamberlain has been commanded by the Queen to invite us to the wedding.

I'm honoured and Amy is outrageously excited, but there's a problem. If Leinster make it through to the semi-final of the Heineken Cup, there's a clash of dates.

We decide to play it by ear and it goes out of my mind as Ireland try to muster some form in the Six Nations. In Cardiff we're the victims of a brutal call by the touch judge, which gifts Wales a try and changes the momentum of the game. We lose by six.

We have England in our final game. Not for the first time, they're coming to Dublin with four wins from four and a Grand Slam in their nostrils.

*

Seventy-five per cent of the time, Johnny Sexton reckons he's right. He says that when it comes to the rest, he'll *argue* that he's right. A collector's item is a full apology, total acceptance that he got something wrong. He says it's good to argue. And I say, yeah, but shouting matches don't do anybody any good.

There's a bit of Roy Keane about him – world-class vision and a mentality that is stubborn and utterly uncompromising in pursuit of excellence and trophies. He's built differently. He's a perfectionist and a deep thinker, encyclopaedic in his knowledge. He doesn't just know his own role, he knows everyone else's, too. He never gets a call wrong. Apart from the shots at goal that any kicker can miss, his only errors are the very odd stray pass or trying to do his job too well and forcing something.

The scale of his desire is one of his stand-out qualities: one of the things that makes him great and – sometimes – volatile. It's not in his personality to concede anything to anybody.

On the Thursday before we take on England, we're working on a training-ground move designed to draw their defence and put somebody through a hole. But it's not happening. He's taking too much out of the ball, taking it too close to the gain line. So I let him know he needs to give it earlier.

'Johnny! You can't take that much out of it – we need time to be able to play!'

He's not impressed. 'You just need to fucking hold on to the ball!' he shouts.

I have a cut back at him: 'You know you *can* be wrong! It *is* possible!'

It kicks off from there. It turns out he's been bottling up a grievance for weeks after I had a pop at him during the game in Rome, for lack of subtlety in a pass. But, like my little spat with Shaggy, it blows itself out and it sets a tone.

When we play England, Sexto is on fire. He mixes up his game brilliantly, runs when it's on and kicks when he needs to. The general feeling is that England are going to do a job on us and win the Slam, just like they did in 2003, but they can't live with our pace and intensity.

Sexto has already put us 9–0 ahead when he sizes up an opportunity and does what England are least expecting. Instead of building a lead with a kickable penalty he taps and goes on their 22 and gives it to Tommy Bowe, who side-steps Ben Foden to score.

We play at the kind of tempo that has been missing for too long. Seven minutes into the second half we're back inside the England red zone. We're moving right to left. Donners tries to hit Keith Earls with a pass that could have put him clean through, but the ball is knocked backwards under the weight of Louis Deacon's tackle. It drops at my feet. I drive low past Danny Care, then motor for the line, Nick Easter running hard from my right, but too late to stop me.

It's my twenty-fifth championship try, one more than Ian Smith of Scotland, who set the previous all-time high in 1933. Individual accolades don't normally float my boat but this is a bit different. It's a pretty cool record to break and it's an emphatic way to finish the Six Nations. We win 24–8 – Ireland's third-biggest winning margin against England ever.

*

My shoulder problem is manageable during the championship but it flares up again back at the Aviva when we play Leicester in the quarter-final of the Heineken Cup. Three minutes into the second half, Alesana Tuilagi, the Samoan bulldozer, comes tearing up his wing. I move in to take him down, right shoulder into his gut as hard as I can. It's like hitting a concrete wall. I'm bounced back five metres as he steamrolls his way over the top of me.

Immediately I get a stinging pain down my right arm, followed by numbness and weakness. I go hiding for a minute, avoiding contact to give it time to dissipate.

We win 17–10, the decisive moment coming when Isa makes something out of nothing and cuts through them. It's a try typical of a sensational player and it puts us in the semi-final again.

The day after the game, my arm is hanging off me. I've no strength on my right side. If I had to throw a pass off it, I'd struggle. And the stingers keep coming, match after match.

The victory over Leicester means I can't go to the royal wedding. Amy is disappointed but she knows rugby comes first. She's listening to a radio phone-in when a caller asks why she doesn't go on her own. I tell her that's exactly what she should do – represent the two of us, show that the invitation was appreciated. So she goes and really enjoys her day.

The following afternoon, we play Toulouse in the Heineken semi at the Aviva. We're ahead 13–10 just before the half-time break when Dave Pearson yellow-cards me for playing the ball illegally at a ruck. By the time I come back, Louis Picamoles has scored a try off the back of a scrum and we're trailing 20–16.

I feel guilty sitting in the bin while the lads are left to cope with the onslaught. When the purgatory ends I'm determined to make amends. Thirteen minutes later, I get on the end of a great team try, squeezing between Vincent Clerc and Census Johnston. I'm only the last cog in the score but my guilt is lessened all the same and it vanishes completely when Sexto kicks us home, 32–23.

Our road to the final has seen us overcome the reigning French champions, Clermont, the French champions-elect, Toulouse, the French championship semi-finalists, Racing Metro, the English champions, Leicester, and the English champions-elect, Saracens. It's been a tough journey and at the Millennium we face another formidable side, Northampton.

The Saints have won eight out of eight in the tournament

but they're deemed the slight underdogs and they relish the tag. With Kearns on the long-term injury list, our team is unchanged from the semi-final: Isa Nacewa; Shane Horgan, Brian O'Driscoll, Gordon D'Arcy, Luke Fitzgerald; Johnny Sexton, Eoin Reddan; Cian Healy, Richardt Strauss, Mike Ross; Leo Cullen, Nathan Hines; Kevin McLaughlin, Sean O'Brien, Jamie Heaslip. Replacements: Jason Harris-Wright, Heinke van der Merwe, Stan Wright, Devin Toner, Shane Jennings, Isaac Boss, Ian Madigan, Fergus McFadden.

In every area in the opening half, we are dominated. Scrum, breakdown, defence – they win every contest. Even when their loosehead prop, Brian Mujati, gets sin-binned, they don't break stride. They shove us off our own scrum with seven men and win a penalty.

At half-time it's 22–6, and three tries to nil. We're shell-shocked and confused.

In the dressing room, I have a few words I want to say and so does Leo, but Sexto gets there first. The competitive animal is unleashed and the positivity comes flooding out of him.

'Listen,' he says. 'We're not fucking lying down here! Imagine how incredible it would be to come back from sixteen points down – that's what the great teams do in sport!'

He talks about Liverpool – three–nil down at half-time in the Champions League final and coming back to win it. He's at his belligerent best. He believes completely: 'We can do this! We just need to get our shit together and it'll happen.'

The analytical stuff is left to Joe. He makes one substitution, introducing Jenno at openside flanker, and it works brilliantly. Three minutes into the second half we start asking some questions. I collect a ruck ball and get across their 22, then Jamie puts us into striking range. Eoin Reddan keeps pressing, keeps finding guys to attack their line: Isa, me, Seanie, then Sexto, wide on the right. He gets over in the corner and converts his own try.

We've got a sniff of it and Northampton go into their shell. They just want to hold what they have. Nine minutes later, Sexto scores again and converts that one, too. It's one thing talking big, but backing it up like that is properly impressive.

When he puts over another penalty, we've turned a 16-point deficit into a one-point lead. They're wilting and we're stubborn as hell. The pack that dismantled us in the first half is now wasted. In leading the fightback, Seanie O'Brien is an absolute bull, but this is a collective thing. Everybody's found their best stuff.

When Hinesy crashes through for our third try, it's done: 27 points without reply. Going into the closing minutes we're 11 points clear and freewheeling. People forget finals all the time, but they remember comebacks like this. We are double Heineken Cup winners and it's a class feeling, being part of it.

At Cardiff airport, we take turns to lift the trophy in front of all the Leinster fans waiting to fly home and there's a massive cheer every time. For us, being two-time champions is special, because every sport has any number of big winners who showed up once and then faded back into the pack. You've got to come again. And when you do, the level of satisfaction runs a little deeper.

In the check-in queue we see Pat Kenny, my *Late Late Show* tormentor of 2004, who's been over for the game. The lads are insistent. They hand him the trophy.

'Lift it up, Pat!'

He smiles. He shakes his head. He's given to understand that he actually doesn't have a choice in the matter.

As he raises it up, he gets soaked from all sides. The lads empty cans of the tournament sponsor's finest all over him. Shaggy and our scrum-half Paul O'Donohoe get him into a king's chair, with the trophy still high over his head and the beer still coming at him.

A week later we play Munster in the Magners League final at Thomond Park. Seeing us win the Heineken only adds to their intensity. The memory of the 30–0 earlier in the season doesn't do them any harm either. They're hungrier and more clinical; they win 19–9. We've no complaints and the Irish management are delighted. The way they see it, they need as many happy players as possible going into the World Cup in New Zealand.

Back in 2008, Leinster won our first competition in six years – the Magners League. We'd begun that season aiming high on all fronts, but failed to make it out of our pool in Europe. Three weeks later, after Munster had won their second Heineken Cup, the slagging from the likes of Rog was inevitable. The Heineken was everything and the Magners was a lucky second.

Now, with the trophies reversed, Rog finds himself in the same Portuguese holiday resort as some of the Leinster lads, still buzzing after the big day in Cardiff. Rog and his good friend Mick O'Driscoll are there for a week in the sun with their families. He's relaxing by the pool when a waiter approaches, carrying a tray. Resting on it is a glass of ice and a bottle of Magners – sent over by Lukie and Ferg, who are putting away a few bottles of Heineken on the other side of the pool.

There's a message with the bottle and, according to

eyewitness accounts, the great man of Munster smiles as he reads it: *Well done on the Magners, Rog.*

*

The Ireland squad is back in camp at Carton House, Maynooth, in late June and I'm in decent shape: body fresh, head in a good place. We do a contact session in our first week and straight away I get a ridiculous stinger. The injections I've had to relax the muscles in my shoulder prove futile. After the first hit at the first ruck, the pain shoots down my arm. I'm disgusted.

Already? You're kidding me!

I know it's bad – and that it's getting worse. A few weeks after the stinger I go to see Ashley Poynton for a scan and he says I've got accelerated degeneration in the C5/C6 disc in my neck. The disc is bulging and I've got osteophytes, or bone spurs – an enlargement of the normal bone structure into the nerve channel. In plain language, the shock absorbers in my neck are worn down. The bone spurs keep jabbing away at the nerve and causing the stingers. The more hits I take, the bigger the spurs grow.

It's been two years since Ashley first mentioned the word 'fusion' to me, but now it comes up again. I tell him I'll think about things after the World Cup, but in the meantime I need reassurance from him that playing in New Zealand is not going to do me untold damage. If he tells me that it's unsafe to play, then that's it: I'll retire there and then. I desperately want to play in the World Cup but I'm not stupid. I have a life to lead. There's a bigger picture in all of this. Rugby is very important but it's not the be-all and end-all.

I look for clearance and Ashley gives it to me. He says I'm not putting myself in danger by playing on. After I hear that,

I reckon I can deal with everything else – it's all about managing the situation. I need to cope with the discomfort, and I have to come up with a way of training that gets me in shape for the games but doesn't put stress on my injury.

When I tell Dad I'm good to go, his reaction is unsettling. 'What about the stingers?' he asks.

I tell him Ashley talked again about a fusion operation – something I'll have to think about after the World Cup.

'Whoa, whoa!' he says. 'If that happens I would not be happy.'

The forcefulness of his response gives me a jolt. It's not so much the doctor in him that's speaking, but the worried dad. The last thing I want is my parents stressing, so I play it down. Anyway, I can't imagine a scenario where I'd go through with a fusion and keep playing. The way I see it, if my neck is bad enough to need it, it's going to be an operation with the rest of my life in mind – not something that gives me another season in rugby.

So I put it to the back of my mind and go back into camp.

We have four warm-up games on consecutive weekends in August.

We lose 10–6 against Scotland at Murrayfield.

France beat us in Bordeaux, 19–12.

The French come to Dublin the following weekend: they win 26–22.

Next, England roll up, outmuscle us and win 20–9. For us, the worst thing about the game isn't the scoreline: it's the sight of David Wallace leaving the pitch on a stretcher, out of the World Cup with a serious knee injury.

I play in just one of the four friendlies – the loss to the French at the Aviva. It's a good thing and a bad thing:

the shoulder improves, but I'm concerned about match sharpness.

Outside the camp people are beginning to panic about four defeats on the trot, but the upside is that we've spent time together and the bond between us has never been stronger.

That camaraderie only increases when we land in New Zealand and head for Queenstown, in the south-west of the South Island. It's the adventure capital of the country and it does wonders for us. We try the hilltop luge run, some guys are up for a bungee jump, and top of the pile is a helicopter ride over Milford Sound, landing on the Mount Tutoko glacier. Some of us have been told about the famous mouth-watering Fergburger restaurant by the Leinster prop Heinke van der Merwe and it does not disappoint. We train hard but we have a good night out, too. We relax, we enjoy ourselves, we're dying for a cut off America in our first game. We want the kind of clinical performance that boosts our confidence levels and obliterates the memory of August.

It doesn't happen. In New Plymouth, we're loose, wasteful, unconvincing in a 22–10 win.

It's not a lot of feelgood to bring into game two, against Tri-Nations champions Australia in Eden Park. We haven't put in a really big performance since beating England in the Six Nations, and you have to go back a long way to find the one before that. In the days leading up to Australia we talk about how we're capable of putting it together when the mood strikes us. Lack of consistency has always been our problem, the thing separating us from the great teams – we dip below our standard far too often.

But there are some weeks when you just know that things

are right and this is one of them. We have a fantastic intensity. Before we go out, Geordan Murphy and Shane Jennings say a few words about what victory would mean. It's all the more powerful coming from them because they haven't been picked in the twenty-two and yet they're as psyched as the rest of us.

We have the support of a huge Irish crowd and also the backing of all of New Zealand. We stifle Australia right from the first whistle. Our defence is ferocious and unrelenting. Our forwards choke the supply of ball to their backline. Their dangerous runners can do nothing.

Sexto puts us 9–6 ahead with two penalties and a drop goal. He slots in alongside me when Rog appears for an injured Darce. We're untested as a midfield partnership but we're solid all the same and our forwards are in riotous form. They win two penalties and Rog lashes them over. We're 15–6 ahead and in Rog we've got a master at shutting things down from a winning position. It's a day when everything just clicks and the win leaves us in control of the pool.

In the post-match TV interviews, I'm just the warm-up act for Rog. I'm proud but restrained. He's emotional, searingly honest, box-office gold. After a very impressive thirty minutes off the bench he's in a happy place, but once he starts talking, the pain he felt over not starting the game pours out of him.

'I'm done with Ireland in a few weeks,' he announces, which comes as news to the rest of us.

In our group, nobody gets away with making a big statement like that on national TV without having the piss ripped out of him. Rog dishes enough of it out, so he knows he has to take it as well. And I take great pleasure in flagging up a couple of inconvenient truths for my good buddy. 'Sorry,

Rog. You're under contract, by the way! You can't just retire – the Union has you by the balls!'

And anyway, when he's playing so well, why would he even want to walk away?

Deccie rests most of the usual starters for the Russia game and Rog is brilliant with the boot. When the team to play Italy is named, he stays in and Sexto drops to the bench. I can tell it's devastating for Johnny, but in this kind of scenario you don't like to intrude on personal disappointment, other than saying, 'Hard luck' – it's what can happen when you've got two unbelievable competitors going balls-out for the same jersey.

When we put Italy away – 36–6, a fair statement – we're one win away from a World Cup semi-final and Wales don't hold any fears for us. We know them, they know us – it's a matter of who brings their A game.

At the Westpac Stadium in Wellington, Wales explode out of the blocks. They run at us hard and we've got no answers. They come blasting through the gain line and score after a couple of minutes through Shane Williams. They chop-tackle our big runners and get up a head of steam. Their game plan works like a dream.

We get it to 10–10 just after half-time when Keith Earls scores, but we make too many unforced errors and they pull away. We concede a sloppy try to Mike Phillips down the short-side of a ruck, then another soft one when Jonathan Davies finds a gap in our defence and gets over way too easily.

Once they go two scores ahead it's good night. We have mountains of possession and territory but we're devoid of ideas, or the cutting edge to open a tight defence. Our attacking play lacks cut and thrust. It's not the kind of frailty you generally find in World Cup semi-finalists.

For all of us, it's a sickening feeling of an opportunity lost. For some of us, including me, it cuts a little deeper because I know I can't get it back. It's gone for ever – I'll never play in another World Cup and I'm disgusted.

I'm also physically shot. It's the worst I've been since the problem first arose – even as the game was going on and the impact of the collisions was weakening my right side, I was talking to myself:

This is ridiculous!

I can't go on like this!

For two days I can't switch off. It's the biggest disappointment of my career. Some of the lads go for a drink, but I've little interest.

We go home and there's a few hundred people at the airport, applauding us as we arrive. Seeing them there makes me uncomfortable. I know they're still feeding off the victory over Australia, but we didn't back it up. We failed. Beating Australia and then losing in a quarter-final – like other Ireland teams before us – is nothing to be proud of.

*

A week later I have more scans on my shoulder, and then myself and Amy go on holidays to a friend's house near Marbella.

Spain is supposed to be a retreat; it's anything but. I've got a hundred different things in my head. A few years before, I'd thought that the World Cup in New Zealand would be where it all finished. A dozen seasons as a professional, four World Cups – it felt like an ending.

But now I'm not ready to let it go.

I take phone calls from the specialists about the results of my scan and the fusion operation is higher up the agenda.

There are more phone calls from my dad. He knows what a fusion entails, and he tells me that if I have it done, his advice would be that I give up rugby.

He's so honest and so clear in his mind that the questions start flooding my brain.

Is this the end?

Have I played my last game?

'Your dad is right,' Amy says. 'Listen to him.'

Retiring looks like the sensible option, but I'm not ready to give up rugby. I still love it. And I don't know how to replace it in my life.

So I sit by the pool and fret.

12. Fusion

'It's pretty straightforward,' says Ashley Poynton. 'You're not safe to play until something happens.'

It's Monday morning, 24 October 2011. I'm in Suite 16 at 69 Eccles Street and the room is full of medical men. There's Ashley and another surgeon, Keith Synnott, and the Leinster and Ireland team doctors, Arthur Tanner and Éanna Falvey.

I feel a few different emotions, but the biggest is relief that they're taking the decision out of my hands. I'm not stupid – I'm not going to put myself in danger if an expert in the field tells me I can't carry on as I am.

By 'something', Ashley means the fusion operation. He spells out the procedure in detail. Like any spinal specialist, he's got your life in his hands so he's got to make sure you understand what you're agreeing to. He goes through the things that could possibly go wrong but, like most people in this situation, I'm not overly keen on thinking about the worst-case scenario. All I want to know is, am I going to be better after it? Will I be able to carry on playing?

The day after I spoke to my dad by the pool in Spain, Arthur had called me. There were plenty of examples, he'd said then, of players in different sports having fusions and carrying on with their careers, uninhibited. Rory Best, for one.

And now, across the road from the Mater Private, Ashley makes up my mind for me.

'There's no reason that you can't come back and be perfect,' he says.

With career-threatening injuries, there's no room for 'I wonder . . .' You've got to be positive from the beginning if you're going to get through the rehab. As soon as I hear the words come out of Ashley's mouth, my head is filled with optimism.

I'll be fine.

I'll back myself to come back.

I don't want it to finish here, in a hospital consultant's office – walking off after one of the biggest disappointments of my career and then announcing, six weeks later, that I'm done.

There's a Lions tour to Australia less than two years away. It would be a big ask to be part of it, but it's something to shoot for, a target in the distance. For a while I've been thinking that winning a Lions series after three losing tours would be some way to go out – and if I didn't have my post-rugby future clearer in my head by then it would be a sorry state of affairs.

Dad speaks to Arthur and Ashley and they put his mind at rest. I'm booked in for the operation, three weeks later.

Leinster sets up a press briefing in between and nobody asks a searching question about the nature of the procedure I'm having, so I let them run with the shoulder-surgery line. A nerve problem. Pain running down into my arm. Six months to recover, probably.

The average Joe doesn't know what a discectomy or a fusion is and I'm not particularly keen to go all technical, or to cause the mothers of rugby-playing kids some undue alarm. *O'Driscoll to have neck fusion surgery* is not a headline they need to read. *O'Driscoll out of Six Nations* covers it.

Amy brings me in on the third Wednesday in November. As we're driving around the hospital looking for a parking space, a member of staff spots us and offers to help. She puts in a phone call and hangs up, looking pleased. 'You're grand,' she says. 'There's a space reserved for you in the mortuary car park.'

Lovely.

Up in the room, Ashley tells me how it's going to go.

First, a horizontal incision, about three centimetres long, on the left side of my neck. He brings his finger across: 'Just here.'

'Why on the left?' I ask. 'The issue is all on the right side.'

'Yeah,' he says. 'I'm gonna come in on the left because I'm left-handed.'

I wonder if he's kidding me, but I notice he's using his left hand a lot and I figure it's not something he's going to joke about.

He says he'll have to get around my windpipe and gullet, then come straight down onto the front of the spinal cord, where the problematic disc is. He'll use an electrocautery machine with a blade to cut through the soft tissue and the different layers along the way – fat and muscle.

Once that's done, he'll be able to get to the spine, identify my cervical C5/C6 disc by X-ray, take it out, then spread the bones apart. After that, it'll be like soldering together the two vertebrae. First, he'll drill away the bone spur that's growing in towards the nerve and giving me more grief. Then there's the reconstruction – a hollow plastic block, six or seven millimetres wide, filled with bone dust taken from the spur, with a little collagen mixed in to give it some structure: over time, this will grow into a new bit of bone connecting the vertebrae. Next, a plate across the bridge between C5 and C6, secured with four titanium screws.

Finally, he'll close me back up. Job done.

I sign on the dotted line.

'See you at two o'clock,' he says.

When the time comes, he's got Arthur scrubbing for him. They go way back: when Ashley was a medical student in the Adelaide teaching hospital, Arthur was a general surgeon.

The anaesthetist puts a drip into the back of my hand and I ask her how long it'll take to knock me out.

'Under two minutes,' she says – the last thing I can remember before the fuzzy, warm feeling takes hold and the lights go out.

When I come round, after an hour and three-quarters, they tell me it went very well and I start feeling good in no time. Later, when the nurse brings me some tea and toast – with full-fat butter – I demolish it.

Around 8.30 p.m., Ashley pays me a visit. 'Move that arm!' He smiles. 'Good! Now move your legs.'

I wake up the following morning feeling the difference straight away. No pins and needles, no pain.

A text arrives after Amy brings me home in the afternoon. It's from one of the lads in Clontarf, who's just become a father. *This is your time to be pregnant. Take full advantage!*

*

I do practically nothing for the first ten days, except get spoiled by Amy.

At half ten one night, the buzzer goes outside. There's a camera at the gate and when I check the security screen I see a kid standing there. He's twelve or thirteen. I recognize him from a few days previously: he called hoping to get a jersey signed. I was just out of the shower and I asked him to come back some other time. I wasn't thinking of 10.30 p.m. in pitch darkness.

'Hi, I was here before,' he goes. 'Will you sign that jersey?'

'I'm in bed,' I fib. 'It's half ten at night! Sorry, but you'll have to come back again.'

'Will you be there at three tomorrow?'

'Ah, I don't know. Maybe.'

'Okay, bye.'

It's raining outside. I hang up, and then guilt gets the better of me. I open the gates and he comes in.

You can't really expect a twelve-year-old boy to understand that I give as much of myself as I can when I'm out and about, and that – no more than anyone else's – my home should be my sanctuary. But there's a car parked outside with one of his parents at the wheel, somebody who clearly thinks it's okay to knock on the door of a private residence at any time of the day or night, just because the person living inside happens to be pretty well known.

I get a lot of enjoyment out of signing an autograph or getting into a photograph to make a kid's day. Even after all these years, it still feels mad to think it can have that effect – and any kid who asks nicely will get my very best signature.

I remember pulling into my parents' drive in Clontarf one day and seeing two youngsters running up, brother and sister.

'Excuse me, Mr O'Driscoll,' the boy said, 'sorry for bothering you, but can I please have your autograph?'

First I thought, *Who's Mr O'Driscoll?* Then I wondered if there was a hidden camera in the garden, because that level of good manners isn't exactly the norm these days, more's the pity.

The comments that come out of young mouths aren't always guaranteed to make you smile. Once I was shopping in the local Dunnes Stores when a little chap approached.

'Please can you gimme your autograph?'

'No problem.'

'Will you be in your house at Hallowe'en this year?'

'Yeah, I should be.'

'Okay. Great. It's just my friend lives on your road and he called in last year, trick or treating.'

'Yeah?'

'He said you were definitely in but you never answered.'

Needless to say, only Mr Simms himself rivalled me for sweets that Hallowe'en night.

Now the kid with the jersey gets his autograph and a friendly request: 'If you want something else signed, ask me after a game some time, okay?'

*

Confined to the house, unable to drive, I try to busy myself with stuff I've been putting off – like going through my post.

Dear Brian,

In some ways, it is with a heavy heart that I write this. But regardless of what happened in Wellington, I believe that Ireland are the No. 1 team or a close second in the world – all things considered. You owe the Irish Nation nothing.

Right now, your job is to RELAX and make lots and lots of young 'O'Dricos' for Ireland with Amy, your beautiful and intelligent wife who the whole country seems to love. Bless you both in the radiant and amazing years that lie ahead of you.

What a rugby adventure it has been – and it's not finished yet, Brian! Before you ride off into the sunset, there is still the one little matter of regaining OUR Six Nations crown and the small task – for the first time in Irish history – of slaying once and for all the mighty All Blacks.

Despite the latest setback, I trust that both will be accomplished.

All the best . . .

Dear Brian,

I'd like to wish you the best of luck with your surgery. I hope it goes well and that you make a swift recovery.

I have enclosed a picture of you and the lovely Amy for this reason: I'd like to get the coat for my wife that Amy is wearing in the photo. My wife was admiring it, saying how nice it was, so I decided to cut it out and one day try to get it for her as a present. So with Christmas coming up, I said I would get the ball rolling.

I would very much appreciate if you would ask your wife for details and hopefully it doesn't put you out too much. I looked online to see if there was any way of emailing Amy or anything like that but there didn't seem to be. My details are at the top of the page. If you can help me out I would be very grateful.

Best wishes . . .

I like to do what I can – and Mum and Sue do a brilliant job in helping me. Most of the people writing are really sincere and you come to recognize the others – the ones looking for signed pictures to flog for a few quid online. Usually they'll chance their arm and ask for four or five. Some don't even bother to disguise the fact that the same photocopied letter is going to dozens of others.

Dear **Brian**

I've been a huge fan of yours for a number of years. I would very much appreciate it if you . . . etc

Once you start signing stuff for the eBay operators of this world, the ones who end up losing out are the good causes who can make some money from charity auctions.

*

Twelve days after the operation, Amy takes me to the Leinster training ground, five minutes down the road. I get myself on a stationary bike and start thinking about the time frame for my comeback. I've been told four to six months, and any rugby player I know is going to look on the more optimistic side of that guesstimate. As I turn the pedals I'm thinking that if it's more four than six, I'll be in the running for the quarter-final of the Heineken Cup, if we get that far.

We're looking pretty good when the lads do the double over Bath, on back-to-back weekends in December. A six-point lead at the top of our pool is a decent reason to let the hair down at our Christmas party the night after a 52–27 win at the Aviva. Not that we need one, though: these are the nights when you build Heineken Cup success.

It's a fancy-dress gig at a club down in Carlow, Sean O'Brien country. Some of the lads go all out – Ferg McFadden and Fionn Carr are worryingly convincing as the Williams sisters, Serena and Venus.

Four of us get a taxi down together after an RTÉ sports awards show. Isa goes as some kind of furry dog, with the whole body suit. Leo's an elf. I help Shaggy do his make-up, the war paint that transforms him into Adam Ant, eighties pop icon.

I put on my blond wig and pink shirt, and once we get there it's only the younger lads – the ones with absolutely no interest in Irish politics – who don't cop my look.

'Who are you supposed to be?'

'Isn't it obvious?'

'Ah . . .'

'You're only showing your ignorance! I'm Mick Wallace.'

By the end of the night there's carnage everywhere, but as a team we're all the better for the blow-out.

*

Christmas with the Hubermans. An incredible lunch is served and then it begins: the great Huberman present-opening ritual. A two-hour extravaganza, one gift at a time, each one to be savoured and salivated over.

'Okay, next! Amy for Paul!'

'Looks interesting!'

'Beautifully wrapped!'

'Here you go!'

'Thanks!'

'Nice shirt!'

'That colour really suits you!'

'Cheers, Amy!'

'You're very welcome!'

'Right . . . Let's see. Here we are, we'll go with this one next. Mark for Mum . . .'

'No, hang on, let's open this one first.'

And so on.

Over in Clontarf, a couple of hours later, we O'Driscolls rip the paper off our presents like wild animals.

'This is yours.'

'Dad! One of yours here.'

'Great!'

'Who's this for? Doesn't say.'

'Open it and see.'

Amy is aghast. 'No one's paying any attention to who gave what!' she says.

I tell her other people's Christmases never cease to surprise. We had Christmas dinner with her family last year, my first as a married man. Now, the turkey and ham are served up to us in Park Lawn.

After a great meal – and a couple of glasses of wine – it's time for the annual O'Driscoll Christmas-night quiz, featuring teams of three drawn from a hat, with Mum in the Anne Robinson role and lots of cousins over.

Every year we all pray that we'll come out of the hat with my cousin Carol's husband, Kev – a quiz genius. Jules strikes it lucky this time, along with Sue's husband, Mal. They're a crack team and they blow everyone else away. We're second. My team comes second every year.

Me and Mal stay up late talking and finish solving the world's problems around about half three.

Three days later, I finally step up to the plate as first-time babysitter for Jules and Tomás's three kids – my goddaughter Katie, Aoife and Sean. They're all mad about Amy. We take them out for the afternoon and – like the childcare novices we are – forget to bring a bag for contingencies.

'I went to the toilet in my nappy,' Sean announces, as soon as we arrive in town to see a panto.

Amy dashes off to get supplies. She comes back, has a word with Sean and points at me. 'I want *him* to change it,' she says.

I try to defend myself – 'Pick her! Pick her!' – but it's a done deal. My first nappy change.

*

Before the year is out, after a frustrating day at the gym when the right side of my upper body doesn't feel like it's firing, it hits me: I need to refocus – more effort, more sessions.

I need to be more demanding of the strength and condition-ing guys, more understanding of the science behind what they want me to do.

What will this exercise do for me?

What are my targets for this week, next week, the week after?

Write them down and let's make them happen.

Up to this moment I've been pretty conscientious about my rehab, doing everything asked of me and sometimes a bit more. But I've also had one eye on retirement and what comes next, frightened by the thought of being one of those players who hangs up his boots one afternoon – or has the decision made for him – then asks, 'Now what?' the follow-ing day.

I've watched friends and former team-mates struggle to reincorporate themselves in the real world – at least for a while – when the pay cheques from rugby stop hitting their bank accounts. A country in recession isn't the best place to go looking for a new sense of purpose – not to mention a new job.

Without games to prepare for I've been in early at River-view, working through till lunchtime and then leaving – people to see, brains to pick, all kinds of different things on the go.

Too much, too soon.

Part of me has forgotten that I'm still a full-time rugby player.

Injured, but not quite finished.

In need of a plan for life after rugby, true, but getting ahead of myself.

Because any time I talk to the guys who've finished up – even the ones building successful new careers – the same messages keep coming back, loud and clear.

'You'll be a long time retired.'
'Keep bloody playing!'

*

Thursday, 5 January 2012. Den texts me at 7.16 a.m.
Call me when you can.

I'm already up, halfway out the door to the training ground.

'I'm meeting Hego and Shaggy for nosebag tonight,' he says, when I call. 'Y'interested?'

Hego is our mutual buddy Derek Hegarty, a scrum-half for Leinster back in my first two seasons, a good pal and a serious laugh.

I'm keen. Den – ever the man of refinement – books an excellent word-of-mouth restaurant in Ranelagh, Pinocchio. Later, Hego cries off so there's just the three of us.

Four years retired, Den is getting on well in the big bad world outside. He's business development manager for Mainstream, a renewable-energy company with a global presence. People said he quit rugby too young – gone at thirty-one, less than six months after starting all five games in the 2007 Six Nations, one of the best campaigns of all our careers. He could easily have hung in for a few more years, but he went out on his own terms and not many can say that. In the years since, he's been a reliable sounding board for me, wise counsel always there when I've needed good advice.

For Shaggy, it's a tough time. He hasn't played since the end of last season and his knee isn't coming right after two operations. At the restaurant table, he constantly moves his left leg and the discomfort is obvious.

It's only seven months since he finished one of his best seasons on a high, pivotal to our second Heineken Cup win. He desperately wants to play on. He's been a pro for fourteen seasons but he has more to give. The passion is still burning in him, the same desire for us to keep getting better as a team. The negative vibes from the specialists are getting him down, but it's not in him to mope around the place.

He turns up for the early-morning senior players' meetings and you'd swear he was playing the following weekend. He wants the rest of the lads to see he's around, still with the same work ethic, still fighting to get back. And everyone would love to see it, but we want him to be able to kick a ball around with his kids, too.

*

Once the switch is flicked, once I finally cop that I need to dump the stuff that's getting in the way of me returning in the best possible shape, change kicks in quickly.

I allow myself to chill out after a day's rehab, to let the brain do nothing but veg. At the training ground, we up the intensity. I talk to our physio, James Allen, about how far I can push it. Stevie Smith – the strength and conditioning coach who specializes in rehabbing players – is another positive guy who plays a big part in getting me back on track. He brings energy, laughs and huge commitment to every session.

He takes out an iPad and runs two videos side by side on the screen. I see myself, top off, on a lat pull-down – the same exercise filmed from different angles. In the first clip, the whole left side of my body is twitching and firing as I bring down the bar from over my head. In the second, nothing's happening on my right side.

It's not just a by-product of the operation, it's also down to the fact that for three or four years I've spent very little time lifting upper-body weights. I've been doing my own thing, with a TRX suspension trainer, a pulley system that uses body weight to build your core. It's a great piece of kit but it's not going to get enough strength back in my arm and shoulder. Stevie comes up with a programme that has me working predominantly on my right side. I throw myself into it, with a new energy and positivity.

I've always seen the gym as a means to an end, but if there's one thing I've really gotten a lot out of it's sled fitness. You tie a harness onto your back and pull a hundred-plus kilos of weights resting on a sled for twenty metres. It takes eight or nine seconds, with fifty-odd seconds to get the sled in place for the next effort and catch your breath. On a good day you do it thirty times for strength and endurance.

I like it because it almost mirrors my game. Burst. Take a breather. See what's going on around you. Get in position. Go again.

There's another thing: I can't compete when it comes to lifting weights but I'll give most of the lads a run for their money on the sleds.

On the second Monday in January I do a session with two of the forwards, Sean O'Brien and Devin Toner. Shane Jennings has been on the sleds before us – a strength session, five twenty-metre pulls with 275 kilos on board on the indoor running track at UCD. Myself and Sean put an extra five kilos on, just to get a fraction ahead of him. If you're staying with Seanie and you're five ahead of Jenno, it's fair going; a small battle won on the road back.

And good for the morale, because in Joe's second season Leinster aren't exactly missing me. After hammering Ulster in the RDS on St Stephen's Day the boys win again at Connacht on the first day of 2012 and rack up another away win in Cardiff a week later. It brings their unbeaten run to fourteen games, stretching back to mid-September. In the number

13 jersey, Eoin O'Malley is playing the rugby of his life. For him, an Ireland career beckons. If it's not Chubbo at outside centre, it's Fergus – another guy in form.

With my thirty-third birthday fast approaching, I watch them in the games and it's like sitting in the passenger seat with a bad driver – always thinking of what's coming next, wondering if they're making the same reads.

Plug the inside!

That's great D!

Maybe you should've stayed off there . . .

As you grow older – when you're giving eight or ten years to the guys coming after your place – the game gets harder and the competition feels tougher. Brian Moore, the England hooker, dealt with rivals for the number 2 jersey by blanking them completely. I'm not from that school – not many are. If there's a chance to improve the team by passing on some knowledge to the players coming through, I feel you've got a responsibility to do it.

But, still, the more the team prospers without me, the more I feel my return can't come soon enough. Confidence comes and goes in an older player and you have to keep convincing yourself that you're still up to it. But at least there's light at the end of the tunnel and I'm practically counting the hours to my big appointment with Ashley – 16 January, 8 a.m. Two months to the day since the fusion.

I'm hoping for some level of certainty once he scans my neck. I need an achievable comeback date I can work towards – physically and mentally.

What I don't need is for him to keep me hanging on, uncertain – 'We'll see you in another month, just keep doing what you're doing.'

*

On a computer screen in his rooms on Eccles Street, Ashley shows me the plate inside my neck. It jumps out like a hand-gun on an airport X-ray scanner, a startling object that blatantly doesn't belong.

Oh my God! That's actually my neck!

Ashley, though, looks pleased at what he sees.

'That's good,' he says, deadpan. 'It hasn't fallen off yet.'

He's got a dry sense of humour and I'm pretty sure it's a gag, but I don't want to turn my head to check his expression so I take a punt and laugh.

He's happy with the level of bone growth since the op. 'There's grey matter here,' he says, 'but it's coming on very well.'

James Allen is alongside us and I push Ashley for a come-back date. 'I've pretty much written off the Six Nations,' I begin, 'but I need a target.'

'I've seen a good fusion take six weeks,' he says, 'but when you're dealing with necks you have to err on the side of caution.'

When I tell him I'm hoping to be back for the Heineken Cup quarter-final, he asks when it's on.

'The seventh or eighth of April – that weekend.'

'I don't see why not.'

'But I'd need to play a game before it.'

'So, the week before?'

'Yeah.'

'No problem.'

It's supposed to be a day off for me, but I'm so buoyed by the news I head straight for the training ground. I hammer into a fitness session, trying to justify the five-day break in New York with Amy I've booked for the following morning, knowing I'll feel less guilty about enjoying myself on holiday if I hurt myself in the session.

On my first day back from the holiday, Sean O'Brien doesn't miss a trick. 'Jeez,' he says, 'you've put on a nice bit of weight. New York was good to you!'

It's harsh, but the only way to answer it is by sticking it to him on the sleds. I put an extra fifty kilos on board and get our fitness coach, Dan Tobin, to take a video of me pulling it. Then I send it to Seanie with a message attached – mostly for the laugh but also because he's a guy worth getting the better of: *330kgs . . . best of luck in the Plate, kid.*

*

An email arrives from Louise Hart, PA to the IRFU chief executive, Philip Browne, inviting me and Amy to watch the first game of the 2012 Six Nations from the president's box. It's a nice thought.

When we get there, the place is full of alickadoos from the Union. There's something to admire in them giving of their free time, but it's hard – as a current player – not to be struck by how much the game has moved on. I sit there trying to ignore some of the senseless comments and wishing there was younger blood in the positions of influence, retired players from my generation who understand what it takes to compete against the world's best.

The way I see it, a professional game should be run by fully professional people, each one accountable for their work, just as it is on the pitch. I guess without the voluntary work done for the Union, the cost base would rise, but there has to be some way of arriving at a more efficient system of decision-making than leaving it to hierarchical committees.

It would be wrong and unfair not to give big credit to the Union for all the good things it's done – like the central contracts that have strengthened the national set-up and allowed people like me to extend our careers without being flogged for forty games a season. But, still, there's something seriously amiss when the Ireland head coach has to sit down with the IRFU's management committee and tell them what he's thinking about for the next game.

At the Aviva, Paulie leads the team out and Sexto's back in the number 10 jersey, alongside our rising star of a scrum-half, Conor Murray. Ferg's at 13, after Keith Earls pulls out injured. Four months on from the World Cup, we're up against Wales again. And we lose again – beaten by a last-minute Leigh Halfpenny penalty.

People often ask if you feel secretly relieved, or even a touch pleased – watching from the stand as the team get beaten without you. No. Only a liar would claim to enjoy it if the guy taking his place in the team has a complete blinder, because we're all competitive animals, but the honest truth is I feel bad for the lads. I'm an Ireland fan first.

As the championship is played out, I find myself thinking of what they'll be doing at different moments – the captain's meeting on the Friday before a game, apple crumble after dinner, a few sweets in Rala's room later on. And I miss it all something terrible.

13. Back in the Game

For a while I've had the game circled in my diary: Leinster v. Ospreys, 23 March 2012, Friday night. It's two weeks out from the Heineken Cup quarter-final against Cardiff, with a match against Munster in between. It's a tight time frame to get myself battle-ready for the quarters. Tight, but doable.

As the comeback day draws closer, there are the usual setbacks and frustrations that afflict an injured player who's on the outside looking in. Sometimes, when you're so focused on getting one thing right, you end up neglecting another. I've let my core work slip a little, and when my back seizes up I'm bedridden for a couple of days. I need Arthur Tanner to come round and give me a shot of morphine, because the muscle relaxant I'm lumping on isn't making a blind bit of difference. I also have to convince an alarmed Amy that the problem in my back has nothing to do with the neck surgery. She feels I'm pushing things too hard.

I get my facet joints injected to numb the pain, I start hammering the Pilates five days a week – and it all clears up.

Seven days before the Ospreys game I head over to Ashley again, feeling better than I have in a couple of years and pain-free. I'm back lifting decent weights, with equal strength on both sides. He looks at the latest X-ray and clears me to play.

I'm excited but apprehensive, hoping that what I had before will still be there. I know I'll be feeling my way back in – that the confidence won't return straight away, or the match fitness. But at least I'll get the blow-out my lungs need, and in my head anything else will be a bonus.

Get it done. Then move on.

It's a seven o'clock kick-off but my gear is packed and good to go by 2 p.m. I drive through the gates of the RDS at 5.15 and the first thing that hits me is that it's going to be strange not having Shaggy around any more. He's leaving the official announcement for another week but the decision is made. His career is over – the last of my closest friends to call it a day.

The boys from Clontarf are there in force to welcome me back: Dunny, Redser, Robbie Ryan, F. J. O'Driscoll. Leo is also making a comeback, after two months out injured, and he's got a half-decent new partner in the second row. At the beginning of the season we lost Nathan Hines to Clermont Auvergne. Joe fought hard to keep him and Hinesy wanted to stay, but the IRFU wouldn't give him a new deal because he's not Irish-qualified. Now, as a short-term measure because we're running low on second-rows, Brad Thorn has signed on for the rest of the season – as in the World Cup winner with New Zealand and all-round legend. It's a seriously smart piece of business and it's a genuine thrill seeing him put the blue jersey on.

I've got Ferg alongside me in the centre. Chubbo – who has played 13 for most of the season – is on the bench. In fifty-eight minutes on the pitch I make hardly any tackles and touch the ball three or four times but come through it feeling reasonably sharp.

Good enough.

Four minutes from time, the Ospreys get over in the

corner and sneak a one-point win. It's the first time we've been beaten in six months – twenty-one games.

Not so good.

*

It might sound like a bullshit line, it might be a well-worn rugby cliché, but it's 100 per cent true – any time you play you're only borrowing the jersey. Sooner or later, everything moves on.

I look at the strength in the Leinster squad and in my eyes there's only one player who can be fully confident of his starting place – Sexto, now the best number 10 in Europe by a distance. Back when we were starting to get our act together under Cheiks, I felt I was a vital component of the team myself. Six years on, I still think I can add something but I know I'm not as important as I was before. The other guys in my position are really stepping up. Chubbo, Ferg and Brendan Macken from the academy – really good players, all of them, with big engines.

For the whole five months I was out, there was never a time when I saw myself walking straight back onto the team, when I thought, *Right, I'll have that 13 jersey back now, thanks very much.*

Just as well.

Getting through my comeback game reasonably okay is a guarantee of nothing. There are bigger selection tests ahead, and when the team for the quarter-final is named, reputations will count for nothing in Joe Schmidt's eyes.

It's not like I hadn't worked that out already, but coming back into the match-day squad brings it home. A little rusty post-injury? Tough – he expects high standards immediately.

There's a part of me that finds this brilliant and another part that wishes a dozen seasons at a high level would count for something – but it doesn't.

Pilates, stretching sessions at home, way more thinking about my game than ever before – I've never had to work so hard to make myself believe I can still deliver when it counts. I deny myself even a taste of chocolate, I cut out sweets, drink a protein shake instead of the usual late-night bowl of cereal. But convincing myself is only half the battle – I've also got to worry about the guy who picks the team. For Joe, it's not about experience or what you've won in the game, it's about who's training well and playing well.

*

Saturday, 24 March, the morning after the Ospreys game.

I'm rounding up some company for brunch. I call Brian O'Malley – Eoin's older brother. We go way back.

He's up for it. He asks if I've contacted Chubbo. The three of us often sit down together with a few more of the boys.

'Not yet,' I tell him. 'I'm just going to ring him now.'

'He was on to me earlier,' Brian says. 'He's having brunch with Lukie.'

In our world, a gilt-edged opportunity to rip the piss out of someone isn't to be passed up.

'Is that how it is?' I ask Chubbo later. 'Now that I'm back playing, the friendship is finished, is it? We're like Brian Moore, are we? No talking any more!'

He just laughs.

Monday, 26 March. We're at Johnstown House, Enfield, for a mini-camp. I'm in Room 228, sharing with Chubbo.

The quarter-final is twelve days away. First, we play Munster in the league. I've got less than an hour of rugby under my belt and I'm desperate to get eighty minutes at Thomond Park. I'm thinking: *Hurry, hurry! Just give me the game time and it'll all work itself out.*

At Enfield, the plan is for a video session in the morning, after which Joe will name the two teams for a training game. It's how you know if you're likely to be starting at the weekend: pretty much always, the team that trains together plays together.

Joe starts calling out the weekend XV: 15 Kearns, 14 Isa, 13 Chubbo, 12 Darce . . .

In thirteen years as a pro it's the first time I haven't heard my name when I was expecting to be in a team.

As we walk towards the training pitch, I head straight for Chubbo and give him a jokey hug. 'One–nil to you from Room 228!'

Before the training game gets under way, different reactions fight for space in my head. First . . .

I need that game time!

Then . . .

What's he thinking? I'm not going to be ready for a Heineken Cup quarter-final with twenty or thirty minutes off the bench!

And then . . .

Fuck! Is he even thinking of me for the quarters?

A few minutes into the session, Chubbo pulls up with a calf injury that puts him out of the Munster game.

It's a tough break for him. All season he's been the guy in possession, a coming man on serious form. Later on, both of us are left wondering what would have happened if he'd gone to Thomond Park and played well.

I could ask Joe what was in his mind, selection-wise, but he's liable to give me an honest answer. And I'm not at all sure that I want to hear it.

In Limerick, I get my usual mixed bag of a reception. It certainly doesn't bother me, but for a long time I've gotten the vibe that the average man on the terrace at Thomond Park had had his view of me tainted by the blond hair and the extra-curricular activity from years back. Or maybe it's just that the Munster fans need to pick on a few targets when their biggest rivals come to town and I get paid the backhanded compliment. My strike rate has been pretty good over the years in this fixture.

I've taken stick there in the past for wearing warm-up tights before kick-off, the very same ones that Munster players like Rog often put on at training. When I run out without them, a guy near the touchline notices: 'Where's your fucking tights, O'Driscoll?'

Fair enough, I can get a kick out of that, too.

In front of a full house, we win 18–9 to go 10 points clear at the top of the league and I get my eighty minutes.

A week later, we reach another Heineken semi-final – our fourth in a row – by beating Cardiff 34–3. There's a couple of tries from Kearns, one from Isa and I finish off a move that ends up getting voted our try of the season – a training-ground play from a lineout that comes off like a dream. Sexto creates the hole with a sublime pass behind himself, Lukie runs through it and I'm on his shoulder when the cover closes in.

People get off your back when you score tries, but my mum could have run this one in. For me, there's more satisfaction in seeing the pass inside to Kearns that opens them up for his second try.

We get Clermont Auvergne in the semis, away. And we've got four players who believe they should be starting in the centre – Darce, Ferg, Chubbo, me. Some feel more secure than others, but Joe still has us guessing. We don't know where he's going, what combination he's leaning towards. I turn up for training and I feel less confident of my place in the Leinster team than I do with Ireland. I feel like knocking on Joe's door and asking some questions:

Where do I stand with you?

What do I need to improve?

Nine days before Clermont, we're down to play Ulster at Ravenhill. Darce is being rested after cutting his eye, but he's going to be fine for the semi. On the Monday, Joe calls out the backline for the training team: 15 Kearns, 14 Dreamboat, 13 Chubbo, 12 me, 11 Lukie, 10 Sexto, 9 Redser.

For the second time in three weeks I'm left feeling concerned, convinced I need a big game to make the Heineken Cup team. I'm trying to fight the negativity in my head, but I can't help questioning whether Joe rates me as much as other coaches have in the past. Even when I had the confidence wobble back in 2008, I never had the impression that Michael Cheika doubted me. But now I'm thinking that if Eoin goes well at 13 – a week out from the semi-final – why shouldn't he keep his place after being in the team for most of the season?

For years I've been carrying around the badge of never having been dropped, hoping to get through my whole career without it happening. And now it doesn't seem like such a big deal any more. I figure that if it did happen, I could handle the blow to my pride.

Provided I got back in.

We beat Ulster, making it six from six for the season against the other Irish provinces. I end up playing 13, after Chubbo pulls up in training again.

For him, it's not a remotely funny situation, but he jokes about it anyway.

He says I can take the pins out of my voodoo doll now.

*

At the Leinster awards ball twenty-four hours later, there's a photograph of Shaggy I really like, projected onto a giant screen behind the stage. The picture is taken from behind and shows him with his hands on his hips, his wrists taped in the particular way he likes, the number 14 on his back. Very him.

I sneak away from our table and surprise him by inviting him on stage for a Q & A. It seems weird – close friends chatting in front of four hundred people – but there are moments when it feels like it's just the two of us.

I've a fair idea how he's going to answer every question –

'Do you think the hard days and the disappointments made the victories all the sweeter?'

'Definitely.'

– but other people need to hear it because he was a massive part of getting us there.

*

Sunday, 29 April 2012, Stade Chaban Delmas, Bordeaux. Heineken Cup semi-final: Clermont Auvergne v. Leinster.

It's a decade since a French team was beaten in a home semi-final, but statistics and milestones can be overrated. If they're going to take our title away from us, they're going to have to earn it. They know that well enough, but we need to put down a few markers early on, just to ram the point home.

When you're able to smack someone early, you're hoping

it'll put a little screw in their head. You're thinking maybe they'll be a fraction off the next time, remembering what the last hit felt like. It's a psychological one-up, a means to an end. Only the meatheads really understand the psychological effect of forcing a penalty scrum through sheer pressure on the opposition front row. For the rest of us, the big tackle is the nearest equivalent.

Four minutes in, I take an educated risk reading one of their plays off a lineout. Brock James, their 10, throws a flat pass to Aurélien Rougerie to give them some go-forward. As he takes it I hit him square on the chest with a good shot, just to let him know he's not going to have too much time on the ball as the game wears on.

Half-time: Clermont 12, Leinster 6. We know we're up against a serious team and after forty minutes maybe their best player is Hinesy.

In the dressing room, Sexto suggests running with a line-out play we haven't used in more than five months and says we'll score off it if everyone does their job right. One minute after the restart, the opportunity arrives.

We're ten metres inside their half when Richardt Strauss finds Leo at the top of his jump. He's challenged in the air, he nearly loses it, but he recovers and gets it down to Mike Ross, who shifts it quickly to Isaac Boss. Next it goes to Sexto, then me. I make five metres and Brock James hauls me down by the neck.

Wayne Barnes signals a penalty but plays advantage and we're all set up for the play. Bossy collects it from the base of the ruck and moves left to Richardt. We pull four of their defenders across, then Richardt fires the ball straight back inside, in the same direction it came from.

It whistles past the referee's chest and catches Clermont

stone cold. There's a massive hole and Kearns rockets into it, with Cian Healy and Shane Jennings running support lines left and right. Kearns makes fifteen metres and finds Cian in an acre of space. The try is converted by Sexto and now we lead by one.

Five minutes later, it's four. Kearns again – from forty-five metres out, he catches a ball close by the left touchline, looks up and lands a drop goal. Sheer brilliance.

We exchange penalties: 15–19. We feel like we're worth more than our four-point lead. Sexto hits another penalty that looks good, but the TMO rules it went over the top of the upright. We've got fantastic support around the stadium, but their fans are the loudest in France. When Clermont up their intensity and lay siege to our line, the atmosphere is ridiculously intense.

They pick and drive, use their big hitters to open a few holes. They put us under enormous stress but we keep scrambling and wrapping them up.

Good defence is built on trust. As Clermont keep coming, I'm in Darce's ear – not that he needs to be told after all these years. Unless he's going in to steal ball, I want him beside me – hunting on my inside all day long. If he goes to a breakdown, he needs to slow the ball and make it a four- or five-second ruck, enough time for us to get a couple of forwards back around to fill his spot in the defensive line. If he commits himself and it's a one-second ruck followed by fast ball into the hands of a speed merchant, like Wesley Fofana, we're in trouble.

Total trust – that's what I need in Darce, especially against a centre partnership as lethal as Fofana and Rougerie. And it's what I have. I know he won't switch off if he makes a big tackle. If one of them steps me on my inside shoulder, I know he's going to clean that up. Once you start worrying about a class player stepping inside, he'll gas you on the outside just as you're hedging your bets.

Two minutes left. Julien Bonnaire, their big number 6, picks the ball up two metres short. He's got three guys behind him, and as he surges for the line Jamie hits him low and hard. He goes to ground a foot short. Morgan Parra, their 9, whips the ball across and Fofana rockets forwards at the kind of speed that will break any defence, no matter how heroic.

Darce springs off our line and hits him. He turns Fofana's body in the tackle, but Fofana gets over the line and when he jumps back to his feet, his fist is clenched. The crowd goes mental, we are crushed and my heart starts pounding hard.

In the huddle behind the goal I don't feel like saying anything, but the words come from somewhere within me.

'Right, we've got seventy seconds here to get our shit together! We've done it before, we can do this again. We just need to get this kick back.'

On the big screen in the stadium, they are replaying Fofana's big moment. I'm not watching it but somebody in the huddle is and he breaks the good news to the rest of us: 'It's a knock-on!'

They show it again as Wayne Barnes walks around the in-goal area, waiting for the TMO to tell him if it's a try or not. They slow it down and we see Fofana lying on the turf with his right arm over the try line and the ball cupped in his palm. The ball is six inches off the ground but as he brings it down he loses control and it falls out of his hand.

I can't believe how lucky we've been. Even before the TMO reports back to Barnes, Sexto is marching around our forwards like a man possessed: 'Big scrum! Big scrum! Big scrum!'

There are sixty-eight seconds left in the game. The scrum is reset and they win a penalty off it. With six seconds left, Parra taps it and Vincent Debaty – all twenty stone of him – trucks it up a metre short. Another penalty, another tap. This time Parra gives it to Jamie Cudmore, the big second-row. He makes barely half a metre before Sexto rushes up and hits him with everything he has. He's four stone lighter but he slows him up. There are bodies everywhere – it's complete mayhem until Sean O'Brien goes in and gets over the ball. The whistle blows – penalty to us. Sexto kicks it off the pitch and jumps into the open arms of Joe Schmidt, who has made his way down from the coach's box to pitch-side.

When all's said and done, it belongs with the best of our achievements, but we celebrate like a team that knows it won't count for anything unless we follow it up in the final.

Photographers come on the pitch, looking for the usual snaps.

'Give us a thumbs-up!'

'Pump your fist!'

I've obliged them in the past but I don't feel like forcing a reaction just for their benefit: *That's your picture – that's not what I wanna do!*

It helps that some of our supporters are close by – it means we can show our appreciation without going on a lap of the pitch and looking like we're milking it. Time enough for that if we do the business at Twickenham.

The walk to the dressing room feels like a country mile. When we get there, Joe is beaming. He's not a man to hide his emotions but it's clear as day that winning a semi-final in

France against the club he left – and a team he has massive respect for – means the world to him.

'Jeez, there's a bit of fight left in you still,' he says, smiling, as I walk in.

It feels good to hear him say it. I'm not chopped liver yet.

They don't come along every day, big wins like this. On the emotional Richter scale, it's right up there. Any rugby player will tell you it's the body-on-the-line performances that give the biggest feeling of satisfaction, that warm feeling when you're on a different level from everyone else. And when you're coming near the end of your career it scares you, because that feeling is like a drug and you don't know how you can ever replace it.

When I talk to my sister Sue on the phone twenty minutes after the final whistle, she's so excited it's as if she's played the game herself. Jules calls me and she's a little calmer, already talking about going over to London for the final. At Twickenham we'll be up against Ulster, who, after knocking out Munster at Thomond Park in the quarters, have just beaten Edinburgh.

Back in Dublin, we go for a few beers. You should enjoy the ones that really matter, and at McSorley's in Ranelagh we don't even talk about the game, we just revel in each other's company.

At half one I hit the wall, put down my beer and head for a taxi.

*

I've always felt like I need a high level of fitness to really have an influence. With five games under my belt since the surgery, I am match-hardened again and far more confident in my ability. And then – bang – on the last play in a training session late in the week before the final, I feel a pop in my knee when I plant my right foot and turn.

It's bent, it won't straighten or bear weight. I'm driven off the pitch, and a few hours later I'm in Santry with Ray Moran, the knee specialist who gave Skiddy the bad news a dozen years back.

'You've torn a decent chunk of cartilage off,' he reports, after seeing the scan.

He says I've got two choices.

1. Rehab it for a week and hope it holds up for eighty minutes.
2. Get keyhole surgery, first thing in the morning, and hope for a fast recovery. Once he has cut away the piece of cartilage that's flapping around, the injury will be gone. The problem is, it normally takes three weeks for the knee to recover.

The final is eight days away. I decide to try option 1, but I need some early hope that it's going to give me a shot at playing.

There's no time to lose, so our physio, James Allen, arranges a session in the pool at Riverview for six the following morning. If that doesn't go well, it's onwards to the operating table. I call him at 5.40 and tell him the session is going to be a waste of time. The knee has seized up. I can't put any weight on it at all.

'Listen, let's go straight to Santry,' I tell him.

He rings Ray Moran and I'm on the table at 7.15.

Afterwards Ray tells me I won't do any more damage if I try to play on it – it's just a matter of sucking up some pain and hoping I'll be mobile enough to start.

Kearns is sweating just as hard about his own place. Later

in the day, he brings some ice round to the house for my knee. He's not in the best of form. His back keeps coming at him, but he knows the pain of not starting a third Heineken Cup final in a row would be infinitely worse. He was on the bench in 2009 and injured for the 2011 final.

He's got the Ireland rehab physio, Brian Green, with him, and it's news to Greeny that I've had the knee op. His eyes widen and he's practically drooling by the time I've told him about the cartilage.

'You need to get active on that as soon as possible!' he says. 'Get the knee straight, keep icing it every half-hour! Don't lose any muscle definition!'

He says he rehabbed the exact same injury with Shaggy, and I need to do this, this and this.

'Jaysus,' I tell him, 'you're actually getting off on my knee – it's perverted!'

But I like what I'm hearing and I like it a lot more when it starts feeling better as I lie on the couch with a Game Ready ice-water therapy machine strapped tight.

On the Saturday evening, I'm at home watching the Pro12 semi-final against Glasgow, our last game before Twickenham. Eoin O'Malley starts at 13 and he's doing his chances of making the final no harm, until he hobbles off in the forty-ninth minute. The following day Arthur Tanner tells him he has fractured his tibia and ruptured the cruciate and medial ligaments in his knee.

For Chubbo, it's beyond cruel. For Joe, it's a serious problem. With a second man down at 13, he gives me until Thursday to prove my fitness.

On the Sunday, in the gym at Riverview, I work with Greeny on getting my leg-movement patterns operating again. I do a 10K cycle on an exercise bike, and at the end of the session I try a little trot, up and down the hall. I start cautiously but the confidence builds with every step and now I know I'm in with a fighting chance.

Greeny looks on and throws out one of his trademark lines, his American accent conveying the excitement he can't help feeling when he's hell-bent on pulling off another medical miracle: 'That feels *good*, right?'

'Yeah,' I tell him, 'it feels *really* good.'

On the Monday I go running on an anti-gravity treadmill designed by NASA, a phenomenal machine that allows you to run on as little as 20 per cent of your body weight, then to step it up as you feel stronger. We weren't even aware that there's one in the country, but a guy phones up out of the blue and it turns out his gym is four doors down from my parents' surgery in Clontarf.

With the knee strapped, I'm back training with the lads on Thursday, seven days after the injury and right on cue for Joe. When he names his team, I'm not the only man relieved to hear himself in it: Rob Kearney; Fergus McFadden, Brian O'Driscoll, Gordon D'Arcy, Isa Nacewa; Johnny Sexton, Eoin Reddan; Cian Healy, Richardt Strauss, Mike Ross; Leo Cullen, Brad Thorn; Kevin McLaughlin, Sean O'Brien, Jamie Heaslip. Replacements: Sean Cronin, Heinke van der Merwe, Nathan White, Devin Toner, Shane Jennings, John Cooney, Ian Madigan, Dave Kearney.

*

Brad Thorn is one of the most focused, impressive players in the game but, like most All Blacks, he's not too big on spending time analysing the opposition. It's not arrogance on his part because he's a humble man. For me, there's a balance to be struck and you need to identify the opponents' core plays, but Thorny has an innate, hard-edged confidence that once our own game is right the rest will look after itself – so let's just get on with it, right?

Sexto has the same relentlessly positive mentality and he keeps driving it home as the game gets closer. 'Let's play! We're here to play!'

I look at the footage of Ulster doing laps of honour after beating Munster and Edinburgh on the way to the final and I see a little of ourselves before success came along. I remember the triumphant stroll we took around the Stadium Municipal in Toulouse, a couple of weeks before Munster blew us away in the semi-final of 2006.

I notice the embroidered Ulster jerseys, specially produced for the semi against Edinburgh at the Aviva, and the picture of them standing in front of a massive banner that reads 'TWICKENHAM 2012'. They're a fine team, no question, but I wonder if there's a part of them that's happy – even subconsciously – just being there.

In the first half, my knee holds up fine and Seanie O'Brien is absolutely on fire. First he bludgeons his way over for a try that puts us in front, then he runs onto a nice offload I get away one-handed and almost makes the line. Redser whips it across before they've had a chance to recover their shape and Cian's power does the rest.

I watch Ulster come back out for the second half. They're only 14–6 down, but I can tell from the way they walk out of the tunnel that they're a beaten team. I'm not big into body language but, from where I'm standing on the pitch, waiting for them, it's blatant.

Five minutes in, our pack mauls them from the 22 virtually to their try line. Nigel Owens runs under the posts for the penalty try and it's pretty much game over.

Thirteen minutes from full-time, a cramp in my right calf is killing me and both sutures have opened up on my knee. Arthur Tanner leads me to the tunnel to deal with the blood injury and Dave Kearney comes off the bench, but I'm desperate to go back on. I'm not bothered about the blood on my knee – I just need five minutes to get the calf loosened. After the season I've had – six games in seven long months – I want to see this one out. I want to be on the pitch when it's done, still in my jersey. It's Joe's call to make, but if he needs to hear from me that I'm fine to carry on, I'm more than ready to grab the microphone and get in his ear.

There are seven minutes left when he gives the all-clear for me to go back on and I relish every one of them. When Ferg converts Sean Cronin's try from under the posts, the clock is in red and the score is 42–14.

I wrap an arm around Brad Thorn as Leo and Jenno lift the trophy together, the boys who came back from Leicester and helped to raise the bar for us all. It's typical of Leo – comfortably the best captain I've played under – that he would share another big moment in such a generous way with another of the older brigade.

Three in four years: it's something to be proud of. The following day, as I'm coming out of a shop in Donnybrook, a bunch of Leinster diehards fresh off the ferry and still wearing their blue jerseys rush across the road. Seeing what it means to them gives me a massive buzz, and almost every person I pass on the street has something to say about the game. It feels like the whole Leinster thing has gone to a new level.

Some of the papers go a bit overboard in their reaction, but we'll take the plaudits – it's not so long since we were getting it in the neck. For me, there's huge satisfaction in being a three-time Heineken Cup winner because it's such a hard competition to win. For some reason I keep thinking of the caption that comes up on Sky Sports under Graeme Souness's name whenever he's on as a pundit: *European Cup winner 1978, 1981, 1984.*

Three feels like a good number.

There are some texts that you really hope will come through after a day of achievement, people whose opinions you value. Rog doesn't disappoint. He's such a competitor it can only hurt him that we've got one more Heineken Cup to our names than the Munster guys – I'd feel the same way if it was 3–2 to them. But it doesn't stop him sending some generous words my way. And, coming from him, they mean a lot.

A week later, we get another chance to put a perfect season in the record books by completing the double. We blow it. After leading the Pro12 league table for most of the year – 10 points clear before the play-offs – we give up the title by losing our third final in a row. We're six points ahead of the Ospreys at the RDS with two minutes left, but Shane Williams kills us with a converted try, his second of the game. Thirty-five years old and no stopping him.

It hurts, big-time. And it takes a little of the shine off the Heineken trophy.

*

'Well,' says Deccie, throwing it out there again, 'would you fancy the captaincy or . . .?'

Four years on from the difficult summer of 2008, it has become a superfluous question. Offered the chance to lead my country – this time for three Tests in New Zealand – I'm always going to accept.

Even after eighty internationals as captain, I can't imagine not wanting to do it any more. I can never hear myself saying, 'Thanks, but you know what? I'm done with it.' Mostly because it means so much – winning Heineken Cups is never less than wonderful but Ireland is the be-all and end-all. Ask a guy like John Hayes – two European medals and 105 caps – and he'll tell you the same.

There's another thing that you come to consider when you're thirty-three years old and still trying to hang in: captaincy gets you on the team. So, the way I see it, if the head coach says he wants me to concentrate on my game, without the extra responsibility, then fair enough. If he drops me off the team completely, that's his call to make.

But, other than that, they'll have to prise it off me.

Deccie says I mightn't necessarily be playing at 13, and would I have a problem moving to inside-centre? I tell him no – on the team is on the team. Twelve, 13 – once I'm out there, I'm not overly pushed about my position. More than likely he's thinking about the future. He has given Keith Earls a run of games in the Six Nations at 13 and Earlsy hasn't made a secret of his preference for the centre over the wing.

The day after the Pro12 final we check into the Queen's Hotel in Cheltenham and the painful memories are unavoidable. It's a strange feeling being back in the place where I learned of Barry's death. After eighteen months of trying to find an answer in the confusion, I had to force myself to stop wondering. After his third anniversary, in 2011, I allowed myself to think about it again, but it never got any clearer. All you can do is remember him fondly and never forget.

Because we didn't get a chance to celebrate the Heineken Cup win, having the Pro12 final to prepare for, the Leinster boys in the Ireland party are given the go-ahead by Deccie to put that right. We find a bar in the centre of Cheltenham and we're the only ones in it. Later on we head towards a night-club, buzzing but somewhat the worse for wear. Before we go near the bouncers at the door, we get into a huddle around the corner and it's like we're having a team talk in the middle of a game – refusing to let anyone see we're less than 100 per cent.

'Show them nothing!'

'No tells!'

'NO TELLS!'

We walk up with our game faces on, calm as you like.

'Evening, gentlemen!' the head bouncer says, stepping aside.

Ten seconds later we kick onto another level and it ends up being one of the really great nights.

A couple of days later, I see Amy in London, where she's shooting the second season of her comedy series *Threesome*. The following morning we fly to New Zealand, for three cracks at the All Blacks.

When Deccie names the team for the first Test in Auckland, I'm at inside-centre, with Earlsy alongside me for the first time. I ask him if I can wear the 13 jersey and he insists that I do. At Eden Park, after eight months without inter-national rugby, I'm shocked by the step-up in intensity. We can't live with them: it ends 42–10.

We suck it up and regroup. Against the really good teams, your focus has to be all about the performance, not the out-come. Once you start thinking about becoming the first Irish team to beat New Zealand, you might as well forget about it. You concentrate on the five minutes coming next and you try to get everything right – rucking, line speed, set-piece, all the things you can control, the pieces that add up to a

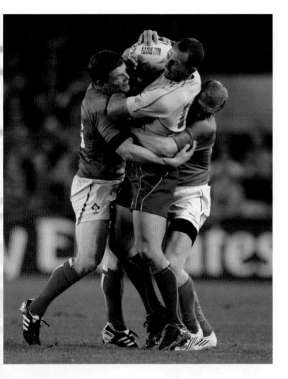

Executing a choke tackle with Keith Earls on Quade Cooper in our group match against Australia in the 2011 World Cup. That sort of defending was the key to our victory (*Dan Sheridan/Inpho*)

Celebrating with Rob Kearney after my try against Italy in the last group match of the 2011 World Cup. Our victory secured our place at the top of our group. Losing to Wales in the quarter-final was a sickening blow for me: I knew it was my last World Cup (*Dan Sheridan/Inpho*)

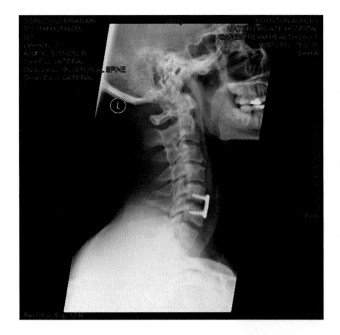

An X-ray of my neck, taken after Ashley Poynton performed a fusion of vertebrae C5 and C6 at the end of 2011. You can see the plate that holds the vertebrae together and the screws that keep the plate in place. I had previously taken the view that I'd sooner retire than have a fusion, but when Ashley told me it was not safe to play on without the surgery – and that I'd be able to play on without ill effects afterwards – I was happy to go ahead

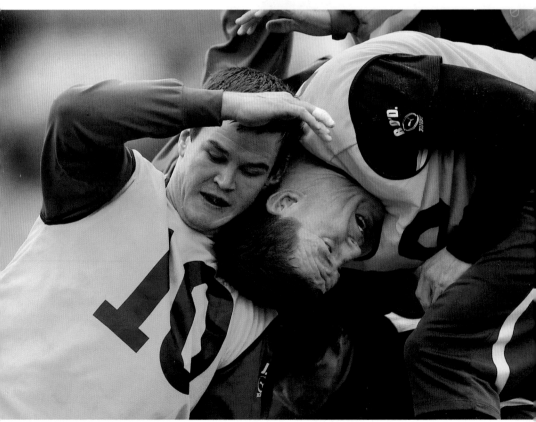

Locking horns at Ireland training with Johnny Sexton. We had a few shouting matches over the years, but he always wanted what I wanted: whatever was best for the team
(*Billy Stickland/Inpho*)

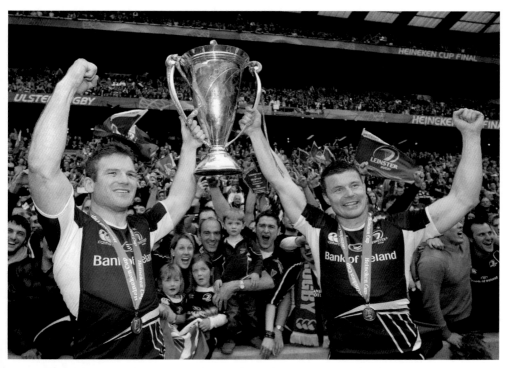

Lifting the Heineken Cup with Gordon D'Arcy in 2012 after beating Ulster at Twickenham for our third triumph in four years (*Dan Sheridan/Inpho*)

With my extended family after the final: my niece Katie, Mum and Dad, my brother-in-law Tomás, niece Aoife, sister Julie, Amy, nephew Sean, brother-in-law Mal, and sister Susan

With Isa Nacewa after his last game for Leinster, our victory in the 2013 Pro12 final against Ulster at the RDS (*Dan Sheridan/Inpho*)

After winning four trophies in three seasons with Leinster, Joe Schmidt took over as Ireland coach – and led us to victory in his first Six Nations championship. Even late in my career, I was always learning from Joe (*Dan Sheridan/Inpho*)

A light moment with Rob Kearney and the Welsh lock Ian Evans at Lions training in Noosa, Queensland, in 2013 (*Billy Stickland/Inpho*)

Lifting the trophy with Paul O'Connell at the end of my fourth Lions tour – and first series win (*Billy Stickland/Inpho*)

With Mum and Dad at my testimonial dinner in London in November 2013

The Italy match in the 2014 Six Nations was my last-ever home international; it was also the day I became the most capped international player of all time. Adidas made a special boot for me to mark the occasion – including shout-outs to Amy and Sadie ('A&S'), Barry ('Face'), Leinster, and UCD ('Ad Astra')

After the Italy match, the IRFU staged a generous on-field tribute, which I was glad to enjoy in the company of Sadie (*Colm O'Neill/Inpho*)

Jumping for joy, into the arms of Fergus McFadden, at the final whistle of the 2014 Six Nations title decider against France in Paris (*Billy Stickland/Inpho*)

Enjoying a quiet beer in the dressing room after winning the championship: another kind of great night in Paris (*Dan Sheridan/Inpho*)

Leo Cullen lifts the Pro12 trophy after my last-ever game. I went off injured in the early minutes, but it was great to end my career with a proper celebration (*Billy Stickland/Inpho*)

performance. You stay in the game – then you move on to the next five minutes and try to do the same.

From numbers 1 to 23, every All Black is completely convinced Ireland cannot beat them – not now, not ever. So we need as many guys as possible in our team who truly believe, deep down, that we can win against New Zealand when they come at us hard with the game in the balance, looking for the chinks in our armour.

For game two, Darce comes back in on a rainy night in Christchurch, sixteen months on from the earthquake that broke up the city. We've already caught a break before kick-off because a high-tempo team like New Zealand will never thank you for a greasy ball on a slow pitch.

We get stuck into them. We lead by a point at half-time. With ten minutes left we're level at 19–19 but a draw is worth nothing to us – against them, it's as good as losing.

Two minutes later they lose Israel Dagg to the bin, but still they find a way to win. With twenty-seven seconds on the game clock, Dan Carter kicks a drop goal from close in and it's curtains again.

For the next six days, the New Zealand media take us seriously for a change and the All Blacks fans on the street come over all friendly – another novel experience for some of us.

We get it everywhere we go – 'We really wanted you guys to win!' – and we smile and bite our tongues.

No, you didn't – don't patronize us!

At Hamilton, in game three, they put three tries on the board in the first eighteen minutes. It's hard, mentally, trying to see a way back when they're in fourth gear and you're stuck in first. It's as poor a game as I've ever played: a 2/10 performance. There are bad passes, balls down, system errors in defence, and almost no positives to put up against the negatives. At 41–0 I just want it to be over but when I look at the clock there are still thirty minutes left. Every pass they make sticks, every offload under pressure goes to hand: it's like a training game for them.

It doesn't seem credible that you can come within a score of winning one week and get totally annihilated by the same opposition seven days later, but when New Zealand get a run on you early they can do terrible things to any team.

'That was fun out there today,' says their captain, Richie McCaw. It's the final ignominy, a horrible thing to hear, because even when you're beaten you want them to walk off physically spent, feeling like they've earned it. The enjoyment is supposed to come afterwards, not during the game.

In the list of career disappointments, it takes a place on the podium.

1. 2011 – Ireland 10 Wales 22
2. 2006 – Leinster 6 Munster 30
3. 2012 – New Zealand 60 Ireland 0

*

Half an hour after I get home, Amy brings me down to the spot at the back of the garden where I proposed to her.

'I've got a present for you,' she says.

She hands me an envelope, and when I open it and pull out the card inside, I'm confused.

'Happy Father's Day,' it says on the front. It's a Monday, the day after Father's Day, but I don't understand why I'm being given this card.

'Look inside,' she says.

I'm still completely thrown as I read the words she has written:

First there were two and then there were three.

I'm very rarely shocked, but I stand there flabbergasted, then panicked. A good panic.

'You mean you're . . .'

'Yes.'

It's a nice moment, a great moment. It's a few more seconds before I really take it in, but when I do it's the greatest feeling I've ever had, hands down. It supersedes any medal.

On holiday, lying on a lounger in Sicily, there's the odd minute when my mind wanders and the embarrassment of the third Test flits into my head, but it never lingers because I'm still buzzing with positivity.

Whoa! You're going to be a dad!

14. Get In!

Another year, another pre-season. I'm walking onto the pitch at UCD for the first training session of 2012–13 when I'm overtaken on both sides by a blur of young lads. They're like greyhounds leaving the traps and Cian Healy is out in front.

Cian is twenty-four years old, a seventeen-stone prop forward and a modern pro from head to toe. When you're twenty-four, you don't worry much about warming up before training. You don't worry about a whole lot. He runs past me and puts boot to ball as hard as he possibly can, without a single thought for his hamstrings or his calf muscles. There's a violent thud as he whacks it sixty metres downfield, then chases after it.

I don't even need to see him kicking it to know it's him. We spend so much time together on the training ground that the sights and sounds around us become second nature. We can look at a ball in flight and identify the guy who's kicked it just as surely as if his name is written on it.

Ferocious thump? Wobbly trajectory? Prodigious distance?

That'll be Cian.

And I smile to myself, because I used to be able to run onto a pitch and do things like that without having to limber up first. I look around and I'm not the only one. We older players are like desktop computers that take time to start up. The young guys are like tablets – ready to roll in the blink of an eye.

My engine is slowing down, but my desire to win is as

sharp as ever and that's what gets me through. I still get a perverse kick out of listening to people trying to put me on the scrap-heap, knowing that I have it in my locker to prove them wrong.

Training still excites me. The quality of Joe's coaching, the buzz of the dressing room, the class we have in the squad and the trophies we've won: it's a privilege to be part of this, for however long I've got left. I tell some of the younger lads that I'm not sure what I'm going to do beyond this season and their reaction is heartening.

Ian Madigan says I'd be crazy to give it up.

'Back into the real world?' says Ferg McFadden. 'Don't be stupid!'

It's nice to hear them say it, but when you get to a certain age you start wondering about how you want to bow out. We're nearly all the same in professional sport: we want to go with our reputations intact, for people to remember us for good reasons. But public perception is not something you can control, and the things you do when you're past your best can be sharper in the public's memory, especially if the story pumped out by the media is about a fall from grace.

No, we all want to leave the game like Lawrence Dallaglio. His last day in rugby was in front of eighty-two thousand people at Twickenham. He captained Wasps against Leicester in the Premiership final of 2008 – and he won. Out on an unbelievable high, with the photograph of that moment still in people's memory all these years later. Another trophy in the air.

As a season full of possibility begins, I think about a fourth Heineken Cup, a second Six Nations championship, a winning Lions tour at the fourth time of asking – back in Australia, where I played in my first – and I'd take your hand off for any one of those. If that was the end I'd go with gratitude.

Isa has also been thinking about the endgame but, unlike me, he's come up with an answer. He's contracted to Leinster until the summer of 2014 but he tells me he's leaving at the end of this season. He's got three young kids and it's time for his family to go home to New Zealand. As much as I hate the idea of playing for Leinster without him, I understand his reasoning and he's got nothing left to prove.

*

In our sixth game of the season we play Munster in the Pro12 and it's like a starting pistol going off to mark a big step-up in intensity. We edge it 30–21, an encouraging performance and also, for me, a lucky escape. I score our third try and I'm blessed I don't break my left ankle when contorting myself over the line.

A week later we play Exeter in the first round of the Heineken Cup. I try to convince myself that the ankle isn't an issue, but in my head I don't feel fully right. We win 9–6 and I'm flat.

In round two we go to Llanelli to play the Scarlets and things don't get any better. We're 14–3 ahead and in control of the game when my opposite number, Gareth Maule, does me on the outside and scores a try that brings them back into it. We go on to win 20–13 but I'm seriously bothered by Maule's try and the quality of my attempt to stop it.

I'm slow to react to the danger in the first place. I'm all right foot, because subconsciously I don't trust the left ankle. When I get myself into position to make the tackle, I slide off him. I have him in my sights and I let him go: a killer. And the thing is, Maule is a decent player but he's only filling in for Jonathan Davies, the Wales 13 and a big contender for the Lions tour. If it had been Jonathan on the ball, I doubt I'd have even got close enough to him to make a tackle. He'd have been gone.

I'm a confidence player – most of us are. So there are questions in my head: *Was the slow reaction down to the ankle? Or are you just looking for excuses?*

I have a talk to myself before we play Cardiff in the Pro12 a week later. When my back has been to the wall before, I've come up with something. Cardiff have Leigh Halfpenny at full-back, Alex Cuthbert on the wing, Jamie Roberts in the centre and Sam Warburton in the back row – all great individuals – but we bury them. We're 21–3 ahead inside the first quarter. I get my hands on the ball early and do some damage. A break, a hand-off, a scoring pass. It all feels good again.

You haven't lost it, son! It's still there!

After twenty-two minutes, my ankle buckles and I hit the floor. The pain is nasty. I shout out and beat the ground as the physios attend to me. I get up and try to carry on but it's no use.

There are degrees of slagging in our dressing room. There's the normal day-to-day stuff and then there's the premier-class piss-taking especially reserved for guys who are howling in agony on the pitch one minute and then right as rain the next.

'Welcome back, Lazarus!'

When I get home, the pain has eased and I can put weight on my ankle again. All well and good, but I'm not looking forward to what might be coming my way when I breeze into training like nothing ever happened. The masochist in me makes me watch the incident again, just to steel myself for the abuse. Amy tells me not to torture myself, but I can't help it.

'Oh my God! There's an Oscar-winning performance right there!'

When I get my ankle scanned it's almost a relief when I'm told there's an issue. I haven't turned into Sergio Busquets. The problem is called syndesmosis – ligament damage above the ankle joint. I have a choice: struggle on and maybe get back to full fitness, or have an operation and miss twelve weeks.

The smart move is to go under the knife, so as not to lose the whole season. I tell myself I'll come back as a fresh player in time for the Six Nations – fit and firing at the most critical time of the season. I'll be closer to 100 per cent capacity when I've become used to surviving at 85.

Another reason to still believe.

*

When the news that Amy is expecting reaches the papers we get a letter through the door from an elderly couple in Dundrum.

It starts off with some nice comments about the baby and the excitement we must be feeling at the prospect of becoming parents in the spring. Then it cuts to the chase: they want to sell us their house.

> *Ours is a beautiful six-bedroom family home on three-quarters of an acre with its own tennis court. We felt that at this time in your lives, when you'll be looking for a lovely family residence, you might be interested in putting in an offer before we put it on the market. At the height we rather stupidly turned down an offer of €6 million but . . .*

The bottom line is that they'll knock it down to us for a snappy 1.8. Sometimes you can only smile at the way people think.

'Is ours not family enough?' I ask Amy.

We love our own home and we're already getting the nursery ready. Mind you, the idea of giving Dunny another beating on a tennis court out the back isn't the worst thought ever.

*

In my absence after the ankle surgery, and with Paulie also on the injury list, Jamie Heaslip captains Ireland in the autumn internationals against South Africa, Fiji and Argentina. It's tough missing out on Test matches, and I also have to sit through the pivotal games in our Heineken Cup season. We come off second-best to Clermont, home and away.

I return from injury a fortnight ahead of schedule and appear off the bench in the penultimate game of the group stage, a win over the Scarlets in the second week of January. We don't have a lot of swagger, but with one game left to go, we're still alive, just.

The Six Nations is a few weeks away. Deccie phones me, like he always does before the championship, and asks if we can meet at the Four Seasons Hotel in Ballsbridge for a chat. Same as before, only this time I've got a different vibe. I can feel it in my bones that my days as captain of Ireland could be coming to an end.

I see him in the lobby and then we go up to his room.

'How's everything?' he asks.

'Grand, grand. Good to be back playing.'

'The ankle's okay?'

'Yeah, no bother.'

As usual we bounce around the houses before he gets down to it. But this time it feels a little bit more stagnant.

'Listen, there's no easy way of saying this, but I'm not going to go with you as captain.'

'Okay . . .'

I don't feel the need to ask him why, but I do have one question. 'Who are you going with?'

'Jamie did a good job in November, so I'm sticking with him.'

'Okay.'

Fair enough, I can see the logic. Jamie's going to be around for the World Cup and I'm not. There has to be a changing of the guard some time, but I'm still disappointed and hurt. Not so much by the decision, but by the explanation.

'You haven't played much rugby and I want you to be able to concentrate on you and nothing else,' he says.

There's a part of me that feels like telling him what he's saying doesn't fly. I've gone into the championship in the past with not a lot of rugby under my belt and I've delivered . . .

Eighty-three times I've captained this side. Don't worry about me. I'll get myself right.

But I let it go.

It stings, though. For so long, with Ireland, I've felt a certain level of ownership. You don't lead a team through so many Tests without it becoming part of you.

Deccie gives me the option of putting my own twist on the story – to save face. He says if I want to make it look like it's my decision to step away, then he'll go along with it.

The suggestion doesn't sit well with me. Why would I want to save face? There's nothing I want to hide. You have to live your own emotions – good, bad or indifferent. Anything else is just false. I've got no problem if people can see I'm upset about the decision. I've been captain for the guts of ten years and I've relished the responsibility. It's been an honour and I'm not going to pretend that it doesn't bother me now that it's gone.

At the official announcement, Deccie says it isn't necessarily the end of it for me as captain, but we both know that's nonsense. Once it's gone, it's gone.

*

I line out for Leinster four days later. We get a winning bonus point against Exeter in our last group game in the Heineken Cup, but it's too little, too late. Clermont top the pool and Munster pip us to the last spot as second-best runner-up, courtesy of a bigger try count, 14–12. We drop into the Amlin Challenge Cup, the secondary competition. We're playing for the consolation prize.

We haven't had the crazy hunger of previous seasons. Maybe you can't repeat that kind of desperation year after year, when you've won three titles. You've got to bring other things to the table and we've lost some of our killer instinct against the very best teams.

In the background, the drums have been beating for months about Sexto's future. He's been negotiating a new contract with the IRFU. He's very, very keen to stay but only if the Union offers him a fair deal – and the talks have reached an impasse.

A week after we bow out of the Heineken Cup it's announced that we're losing him to Racing Metro at the end of the season.

It's like getting a knee in the groin just after a kick in the guts.

*

When we meet up at Carton House to prepare for the Six Nations, I'm feeling strange and self-conscious, wondering how others are viewing the change of captaincy.

Are they looking at me differently?

Nobody bats an eyelid: it's no big deal.

I make a beeline for Jamie and congratulate him. I tell him I'll carry on being as much of a leader in the set-up as I can be without stepping on his toes.

I'm still feeling a bit low, but I'm not spitting out the dummy. And sometimes it's good to have a little ammunition in your head, an extra reason to pull out a performance. Not that I'm running short of incentives: every four years the Six Nations is the tournament that decides most of the places in a Lions touring party. You go head to head with the guys who are after the same spots in the knowledge that the head coach is watching and every rugby writer in Britain and Ireland is playing Lions selector, week after week.

It's been four years since I first sat down with Enda McNulty, a couple of months before the best run in my career. I've stayed working with him, although his role has changed somewhat – now it's largely about helping me to organize my life and my time so that I can be as prepared as possible. He's been brought on board by the Ireland management, too, and we talk at Carton House in the week of the Wales game. We order coffee and sit in a quiet spot by a wood-burning stove.

I make it pretty clear that I'm not in a brilliant place mentally. I'm worried that if I'm not physically sharp, completely injury-free, I won't do myself justice in the Six Nations and my chances of making the Lions squad will suffer. I'm not even super-sure that they're going to start me in Cardiff: maybe it's all in my head but it doesn't feel like I'm being involved as much as before, captaincy or no captaincy.

Enda tells me I'm looking too far forward. 'We need super-short-term focus here,' he says. 'One week. One game. It only takes small things to turn it around.'

*

The Millennium Stadium is my favourite ground. It's full of noise and good memories. I'm so used to leading out the team on days like this, it feels a little weird. I walk out second-last in the line and then I wonder where I should stand for the anthems.

I take up a spot between Darce and Donnacha Ryan, the Munster lock forward. When the game begins I wait for a moment that feeds my confidence, knowing that sometimes in the Six Nations it can be a long time coming. These games are cagey. Breaking down a defence has become a science in rugby.

In the eleventh minute we're moving right to left away from the ruck inside the Welsh 22. It's a three-phase set play. Sexto hits me with a pass – fires it out in front of me – and as the ball is in the air Rory Best comes trailing up my inside.

It causes a millisecond's hesitation in the Wales defence. More often than not in training, I've cut back inside, looking for Rory. But I see Jonathan Davies having a little nibble on Rory's run and I keep going.

He checks himself, ever so slightly. He's such a good rugby player and so quick across the ground that if he leaves Rory alone then he closes down my space and kills our momentum stone dead. But the nibble buys me a yard and it puts Alex Cuthbert in no man's land, unsure whether to go for me or for Simon Zebo, who's holding a straight line on the wing.

As Davies and Halfpenny get to me, I slip a blind pass out the side door to Zeebs. It's an anticipation pass. It's thrown in the hope that the guy is where you think he is. And it comes off. Zeebs takes it five metres short of the line and curls around behind the posts.

For forty-three minutes Wales can't live with us. Cian batters his way over for our second try and then early in the second half I add a third from a good eighteen inches. It's a try that gives me great pleasure. I know – from having worked with him on the Lions – that Wales's defence coach, Shaun Edwards, would have made note of my predisposition to get involved in pick-and-jams close to the line.

We're 30–3 ahead when the kitchen sink is thrown at us. We dig in and hold on: 30–22. I'm named man of the match, the kind of plaudit that matters a little bit more when you haven't had one for a while.

It's nice to know I can still mix it, that I still belong at this level.

*

We're one from one and England are next up, in eight days' time, but it's a long way from being the most important February date in my calendar. We're expecting our first child to be born at the National Maternity Hospital in Holles Street on 14 February, the Thursday after the game.

My pal Redser is also an expectant father. We speak on the phone and he makes my heart jump when he tells me that his wife Katie is also due to have her first child on Valentine's Day at Holles Street. What are the chances?

Thanks to Mick Kearney, the team manager, I still have my own room at the Shelbourne Hotel, where we stay in the run-up to home matches – normally a privilege reserved for the captain. It's an act of generosity that makes a big difference to me. On match day – Sunday, 10 February – I'm about to go down for breakfast when my phone starts buzzing on the bedside locker and Amy's name comes up on the screen. It's 8.05 a.m. She never calls this early.

Her voice couldn't be calmer.

'It's on,' she says.

'*It's what?*' I'm completely thrown. And I can't believe how calm she is.

'We're going to have the baby this morning,' I hear her say.

I'm not exactly Mr Emotional. It's a running joke in our house that I don't go overboard in my reactions.

Amy's different. She gets excited over the smallest things. I hear her on the phone and it's like there's been a major calamity somewhere: '*You're not serious! Oh my God! That's awful!*'

'What's wrong?' I'll ask.

'My friend hasn't seen her cat in three days.'

But now I'm welling up. And she's ultra-calm.

'Listen, this is what's going to happen. You're going to come in, we're going to have the baby, and then you're going to head back and play the match.'

I ring Mick Kearney. 'Mick, can you come down to my room? I need to have a word.'

When I tell him the news, he gives me a hug and wishes us luck.

I grab some fruit on the way out the door of the Shelbourne. None of the lads are about. Just as well.

It's only half a mile to Holles Street, but there's a taxi at the nearest rank and I jump in.

'Ah, Brian. Howrya?' says the driver, a friendly Dublin woman.

'Great, thanks. Could you give me a spin down to Holles Street?'

'Of course, love,' she says. 'Is everything all right with the baby?'

'Ah, yeah – just a check-up!'

On the morning of an Ireland v. England game . . . highly believable.

When I get there, it's a whirlwind. Before long I'm looking at our beautiful baby girl, wrapped up in a blanket, in her mother's arms. They bring us to a recovery room and give us our moment – just the three of us. It's all happened so fast that I'm struggling to take it in.

A nurse asks if we've got a name picked out and Amy looks at me.

'Yeah, I think we do,' she says.

Hello and welcome, Sadie.

We call our families and they're overjoyed. Pretty soon it's midday – kick-off is in three hours. I'm thinking I need to hit the road, but it's best that Amy sends me on my way herself.

She reads my mind, not for the first time. 'You'd better head back,' she says.

It wouldn't be right to agree too quickly. 'No, no! I'll stay for another bit!'

Five minutes later, she says it again and I float out of the place.

In the back of a car the IRFU have sent to bring me back

to the Shelbourne for the pre-match meal, I have just enough time to ring the lads and tell them the news – Shaggy, Den, Dunny, Redser, Damo. I can't get hold of Skiddy, so I text him.

Back at the hotel, the boys are unaware I've had to go to the hospital. True to form, Deccie had been vague about why I wasn't at our walk-through in St Stephen's Green that morning.

Rog is first to ask. 'Everything okay?'

'We had the baby this morning – a little girl.'

'That's brilliant!'

I meet Shaggy at the ground and both of us have the biggest smiles. He has bought us a couple of Montecristo cigars. He hands me mine. 'These are for later,' he says.

I'm buzzing but I'm in a daze. I'm not my usual vocal self in the dressing room beforehand and it takes me half an hour of the game to snap out of it.

You're playing a Test match here – come on!

We're in a real battle. Tight defences, little space, a contest decided by penalties. Owen Farrell puts England 12–6 ahead after sixty-six minutes and that's how it stays.

The fact that a Grand Slam has gone barely registers with me. I'm still in my own little world – but aware that I can't just pick up my kit-bag and walk out of the dressing room. I have to live the defeat a little with the lads, even though all I'm thinking about is seeing Amy and my new Sadie. In any case I need to wait for the crowds to clear before I can get back to the hospital.

It all gets more real on the journey to Holles Street. I get there at half six and I'm allowed to stay until 11 p.m. Then I head across town to wet the baby's head in Hogan's of South Great George's Street – me, Dunny, Shaggy, Den, Victor,

Gary Lavin and Joe Carbonari, who's over from New York. There's a bottle of champagne, a toast to Sadie. I've left my Montecristo cigar behind me but Shaggy pulls out his and hands it over. I don't smoke cigars, but for this day I make an exception.

The crew builds – Brian O'Malley turns up, with Conor Buckley – and some of the lads want to make a big night of it, but after a few more in Bruxelles I make my way back to the Shelbourne.

I've got people to visit bright and early in the morning.

*

Sadie is five days old when we wrap her up, put her in the car seat and head home. We've been asked to do a picture on the hospital steps by some waiting photographers and we've given a polite decline. Our daughter isn't public property.

I'm a relieved man when we pull into the house. I've never driven as slowly or as carefully. And never in my life have I felt so protective of two people.

I flit between my parallel worlds of family and rugby, happier than I've ever been. I go back into camp to prepare for the trip to Scotland in round three of the Six Nations, but there's some turbulence on the way.

Sexto is injured and the presumption is that Rog will take over. He might not be having his best season but his strength of character is phenomenal and there's no better man to pull a performance out of the hat when he needs it.

He comes to me before the team is announced and hits me with a cryptic one-liner.

'The obese woman has stretched her vocal cords,' he says.

I pick up the fat-lady-sings reference but I'm none the wiser.

330

'I've just been given the axe,' he says.

Deccie is giving Paddy Jackson his debut and leaving Rog on the bench. It's a big call. Paddy's a really nice footballer with a good future, but the Six Nations is a savage environment for a young guy who's never played international rugby. Against the Scots, he misses some kicks that could have put us in the clear, but there are other reasons why we're under pressure. We butcher so many chances to score tries we virtually lay out the red carpet for Scotland to come back at us. And they do.

Our discipline goes: 8–0 to us becomes 9–8 to them. Rog comes on for Paddy, and with eight minutes left he tries to pull off a cross-kick that comes slicing off his shin and drops into open country. Scotland are on to it quickly, forcing us to scramble like madmen. Thirty seconds later, we concede a penalty at a ruck; 12–8. Beaten again.

Rog has got such high standards that when he thinks he's fallen below them he's the first one to say it. He fronts up: typical. We have a fortnight to let the dust settle before we play France in Dublin. The night before we're due back in camp I get a text from Rog that shocks me: *Not in the 23 this week, chat later.*

After 128 caps he deserves better. He has earned the right to a proper farewell, but he's not going to get it. He knows he won't play for Ireland again. We all know. And I feel for him.

In the build-up to the France game there's talk about my own time coming to an end, about this being my final home game. I'm thinking, *Maybe, maybe not.* I'm not ready to make a call about the future when there's so much going on in the present.

Amy and Sadie come to the match. During the national anthems I scan their area of the stand and it warms my heart when I pick them out. No matter what happens next, at least my little girl got to see her old man play. We can show her the pictures to prove it in the years ahead.

The heavens open. When you're playing France it's always going to be attritional, no matter the conditions, but the foul weather cranks up the intensity. Jamie scores off a driven line-out after ten minutes and Paddy converts. Then he knocks over two brilliant kicks from distance and we're 13–3 ahead at the break.

But the mayhem hasn't even started yet.

In the second half France come at us; they bring it back to 13–6. All around me there are bodies on the line and I'm not exactly coming through unscathed myself.

I limp out of a ruck with a dead leg.

I get a bad cut on my ear.

I take a big dunt in a tackle and my legs wobble.

The hits are massive and the casualties mount. Luke Marshall is on the floor getting treatment for concussion when France start pushing hard on our line.

Vincent Debaty, their nineteen-stone prop, comes thundering at me and I bounce off him like he's made of rock. When I get up, I stumble back into the defensive line but I'm shook, a sitting duck if only the French realize it.

The rip in my ear gives me a way out – and a way back in again. It buys me five minutes in the blood bin to get my head together.

I take smelling salts on the sideline. I insist to the medics that I'm good to go again. They run the protocol questions for suspected concussion.

'Where are you?'

'The Aviva.'

'Who are you playing against?'

'France.'

'What's the score?'

Expecting the question, I've already looked at the score-board – knowing that if I nail it off quickly it will help me get back on.

'They've just got a try – it's thirteen all! Let me back on!'

Maybe the story would be different if there wasn't so much going on, if they didn't have Luke's situation to worry about as well, but I talk my way onto the field with four minutes left to play. My head is clear enough to know that if this is my last international match at home, then I don't want it to end this way.

With a minute to go, Eoin Reddan falls awkwardly in a tackle and breaks his leg; another man down on a savage day.

There's no last-gasp win to ease the pain. In rugby, a draw is no good to either team.

We haul ourselves off the pitch, exhausted and sore. The promise of early February feels like a long time ago.

*

My pal Mick Quinlan texts me two days later, wondering if I've managed to put myself back together again. I tell him if ever there was a match to make me retire at the end of the season then that was it.

Amy's concerned but says she'll support me if I want to give it another year, as long as I'm physically up to it and not taking any unnecessary risks.

My folks would like me to give it up, all the more so after the France game, and my sisters would probably agree. Some of my friends, too. Maybe the summer would be a good time to get out, Mick says.

On the morning of our final championship game, against

Italy in Rome, I get a lovely text from Dunny. He's not sure whether he'll see me play in the green jersey again and he wants to say something to mark the occasion, if this is the last time. It's a heartfelt message from a friend who, in his own way, has shared the journey with me from the start.

I tell myself the decision would be a whole lot easier if my competitive edge had gone – or even if it had lessened. You read about sportsmen and -women who say they knew instinctively when it was time to go. And I don't feel that – not yet.

We limp on to Rome. We've got a strong squad but it's always going to hurt when you're missing big players, like Paulie, Stephen Ferris, Sexto, Darce and Tommy Bowe, all at the same time. We're not New Zealand, blessed with depth in every department. One of the things people forget about our Slam-winning season was the fact that we suffered almost no injuries.

In the history of the Six Nations we've never lost to Italy, but the gods are sending us messages early in the game. Earlsy goes off injured in the twenty-fourth minute. Three minutes later Luke Marshall follows him into the treatment room.

Just after that, their openside flanker, Simone Favaro, makes a tackle on Ian Madigan. He rolls over on our side of the ruck and just lies there. He flails his arms as if he's trapped and can't move. He's slowing down our ball and hoping to get away with it.

I get in there and give him some shoe, right in the chest. I'm thinking, *Get the fuck out of our ruck!*

My boot is in the vicinity of the ball, but not close enough. I look to see if anyone's spotted it. If they have, I know I'm in trouble.

Romain Poite, the touch judge, has a word with Wayne Barnes. Out comes the yellow card.

It's only the second time in my international career that I've been sin-binned. Two yellows in 130 Tests for Ireland and the Lions – both against Italy, nine years apart.

While I'm sitting in the bin, Luke Fitzgerald comes off injured. He's only been on the pitch for twelve minutes as Earlsy's replacement. Deccie has run out of options in the backline. He moves Peter O'Mahony from the blindside flank to the wing and waits for the next calamity.

Paddy Jackson keeps us in it with some nerveless goal-kicking, but the wheels are loosening all the time. Italy put us away with another penalty a minute from the end: 22–15. We finish fifth in the table. We only just avoid the wooden spoon, on points difference ahead of France.

As frustrating as it is, the disappointment isn't as all-consuming as before. Failure always hurts, but when you've got a baby at home you don't have the time or the inclination to dwell on it. I live it for a little while with the lads and then I park it. When I turn the key in the door at home and step inside, rugby doesn't matter until I walk back out again the next morning.

Two days after Rome, myself and Amy go to London for my testimonial evening at the Dorchester Hotel. It's the first social event we've been to since Sadie was born. And it's a jaw-dropping night, a humbling show of support from two thousand people with a good cause benefiting at the end of it – the IRFU Charitable Trust.

Prince William finds the time to attend. Bono is there. Michael Fassbender, the actor. The Riverdance troupe. Niall Horan from One Direction. Team-mates past and present. All sorts of folk from all sorts of places.

Two days later, the black tie is off and the hair shirt is on. I'm before a Six Nations disciplinary committee for the stamp on Favaro. A five-week ban is cut to three because of my past record.

It's not the worst outcome. It gives me time to recharge before the last push for Lions selection. I can rest and relax and come back fresh. You learn to try and turn every negative into a positive and this time it's not hard. A mini-break at this stage of the season feels like a godsend.

*

Deccie's contract has only a couple of months left to run, and our worst performance in the fourteen-year history of the Six Nations isn't the best argument for giving him a new deal. Four years on from the Slam, we've stagnated. We're in need of new ideas, a different voice to get us going again. These were the circumstances that first brought him in and he's under no illusions about the likely consequences of another poor campaign.

The news comes after what's described as 'an in-depth review process' by the IRFU's National Team Review Group. When it comes down to it, professional rugby at the top level is a cold-blooded business and Deccie suffers the same fate as Eddie and Gats before him.

Myself and Sexto have a word with Joe Schmidt and tell him he should go for the job. We reckon he's exactly what we need. If you fed the requirements into a computer then Joe's face would pop up on the screen in front of you.

He's not sure about it, but we work on him, willing him to step forward. He plays his cards close to his chest and keeps focused on Leinster. We can't win the trophy we wanted most of all this season but there are two others to play for and we go after them hard.

I'm back in the team on 13 April, for a Saturday night in Limerick and a Pro12 victory over Munster that's all the more welcome given that Warren Gatland, head coach of the 2013 Lions, is sitting in the stand at Thomond Park alongside Rob Howley, the backs coach. I know Gats wants to be sure that my body is up to the rigours of a six-week tour, so eighty minutes and the winning try near the end is a reasonable statement.

Two weeks later we take on Biarritz in the semi-final of the Amlin at the RDS and Rob Howley texts me to say he's coming over. It's my last game before the squad is selected, and Howlers gives me a little encouragement when I text him back.

Do I need to have a stormer?!

No, not at all mate.

I take it as a positive.

I've got Ian Madigan alongside me in the centre as we unload on Biarritz in a big way, 44–16. I put in another eighty minutes and score another try, my thirty-third in Europe. As I'm waiting for Mads to kick the conversion, a chant goes up around the ground . . .

'*One more year!*'

There are three days to go before Gats shows his hand – nice of the Leinster faithful to put in a word for me.

Later in the afternoon, Munster go hammer and tongs with Clermont in the semi-final of the Heineken Cup. This time they can't get it done but they give it a serious rattle and Rog is in his element, still pulling the strings at thirty-six. Over a fifteen-year period he has been the best and most influential player in the tournament.

It's a disappointing result but a classy goodbye, the kind of farewell to the fans that he deserved with Ireland but never got.

*

When Joe is named as the new Ireland coach, it feels like a pivotal moment in my own dilemma about retiring or playing on for another year.

He encourages me to give it one more season. He feels I should be Ireland's most capped player. It's classic Joe – subtle. He dangles the carrot and makes me think a year under him with Ireland could be a lot of fun, maybe with a trophy at the end of it.

When the Lions squad is announced the next day, I'm at home with Amy, Sadie in my arms. All the phantom squads that have been picked don't matter a damn now.

Gats sits on stage with his principal lieutenants: Howlers, Graham Rowntree, Andy Farrell, Neil Jenkins. Andy Irvine, the tour manager, steps up to the microphone and starts naming names.

I hand Sadie to Amy, just in case something goes horribly wrong and I feel an overwhelming urge to stand up and kick the furniture. We're just two players into the announcement when my phone beeps with a message from Sue.

Stuart Hogg's picture is on my television as I read her text. *Get in!*

It throws me for a second or two, but it turns out my Sky box is on pause and I'm a minute behind. I say nothing to Amy and just let it unfold.

George North, Scarlets and Wales.
Jonathan Davies, Scarlets and Wales.
Brian O'Driscoll, Leinster and Ireland.

Relief, joy, excitement. Four times I've heard my name called out for Lions tours and the thrill never lessens.

Gats steps up to the podium and announces his captain: Sam Warburton of Wales, skipper of the Six Nations champions.

A little later, Amy hits me with a stat: 'Hey, congratulations! You're the oldest in the squad!'

I'm appalled but she's right. I am thirteen years, five months and three days older than Stuart Hogg, the youngest guy in the squad. He was eight when I flew to Australia on my first Lions tour.

I've never been the oldest at anything before. Ever.

15. One Last Trip to Oz

Under the RDS lights on the third Friday night in May, the score in the final of the Amlin Challenge Cup is Leinster 34, Stade Français 14. For twenty hours, until the Heineken decider the following day, we are the holders of both European trophies; a decent evening's work.

Injured for the game, I walk onto the pitch at the end, happy for the boys but not really feeling part of it, because that's just the way it is when you're wearing an overcoat and your team-mates are bouncing up and down with medals in front of their jerseys. It's twenty-four hours since John Terry – for the second time in a year – lifted a European trophy in his Chelsea gear after watching the games in civvies. Sitting at home earlier in the day, chatting with Amy, I'd thought about heading to Dundrum shopping centre to buy a full Chelsea kit, and whipping it on if we won the Amlin. I thought better of it, though: I didn't want to belittle the Challenge Cup.

The trophy is joyously lifted by Sexto and Isa, our departing stars, in the knowledge that they're not quite done yet.

Eight days later, I'm grateful to be back in the side for our second final of the season, the Pro12. Ulster bring a big following on a sunny day at the RDS for a game we are desperate to win, after leaving three league finals behind us in successive years. It's the most nervous I've been before a game in a very long time: the thought of losing four in a row is unbearable.

We get it done, 24–18. When Sexto's in the vicinity it's not often I get to have the final say, but with the clock in red, I fish the ball out of the bottom of a ruck and punt it into the stand. As it's on its way, Sexto runs forward and embraces me.

He's already preparing for his new life in Paris, learning the language. When he puts his mind to something, he's all in. But his happiness at going out with another trophy couldn't be any greater.

Ten minutes later I'm on the podium with Dreamboat on one side of me and Isa on the other. We're going to miss Isa too, hugely. For five seasons he has been different class, one of the very best I've played alongside during all my days in the game.

Typical Leo, he stands aside and lets Jamie accept the trophy. It's the fourth we've won under Joe in three seasons.

Not bad going for the guy they said wouldn't last.

*

Lions tours are about a lot of things, but mostly they're about getting on the Test team. You weigh up the competition, you back yourself, and the early games are a means to an end.

I look at the four centres in the party – Jamie Roberts, Jonathan Davies, Manu Tuilagi, me – and I rule out two of the potential partnerships on the grounds of balance.

1. Jonathan and me – two natural 13s.
2. Jamie and Manu – two power runners.

Straight away I'm thinking I need to build a partnership with Manu if I'm to make the Tests. The Welsh boys are coming off the back of a Six Nations championship and Jonathan has had a big campaign at outside centre, playing every minute of the five games. Even though me and Jamie went well together in South Africa, I figure the Wales pairing is unlikely to be broken up.

I don't put all my eggs in the Manu basket – there's a bit of talk about me and Jamie picking up our 2009 partnership – but I do see it as a straight contest between me and Jonathan for the 13 jersey.

For the first five games – all of which we win – Gats tries every one of the most likely centre permutations. He starts Jonathan alongside Jamie against the Barbarians in Hong Kong. Me and Manu get our go in the first match after we hit Australia – and we go well. Captaining the side in Sam Warburton's absence against Western Force in Perth, I score a couple of tries – the second after a nice offload from Manu. We defend well. We're solid. We do our chances no harm.

Game three: the Queensland Reds in Brisbane. Jonathan starts at 12, Manu's 13 – but he's off after twenty minutes with a shoulder problem and doubtful for the first Test.

Game four: I pick up another try alongside Jamie against a Combined Country XV. I also tweak my groin, ever so slightly but enough to put me on the easy list.

Game five: a stiff test against New South Wales Waratahs in Sydney, on the Saturday before the first Test. They're coached by Michael Cheika, who, after a couple of seasons with Stade Français, is building a strong side back home. In the week of the game, Cheiks invites me over to his house and we enjoy the catch-up. It's good to see him getting on well, and it's clear how much he wants a good crack at the Lions, but he has to do without the Tahs' big Wallaby contingent, who aren't being risked ahead of the Test series.

For us, Manu's out of the reckoning, so it's down to two from three. I'm thinking I need more game time alongside

Jamie, but Gats says he's resting me. My high-speed metres in the Tuesday game were pretty decent and, with the Brisbane Test looming, he's thinking about the mileage on my clock. On one level I can see his point, on another it feels like an opportunity lost.

Out of sight, out of mind: Jonathan plays a stormer and I have to sit back and watch him from the stand, wondering if my chance is slipping away.

I'm not the only one. Kearns, so impressive at full-back on the 2009 tour, must fear the worst for his own Test chances, looking at Leigh Halfpenny light up the stadium with a 30-point performance – two tries and eight kicks out of eight, every one of them beautifully struck.

Ten minutes before the end of a 47–17 win, Jamie limps off, but it's never a good idea to read too much into other people's injuries, or wonder if they might open a door for you.

In the dressing room afterwards, I call it like it is: 'How good was Jonathan Davies?!'

When maybe the best player on the pitch is the guy wearing your number, there's no point in pretending otherwise: everyone has seen it, everyone knows it. You're part of the big picture so acknowledge it and use it as motivation to drive yourself on.

Jamie's scan shows a torn hamstring, so, with Manu also injured, the partnership I thought was the least likely gets pencilled in by a process of elimination when Gats calls out the Test team: Leigh Halfpenny; Alex Cuthbert, Brian O'Driscoll, Jonathan Davies, George North; Johnny Sexton, Mike Phillips; Alex Corbisiero, Tom Youngs, Adam Jones; Alun-Wyn Jones, Paul O'Connell; Tom Croft, Sam Warburton, Jamie Heaslip.

People can get hung up on jersey numbers, but there's a lot of mixing and matching in the centre. Me and Jonathan – or Foxy, as the Welsh boys call him – train well together, we room together, we get on well and we feel ready for what's coming our way in Brisbane.

*

I look at the Australia team and I don't see the same quality they had twelve years ago. With less than a minute gone their nominated kicker, Christian Leali'ifano, is out cold after a big collision with Foxy, and when we look back later we wonder if the winning and losing of the game came there and then. Without him kicking, they leave 14 points behind them, while Leigh proves he's human by missing one of his six.

He bangs one over from the touchline after big George North blasts through them from miles out, with Foxy on his shoulder and me a few yards further back, sniffing a cheap try. George doesn't need either of us. Once he breaks the first tackle he's running hard for the try line with dancing feet and they can't get near him.

Australia have a freak talent of their own in Israel Folau and his second try – six minutes before half-time and almost as brilliant as George's – brings them back within a point.

Nine minutes into the second half, five or six metres short of their 22, Sexto whips a nice pass across and James O'Connor bites on my decoy line. With the ball winging its way into Alex Cuthbert's hands, I pull up short a metre before colliding with O'Connor and Cuthy scorches through the gap in their defensive line for a class finish near the posts. We lead 20–12.

We're the better team, we should open up and pull away.

But we don't: we go back into ourselves. By the end, with the gap at two points, we need Kurtley Beale to slip when he's striking the penalty that could have finished us.

We've all heard the stories about the 1997 tour – the thrill of being two–nil up against South Africa, with the series won and a freebie week up ahead. In the post-match huddle I remember 2001 and the way we lost the second Test – the momentum swinging after it, the belief surging back into Australia.

'We win this in two!' I say.

When we're sitting on the benches in the dressing room, not too happy about nearly leaving it behind us, their scrum-half, Will Genia, and their captain, James Horwill, come looking to swap jerseys. I watch this friendly little exchange and I think about how times have changed. In 2001 there was no way on earth John Eales or Dan Herbert or any of that crew would have darkened the door of our dressing room with the series in the balance – and it's the way I feel myself now.

Let's just get this done and dusted – we can all be pals then.

A week later, at half-time in the dressing room in the Etihad Stadium, Melbourne, Gats sends the same message. In a defensive game that's all about making tackles, we lead 12–9, four penalties to three.

'We finish the series *here*,' he says. Then he points at me. 'If you're going to do it for anyone, do it for him!'

For forty minutes, we've been tentative, blunt, showing nothing. Ten minutes into the second half, some space finally opens up on the left wing. I've got Jonathan inside me but the pass I need to make is one further out to George, who's flying up the touchline. He's such a freak he can score from there but I hesitate and the chance is gone. I end up throwing an intercept to Folau, which comes to nothing, but I'm kicking myself because I know it's a lost opportunity in a game that's giving up very few chances.

Sixty-two minutes: the pack wins us a penalty just inside their half and Leigh makes it 15–9. Six points: the most horrible lead in rugby when time is running out.

Seventy-four minutes and fifty seconds: Genia collects the ball from the base of a ruck in front of our posts. He moves it left to James O'Connor and it's three on three, ten metres short.

O'Connor is my man – he's got Adam Ashley-Cooper outside him and Joe Tomane on the wing. I've got Jonathan and Cuthy outside me.

O'Connor runs a great line. He cuts left, away from me and towards Foxy – but he's still my man.

I've been in this situation countless times with Darce. It's a big test of a partnership, a question of trust. There's an element of telepathy in centre play and you've both got to believe. You put your faith in one another – even if it looks like a stretch for you to make the tackle, your partner has to trust that you'll get there. It's the beauty of what I've always had with Darce, but you need a guy beside you week in, week out before you're fully comfortable.

It's my second game with Jonathan so I don't know what's in his head as O'Connor runs at us, but he sits a little too long on me. It's like he's not 100 per cent convinced I'm going to make my tackle: for a split-second he hedges his bets between O'Connor and Ashley-Cooper.

As I take O'Connor around the legs, he offloads it into Ashley-Cooper's path. Jonathan's a very good tackler but to get his full bodyweight in front of Ashley-Cooper he needs to be a yard further to the right. He gets an arm on him but there's way too much momentum. Ashley-Cooper runs hard and straight and he's over the line in a flash.

Back in the team after his one-minute appearance in the first Test, Leali'ifano has already kicked three from three, curling them in without a bother. He bisects the posts with his conversion and it's Australia 16, Lions 15.

Six seconds left, they're penalized for not releasing in a ruck, deep in our half. We truck it up to the halfway line. With the clock more than forty seconds in red, they kill the ball again and Craig Joubert doesn't like it.

'Let it go, gold!' he says.

Three seconds later he blows his whistle. Time stands still while everyone takes in what has just happened. I look at the posts, more than fifty metres away, and it comes into my head that maybe the best play is to tap and go and invite another penalty inside their half. The rule book says the opposition have to back away and give the runner ten metres of space before he's tackled. In the heat of the moment, forwards on the defending team can make bad decisions, especially front rows. They'll tackle the ball-carrier rather than retreating: penalty. It's instinctive, like a kid's hand in a cookie jar – often they can't help themselves.

The moment passes. Most guys are out on their feet and it's massively high-risk play. If the illegal tackle doesn't come, you've given up the shot at goal. You're the headless chicken who gave away the game.

Leigh's been kicking unbelievably well, but from this range accuracy is only half the battle. In the eightieth minute of a draining Test match, it's a massive ask to get it there.

Our kicking coach Neil Jenkins runs on with the tee.

Apart from him, I'm the closest guy to Leigh as he lines it up.

'What are his chances?' I ask Jenks.

'He's got the legs if he hits it spot-on,' he says. 'It's just a matter of how clean he catches it.'

You get to know what flush contact sounds like. The instant he strikes it, I can tell it's short. I don't even join in our chase line: if it bounces back off an upright, there are faster guys than me to contest the ball. From inside our half I watch Will Genia blast it off the park.

We feel for Leigh but we don't feel hard done by. We haven't played well. We haven't played.

*

At the Sheraton Hotel in Noosa, a beach resort on the Sunshine Coast, I'm put in front of the media. It's Sunday evening. We've flown up from Melbourne to rest for a few days, away from the hype and the travelling circus.

Flicking through my Twitter feed, I've already read a piece in the *Sydney Morning Herald* announcing that defeat in the final Test would make me the most unsuccessful tourist in Lions history: played nine, lost seven. It's a stat that assumes I'm playing, and the line of questioning from the journalists in front of me assumes the same.

I'm asked about the refereeing. Already in the series I've been pinged at the breakdown a few times, frustrating penalties when I thought I was competing fairly for the ball. The ref in Sydney will be Romain Poite, a guy you never want to be on the wrong side of.

'We're going to try and work with him,' I say. 'That's the big thing – to understand the way they're thinking.'

No more than anyone else, I'm also wondering what Gats is thinking. The big news in the centre is that Jamie Roberts is ready to train and highly likely to start, in which case Jonathan or me will be making way.

We're also going to need a new captain after Sam's hamstring tear in Melbourne. I'm one of two former Lions captains in a pretty inexperienced squad, but Paulie watched the second Test from the stand, after breaking his forearm late on in Brisbane. He's still with us, but in Sydney he'll be wearing a suit. So I weigh it all up and come to the conclusion that I'll either be captain or I won't be playing.

Always you've got to be positive. In my head I back myself to be the guy picked and I figure the captaincy scenario plays in my favour.

We've got Monday and Tuesday off. We're not training until the Wednesday and a fair few of the lads head out on the beer.

I'm tempted. The 2001 me would be in the thick of it, but the 2013 version worries about alcohol in the system even six days before a game. So I go and get myself an ice cream instead and walk past the bar where the boys are ensconced.

On the Tuesday I'm one of a dozen in the gym for an optional weights session. There's a bit of flak flying over the decision to unwind in Noosa rather than go straight to Sydney, but it feels like the right call. In 2001, we were flogged in that final week and you've got to learn the lessons.

Wednesday morning. After a game of table tennis with Owen Farrell, I make for the coffee machine outside the team room. Gats walks over. He's got Howlers with him.

Before Gats opens his mouth, I don't like the scenario, or the serious look on their faces, or the fact that there's two of them in front of me.

This isn't good.

'Can we have a word in the team room?' says Gats.

'Sure.'

It's only five or six paces away but for those few seconds there's still hope. I'm fearing the worst but already computing that if bad news is coming there are different degrees of disappointment.

1. 'You're not captain.'
2. 'You're in the twenty-three, but you're not starting.'
3. 'You're not playing.'

The team room is empty, apart from two banks of chairs, left and right. We pull some around and Gats gets straight to the point.

'This isn't easy, but we don't have a place for you this weekend.'

The last time someone gave me news like this, I was a schoolboy. It hits me in the stomach straight away. It takes all the wind out of me and I can barely get any words out.

'Oh . . . right.'

There's some kind of explanation, but I barely take it in. Something about Foxy having a left foot – 'We feel we're going to need that in the Test match . . .'

We walk back out after what seems like less than a minute. It's getting close enough to 10 a.m., the time the team meeting begins. There's another lounge area away from the rest of the players. I walk up some steps and take out my phone – still in a daze, trying to take it in.

I text Amy first . . .

I'm not on the team.

Then Mum, same message.

I walk back down and the first guy I see hanging around is Paulie. I shoot him a look.

'What's the story?' he says.

'First time in fifteen years I had to have that conversation.'

When Gats starts reading out the team, I realize I'm not even sure if I'm on the bench or not. Alun-Wyn Jones is captain. It's not much of a surprise when he calls Manu's name in the replacements. For me – a centre who doesn't cover other positions – it was always likely to be a starting place or nothing.

Afterwards there are a few consoling words – 'Sorry, bud' – but I've been in enough of these meetings to know that the sympathy of the guys who've been picked is minimal, because every player starting is totally focused on his own stuff. It's brutally clinical, because it has to be, and my disappointment is no more or less than Jamie Heaslip's, also dropped from the twenty-three after starting the first two Tests.

You're one guy in a squad of thirty-five. Fifteen are on cloud nine, another eight are happy to be involved. And twelve more are trying to hang in there – supporting the lucky ones as best they can, with varying levels of success, but not really feeling part of it any more, deep down.

*

On the bus journey to training, I think about the players I've known who became dead-men-walking after being dropped, giving nothing – and then I think about Brian Carney.

After a stellar career in rugby league, he switched codes and Eddie O'Sullivan brought him to the 2007 World Cup. He never even made a match-day squad, but he trained unbelievably well every single day, forever pushing the rest of us and never once dropping his head.

For years I've talked the talk about the strength of a squad being determined by the attitude of the guys outside the first fifteen, and I don't want anyone saying I didn't back it up when the shit hit the fan for me.

I train as well as I can, trying to feel like I've offered something, then I throw myself into a community session with local kids because there's no point in doing it half-heartedly, or sulking your way through it – you might as well launch yourself in deep.

Afterwards, there's a monster signing session – commercial stuff, jerseys the players want signed for themselves, hundreds of pieces. It can be a pain at the best of times, but worse when you're doing it in a depressed state.

While I'm signing, Howlers comes over. 'How are you doing?' he asks.

'I've been better.'

'Okay. Listen – not everyone's training tomorrow. What sort of shape are you in?'

I tell him I'm 100 per cent ready to train.

I know there's a bunch of guys not involved in Sydney going on a big night out. There's a part of me that wants to let off a little steam, too – but I know I won't feel good about myself if Jamie Roberts's hamstring flares up again and they call me back in after a heavy night.

After two beers and a pizza, I head back to the hotel and spend some time with Jamie on the video, talking through different plays, telling him not to pay any attention if Sexto gets a little short with him every now and then, because he can't help himself in the heat of combat.

The news about the team is made public.

On Twitter, I get a sense of the controversy it generates. Among others, Ian McGeechan is kind enough to say he would have picked me, but he puts his finger on the reality as well: selection is a very personal thing and coaches will always differ.

In Wales, it's no biggie: why shouldn't their two centres start, when both are good to go?

In Ireland, it's portrayed differently and the texts from back home start coming through, softening the blow just a little.

*

After training the following day, we fly to Sydney. Amy and Sadie and the rest of my family are there and I've never looked forward as much to seeing them.

We check into the Intercontinental Hotel and I'm rooming with Tom Croft, another guy left out of the decider after starting the Test series in the team. The last thing either of us needs is to be in with a player who *has* been selected – someone whose frame of mind is on a different planet. So we're kindred spirits, nursing our own disappointment, understanding how each other is feeling inside. In a word, deflated.

On a noticeboard in the team room, I find out I'm not needed for training the following morning and it stings when I see it written down.

CAPTAIN'S RUN – MATCH DAY 23

Typically thoughtful, Sean Cunningham in New York books a restaurant for my family in Sydney and picks up the tab. I meet everyone at Doyles in Watsons Bay, and there are a lot of prolonged hugs. It helps that the restaurant is almost empty and my family have no more interest in dwelling on what has happened than me, so we just shoot the breeze for the evening. Surrounded by the people closest to me, the worst of my disappointment fades away.

Up until Wednesday morning, they've had a trip to remember – and I can say the same for myself about a very enjoyable tour. We even got to celebrate Mum and Dad's fortieth wedding anniversary with a barbecue by the riverside in Brisbane.

At Doyles, over a seafood dinner, I have a couple of glasses of white wine but no more, telling myself again that I just need to make it to Saturday night, because stranger things have happened in the run-up to a game – a tweak, an illness, something from left field. Players have got to be in optimum condition if they're called on at the last minute – especially when it's the deciding Test match in a Lions series – and it surprises me that nobody outside the twenty-three is asked to bring their boots to the stadium when Saturday evening comes.

I don't feel like being judged for taking my own boots onto the bus for the non-playing squad members, but there's still a part of me clinging to the faint hope that I might somehow be needed.

In the hotel bedroom, I put on my Lions suit. Over that I wear a blue stadium jacket, padding for the coldest month of the year in Sydney. There are pockets on the side and, before leaving the room, I slip my gumshield into one of them.

Just in case.

*

I've got Kearns alongside me in the stand as the game begins, with Jamie Heaslip just in front – fellow Leinstermen wishing they were down there, too. With ten Welsh guys in the side, Sexto has made a good joke about how pleased he is to be making his debut for Wales, but it's an Englishman who crashes over for a try in the first minute – the loosehead Alex Corbisiero. Early on, our scrum kills them, and when the penalties come, Leigh keeps stretching the lead.

A long time before the final whistle blows, it's obvious that the series is in the bag. I'd have settled for Lions 6 Australia 3, but when Jamie Roberts gets in near the posts with more than ten minutes left, the scoreboard reads 41–16 after the conversion.

I feel different emotions watching it. Foxy has played well, showing some nice touches. Jamie has scored a good try. But I've got to believe I could have had some of those moments myself, that we'd still have won with me on the pitch.

Over the years, though, the game has taught me that it's not about you, it's about the team. You either buy into that or you're never going to be any good to anyone. That said, it doesn't mean that you feel part of it when you're sitting in the stand wearing a suit, because you don't. You can't pretend it's there, that crazy buzz of satisfaction when the whistle goes and you're in front. You can't force it when it's not there.

There's a reason why a competitor like Roy Keane felt he never won a Champions League, despite being given a winner's medal on that incredible night at the Nou Camp in 1999. Through sheer force of will in the semi-final against Juventus, he'd done more than anyone to get Manchester United through. But the yellow card he picked up along the way meant he was in a suit when his team did the business against Bayern Munich – and for him it just wasn't the same.

I don't ask Jamie Heaslip if he's feeling like me, because I don't need to. It's cut and dried: we haven't had a say on the final day and there's no adrenalin rush to be had in the stand. Once you set foot on the pitch when the game is in play – even if it's only a couple of minutes off the bench – you've made some kind of contribution. You've had enough of an involvement to allow yourself a feeling of inner satisfaction. You're part of it.

Still, even though I'm feeling weird about it all, I want to enjoy it with the lads, to embrace them on the pitch. I hug Adam Jones, a top lad who I soldiered with for two Lions tours.

'It's a shame you couldn't have been out there winning it with us, but,' he says.

Amid all the celebrating, I bump into Gats. It's an uncomfortable few seconds, for both of us, but we make the best of an awkward situation and shake hands. I shrug my shoulders, open my hands and smile. The moment is captured by photographers and, while I don't say anything to him, the expression on my face is clear enough: *Hard to argue with your call now!*

'You're just as much a part of this,' he says.

And while it doesn't feel like it right at that moment, a big weight has been lifted off my shoulders. What I'm left with is that I played two of the three Tests in a winning Lions tour. Far better to have won the final Test and not been selected than to have made the team and lost.

After Sam and Alun-Wyn have raised the trophy together, I get to lift it with Paulie: a nice memory because the two of us have had some tough times on tour, especially in 2005. For both of us, though, being part of the Lions has been incredibly special.

In a stadium rocking with delirious supporters wearing red, somebody points me towards Amy. She has Sadie in her arms and I'm so proud of this gorgeous little person, all kitted out in her Lions gear, that I want to show her off to everyone. She comes with me on the lap of honour, wearing a giant pair of earmuff headphones, happy as you like all the way round.

En route I'm stopped for a TV interview by Scott Quinnell, who played alongside me in all three Lions Tests back in 2001. He's a passionate guy, SQ. Anyone would warm to him.

'It's a winning series for you, my friend,' he says, accentuating the positive. 'It's something that you've wanted all your career. How are we feeling?'

I tell him I'm delighted, which is nothing less than the truth.

'I'll always have it on my CV and that's what counts,' I say, smiling.

It's the bottom line.

*

One of the great things about our game is that, once you've picked yourself up from bad news, the boys in the dressing room have an acute sense of timing over when it's okay to have a laugh at your expense.

Two days after the third Test, on the night before we fly home, a crew of us get together for a slap-up meal and a few glasses of wine. We talk about the tour – different moments, the things people said. We laugh a lot. One of the boys mimics the passionate words uttered by Gats at half-time in the second Test. He points at me and delivers the line, slightly different from the way I remember it: 'If you're going to do it for anyone, do it for him . . . because he won't be playing next week!'

Time is a great healer and a little vino can help the mood as well. I laugh as hard as the rest of them.

Alas, like the spear tackle in 2005, the controversy over my omission doesn't go away when I'm back on home soil. The last thing I want to do is feed it, but that's exactly what I end up achieving at the end of August when I agree to a Sky Sports interview with Shaggy, who's making a name for himself as a rugby broadcaster with real insight.

We both know the score: there's only one subject that viewers of *The Rugby Club* want him to explore. So he gets down to it.

'We all got dropped – we all dealt with it in different ways. You'd never been dropped as a professional rugby player – never happened to you. Did you see it coming down the line?'

Sitting in front of such a good friend, even with cameras rolling in a hotel suite, it feels more like a conversation than an interview – which makes it a dangerous setting when you need to choose your words with care. He asks about how Gats told me the news. Then . . .

'Do you resent him a bit, for the decision?'

It's an open-ended question. It's not 'You resent him – *don't you?*'

Sometimes, for your own good, it's best to keep your feelings private. I can have a burning desire to produce my best form against Wales in the next Six Nations – which I do, already – but that's for me to carry around in my head. It's not for public consumption.

There are any number of ways I can answer Shaggy's question so that my life for the next six months becomes considerably easier.

1. 'No, I don't. Tough calls are made in rugby and you have to accept them.'
2. 'Resentment's probably a bit over the top . . .'
3. 'I wouldn't put it like that. Of course it hurt, but . . .'

I go with option 4. Instead of evasion, I offer him honesty.

'Ahm, do I resent him? Yeah, there's resentment – of course. I'd be, ahm . . .' I'm winging it without a script now. I haven't thought this through properly. 'Is he on the Christmas-card list? Unlikely!'

Shaggy smiles – I've said this in jest but again I'm offering something I don't need to. Too much.

'Thanks for your time, buddy,' he says at the end.

I thank and compliment him – 'Well done!' – because he has handled it really well, a natural interviewer. He hasn't set out to draw something out of me that's going to get headlines – I've done that all by myself. I don't need to be told that I've made a rod for my own back, because I know the way it works only too well when there's a controversy in the offing. Open up just a little – one sentence is enough, even one word – and they'll go to town on the back of it.

Sure enough . . .

O'Driscoll: Of course I resent Gatland for dropping me

BOD finally reveals his feelings

Two weeks later, I brace myself for some awkwardness when the 2013 Lions are invited to 10 Downing Street to see David Cameron. We meet up beforehand in a pub nearby and I've got something for Gats in my pocket. I walk over when I see him.

'I don't know if you've heard any stuff about you being off the Christmas-card list,' I smile, 'but congratulations – you're back on it.'

I hand him the card.

To yourself, Trudy and the family.
Have a wonderful Christmas – Brian and family

It's 16 September – a little early, but it's the thought that counts and there's sincerity behind it. On tour, Trudy thoughtfully organized a private room for our families and close friends in the weeks of the Tests, so that we could chat in peace. She was also very kind in having a quiet word with Amy and me in the hours before the game in Sydney, saying how disappointed she was for me. It was appreciated.

Gats smiles and sticks the card in his pocket. Andy Irvine comes over and gives me a big hug. He's possibly thinking a major situation has been defused – which is a bit of a stretch, because I don't get the impression Gats was too wounded by my comments to Shaggy. He's a guy who has never shirked bold decisions. He was the first coach to drop me, but he was also the one who first played me for Ireland, at twenty years of age.

The team that he picked backed up his selection, so no arguments.

But when the dust settles, I'm grateful I've got one season left in me to leave the game on a better note, and maybe show I could have done a job if selected.

16. Beginning the Long Goodbye

As I begin my fifteenth and final season as a professional rugby player, there are three chances of silverware – the Pro12, the Heineken, the Six Nations – and no reason to believe that all three aren't achievable. Then there's the other side of the coin – the possibility that you're pushing it a season too far, running the risk of tarnishing things a little by leaving on a low.

If you're fortunate enough to have the decision in your own hands, you weigh it all up. And once you've rolled the dice and stayed in the game, then you back yourself – one last time. And you hope.

I've thought about Gary Neville, the Manchester United right-back for most of two decades, quitting in mid-season. His decision was made in the dressing-room toilet at half-time when he knew the pace of the game was beyond him, when he couldn't bear the disappointment of letting himself down. It's a tough thing to do, just walking away like that. It's not about the money left behind on a generous contract that's torn up. It's about admitting to yourself and to everyone else that you can't do it any more to anything like the level you need to reach, for your own peace of mind.

For me, there was something admirable about the honesty of Neville's decision. And now, doing another Leinster pre-season, I'm barely able to remember the life I had before, or how my body felt in the morning when there were no twinges or creaks or reminders that it's a younger man's game.

When you're somebody who prefers to look on the bright side, you don't like to think about it ending badly. But some-times it creeps into your head, because even if the mind is still willing and fairly sharp, the body can let you down. And if the worst came to the worst and I found myself sitting on a bench week after week, or unable to train to the kind of standard I've always set myself – the necessary level of intensity – then what would be the point of continuing, other than being a good squad man? To prove myself all over again from the bench? No thanks.

When September comes my hamstring feels so tight I worry it's on the point of tearing. There are certain move-ments on my left side – reflex reactions in training games – that bring instant pain to my lower back and prevent me going full tilt.

I get relief in the evenings after dry-needling treatment from our new head physio, Garreth Farrell, but come the morning I'm back at square one.

Not for the first time, I get a couple of the facet joints on the back of my lower spine injected with anti-inflammatory steroids, but it doesn't make a difference.

I go to see Keith Synnott, the consultant at the Mater Pri-vate who specializes in back surgery. He says that the wear and tear in my back is no worse than he'd expect in a thirty-four-year-old old rugby player. He reckons the problem could be down to a few different things, but that it's not a major issue going forward. There's a somewhat bulging disc between the L_4 and L_5 vertebrae, a common enough complaint.

'It could be that,' he says. 'I can go in and do something, but you might get no relief and you'll have lost three or four months in the process.'

Not exactly what I was thinking of for my one more year.

He studies my scans and comes up with an alternative suggestion – rhizotomy, a procedure that shuts off the pain signals the facet joints send to the brain. Under local anaesthetic, a needle with an electrode at the tip goes in and takes the nerve endings out of the equation. 'You might get relief from it,' he says. 'And if you don't, you're only out for three days.'

It's a no-brainer.

Four days later, I'm lying on a bed at the Mater, feeling the needle go in to deaden the nerves, waiting for the smell of burning that Kearns so helpfully warned me about.

The plan is to target three different sites. I feel the needle twice more, but I can't smell a thing.

'Are you getting any pain down here?' asks Dr Frank Chambers, the guy holding the needle, just as I'm thinking we're done and dusted.

'It's minimal,' I tell him, 'but listen – if in doubt . . .'

He prepares the needle again – once more with feeling.

You take three, you get one free.

*

You don't need to spend a lot of time in his company to tell that Matt O'Connor, the seventh head coach of Leinster during my time, is a very different animal from Joe. It's also clear early on that he's another good fit for us.

We've long been a pretty self-motivated bunch and it's rare enough in sport that a new head coach is joining a team that's winning trophies season after season. Matt's taking over a steady ship, but he's got his own way of steering it. He has a lovely manner about him and a sharp rugby brain. He doesn't really have it in him to pull a player up in Joe's no-nonsense way. If you've messed up, his style is to let you know by taking the piss out of you. And it works: he wins the respect of the squad quickly and the added bonus is that he's hilarious to be around.

In late September, against Cardiff Blues at the RDS, I make my first appearance of the season. Also back in blue are some of Leinster's other Lions – Kearns, Jamie and Cian, who's returning after the savage bad luck of injuring his ankle early in the tour, when he was right in the running for a Test spot in the front row.

It feels strange not having Isa there – I never thought I'd still be playing when the great man wasn't part of our set-up. We're also missing Sexto around the place – his passion, his personality, his good cheer when someone gets a play wrong in training.

For the Cardiff game, Matt gives the number 10 jersey to Ian Madigan, a young gun bursting with confidence and verve who's coming off a big season in Sexto's shadow. On the bench we've got Jimmy Gopperth, another quality out-half, a Kiwi signed from Newcastle after Sexto made his big decision.

We win with a bonus point, 34–20. I play nicely.

The following week I strain my calf in training, feeling the twinge as I turn away from a ruck. I'm out for six weeks: frustrated as hell, but knowing my own body too well to push it now. I'm in the gym at 7.30 every morning, desperate to get back in time for the November internationals and one final crack at beating the All Blacks.

Nobody said the last lap was going to be a walk in the park, but there's a reason this particular rehab isn't as much of a drag as the others – and her name is Sadie. It turns out everything they said was true: the change in your priorities as a couple, the way your whole world suddenly revolves around one person. The love that you have for your child – you just can't describe it.

*

On the first night in November, I drive across the Samuel Beckett Bridge in Dublin's Docklands and there's a totally surreal sight straight ahead. Projected all the way across the spectacular front of the National Convention Centre, the venue for my testimonial dinner, are images of me in Ireland green and Leinster blue, along with graphics listing the key stats of my career. It's mind-bogglingly flattering.

The event is unforgettable. The best thing about it is the significant amount of money it raises for two causes very close to my heart – the ISPCC and Temple Street Children's University Hospital.

I'm interviewed on stage by Keith Wood and we talk about old times. It's eleven years, almost to the day, since I made my first speech as a twenty-three-year-old captain of the Ireland team, a shocker on the night we beat Australia at Lansdowne Road. Now, after the dinner, with 1,140 guests all around me, I'm called to make another speech. It's a prospect that would have terrified me once, but a life in rugby helps the confidence. It takes you out of your shell if you come to the game – as I did – a shy sort of person. Still, I encourage the few nerves I do have, to keep the mind sharp.

I thank all those people in my life who have helped me on my way – my family, friends, team-mates, surgeons, physios, coaches and teachers. It's my chance to tell them how important they've been to me, mostly during the not-so-glorious days. I also get an opportunity to speak about the two children's charities benefiting from the night and the incredible work they do.

*

It's a season of lasts. My fifteenth and last Six Nations, last Heineken Cup, last time to face this team or play at that ground. And it's too much, too soon. In trying to put an early end to the speculation about whether it's definitely, 100 per cent my final season – '*This* is the one more year. There's not going to be another one!' – I find that I've inadvertently helped give rise to something worse: the Long Goodbye. There's a part of me that thinks maybe I shouldn't have been so definitive until closer to the end, but when you're constantly being asked about it you just want to get it out there and off your chest. I *know* there won't be another year, so what's the point in stringing people along and pretending there might be even a small chance?

I spend time thinking about what comes next, but not too much, because to make something of my final season I know I've got to live in the now. Rog has chosen life as a coach, settling down with his family in Paris and working with Sexto every day at Racing Metro – one of life's little ironies. There's some talk about me and coaching but it's not a career that's going to give me the flexibility my family life needs, so I start putting other irons in the fire, trying to make sure I've got some future income lined up by the time the last direct deposit comes through from the IRFU.

Fit again, I drive through the gates of Carton House feeling excited, hoping to play in all three autumn Tests. I know the days ahead are going to be enjoyable, that the level of detail under Joe is going to be like nothing we've seen before at national level. Even with time running out, I'll still be learning new things. After so many years, Ireland camp is an environment that feels natural to me, completely comfortable.

We figure all things are possible in the new dawn. Samoa, Australia, New Zealand – we're hoping for three wins out of three. At a minimum, we want two. But offer us one – against New Zealand – and we'll take your hand off. From the first day in camp, Joe has one eye on a performance in that fixture. It's against the very best teams you measure yourself. You can put down a benchmark for the rest of the season.

He keeps people guessing until late in the week of game one, before asking Paulie to take over the captaincy. He's been on the injury list himself so Jamie – who's been made vice-captain – leads us out against Samoa with Paulie saved for the last half-hour. We win 40–9 and it's a dream debut off the bench for Dreamboat. He scores two tries, and it's nice to have a bit part in the first: close to the Samoan line, a pass to Kearns, which he ships pretty sweetly to his good-looking younger brother, who gets over in the corner.

Game two: Australia. Seventeen minutes in, I've got Cian defending inside me as Quade Cooper carries across the pitch. After analysing Cooper so much, I know he likes a left-foot step and I try to double-bluff him. I show him the outside, expecting him to hit back in.

He reads the situation as he's on the run. He sees from my shoulders that I'm waiting for the step, and he gets the ball out the back door to Stephen Moore, who picks a great line with Nick Cummins in support on the left wing. Moore is hauled down by Tommy Bowe but he makes the offload, and as I watch the man they call the Honey Badger crossing the line I'm already berating myself for over-analysis.

Defensively, we're poor again when Michael Hooper scores a second try seven minutes later, with me in the blood bin. It ends 32–15 and we know Joe's inquest won't spare us.

*

Game three: New Zealand. It's Ireland's twenty-eighth Test against the All Blacks and half of them have been in the years since I first made the team. Only once in those fourteen internationals have I not been named to start – in 2005, the autumn after the Lions tour and the shoulder injury.

Thirteen defeats – some close, some embarrassing, all painful.

Joe gets the Australia analysis out of the way early and pushes on with an intense focus. He'd be an unbelievable poker player. He projects with such positivity that it's hard to know if he believes all of it, but everyone buys into what he says.

As we stand and sing 'Amhrán na bhFiann', I've got one arm wrapped around Paulie and the other around Tommy Bowe and it feels like we're ready to produce a performance. We begin with intensity and accuracy, forcing mistakes. Two tries inside ten minutes, both converted.

Seventeen minutes in: Kearns has his left boot on our 22 when Israel Dagg fumbles a pass from Aaron Cruden and it falls into his arms. He takes off. Half a dozen All Blacks turn in pursuit but none of them are going to get near him. They all give up the chase – except for the number 8, Kieran Read. He knows he hasn't got the gas to catch Kearns and he doesn't try – he runs a line that's all about keeping him in the corner, preventing the easy conversion. Kearns starts moving infield before he hits the line, but Read makes sure he gets only a few metres. Sexto strikes the conversion well but

368

from the difficult angle it clips the left upright. Ireland 19, New Zealand 0 – every point hard earned.

By half-time our lead has been cut, but not by much: 22–7. Joe tells us we need to keep going at them, but they start getting a lot more of the ball. Against the top teams, momentum always swings. We're pushed into all-out defence, trusting ourselves and our system, soaking it up. But it takes its toll.

Fifty minutes. From a five-metre scrum, their 9, Aaron Smith, finds Ma'a Nonu and he runs at us hard. Darce bursts out of the defensive line and brings him down, but it's only a matter of seconds before they recycle the ball and another strike runner has a go. I run back around, in position as the ball is passed to their lock forward, Brodie Retallick.

Sprinting off the line, I think I'm going to catch Retallick blind, but he takes it a split-second before I'm expecting him to and he has just enough time to dip into the tackle. The GPS unit in my jersey records a 19-g hit and I feel every one of them. There's a shaking sensation inside my head as I'm knocked onto my back.

I'm on their side of the ruck, but Nigel Owens knows I'm not interfering with play.

'Okay,' he says, 'you're fine. Fine, fine, fine!'

Under that kind of sustained pressure, any committed defender is going to want to get back into the line, even if he's feeling far from fine. It's like what Shaun Edwards told us on the Lions tour back in 2009: you'd want to have a broken leg to stay on the ground. Once the opposition ball-carrier sees a body or two on the floor, he changes his decision – he sees only the space. A full defensive line sends him a different picture – he doesn't know that one of the guys standing in front of him is there in body only.

I know I'm vulnerable – I'm just hoping none of the All

Blacks have noticed. I hear Sean O'Brien telling me to get back in line, but I'm still not in control of myself and I spit my gumshield out onto the pitch.

After more full-on defence we give up a penalty. As Cruden lines it up, Éanna Falvey comes on to look me over. He has seen me spit the gumshield out and put it down as a sign of possible concussion.

'You're coming off,' he says, firmly.

When we're fifteen points up on the All Blacks, with thirty minutes left?

'No, no! I'm fine!'

He gets me off the pitch. He tells me I have to do a concussion test. I walk off after Cruden makes it 22–10, completely determined to get back on.

Under the stand, I answer every question correctly and pass the test. There are two other doctors on duty – John Ryan and Jim McShane – but Éanna's the senior medic and his mind is already made up. Eight months on from the controversy over me being allowed back into the game against France, he's absolutely insistent.

'No! He's not going back on. I saw him out there and he wasn't right.'

I argue the point with him, vehemently. I argue because I'm a rugby player and the pitch is where we're meant to be, it's where we belong. It's nigh on impossible for a player to have a measured view of his own situation, to self-diagnose and take himself out of the game. We all want to be a cog in something successful. So unless I'm physically unable to carry on, my mentality will always be to go about my business and get myself back in play – unless there's a point-blank refusal to allow me. And when you're on your way to being part of the first Ireland team to beat New Zealand in 108

years, you'll pressurize the people who have your best interests at heart. You'll do or say anything to get back in the thick
of it.

But Éanna won't back down.

And, of course, he's right.

It's not a point I'm ready to concede fifty-five minutes into
a Test match, but no player can be expected to be rational
when the game is going on around him. So it's only afterwards that I'm in a position to see things with clarity and
accept that the decision – always – has got to be taken out of
our hands. Our safety matters a whole lot more than the outcome of any game, a point made forcefully by my dad's first
cousin Barry, a man of principle who resigned as medical
adviser to the IRB, unhappy with its attitude to head injuries.

It's a complicated area, a tough call for medics in the heat
of the moment. More often than not, the coaches will want
their player back on. The evaluation time is short and things
are rarely clear-cut. Only once in my rugby life have I
been knocked out cold after taking a bang to the head. As a
seventeen-year-old playing for Leinster Schools in Musgrave
Park, I put in a hit on the Munster wing Darragh Holt – a big
unit. I looked up and there were people standing over me.

'Where are you?'

'Murrayfield.'

For reasons unexplained, they let me play on – I suppose
the dangers of concussion weren't as well understood, or
taken as seriously, then as they are now. I didn't have a clue
what I was doing. Andy Dunne was the number 10 inside me
and I started giving him a mouthful.

'Come on! Hit me!'

'But we wanna do this play!'

'I don't care what the play is – just hit me!'

'No!'

A couple of minutes later, I was off the field.

Now, on the touchline at the Aviva, I see Cruden missing a chance to cut our lead to nine points, then Peter O'Mahony limping off the pitch after a big performance. And I'm still in Éanna's ear.

'It's not happening, Brian,' he says.

I rip the tape off my wrists, disgusted. I sit back in the dug-out and put my head in my hands, frustrated beyond words. It's so unbearable to watch that I get up and go back to the dressing room to kill some time. Rala's there, getting himself ready for full-time. I pull off my boots, my jersey. There's no TV on, just the sound of roars echoing down the tunnel – pretty loud, but not enough to mean points on the board for us.

After a while Frank Maguire, the Aviva's head of security, walks in with some news. New Zealand have scored; it's a five-point game.

Five minutes later there's a huge roar and now I can't stand not knowing how it's going so I walk back out, in time to see Sexto lining up a penalty with the game clock ticking past seventy-three minutes. It's the chance to make it a two-score game, but he doesn't catch it flush and it misses the right-hand post.

Sixty seconds left: we've got the ball in our hands on their ten-metre line, picking and jamming and running down the clock. I'm in dread of a penalty against us. There's only so many pick-and-jams you're going to get away with without someone going off his feet, or the referee penalizing you for negative play. Especially a referee like Nigel Owens, who wants an open game, who doesn't like one team closing it off at the death.

My head is screaming for a change of tack: *Go to the 10! Do a switch!*

I'm thinking if we change it up, try something else, we can clear the next ruck – and it buys us another pick-and-jam.

Forty-five seconds: another pick-and-jam.

We're going to get penalized here!

Thirty-five seconds: one more.

Thirty seconds: Nigel's arm goes up. Penalty.

Once the ball is back in their hands, for phase after phase, closer and closer to our line, there's an air of inevitability. After almost two minutes of brilliance and belief, Ryan Crotty crosses our line in the corner: 22–22.

For us, the conversion is an irrelevance. A draw might as well be a defeat.

For them, it's a piece of history: fourteen wins from fourteen games in 2013.

Our dressing room is so grim I can't stay in it. There's a wart on my leg I've been planning to get taken off and I have a word with the doc: 'Let's get it done.'

The next time Joe sees us he talks about the seven system errors he picked out in the way we defended the last 100 seconds. And he talks about Kieran Read and the way he kept Kearns in the corner.

'That's what it takes,' he says. 'That's what it takes.'

17. Trust and Joy

There's a creative type in every marketing department who always wants to float an idea too far. When I was young and innocent, I'd reluctantly go along with PR stuff that instinctively made me feel uncomfortable. But with my thirty-fifth birthday a couple of months away, that time is long gone.

Adidas, who've sponsored me for most of my career, tell me they're shooting a tribute video to mark the end of it – part of a campaign they've devised based on a Twitter hashtag, #thankyoubrian.

The plan is to film it in London in December, then show it before my final Test match – all going well, against France in Paris on the last weekend of the Six Nations. It will, says Paul Moloney, their man in Ireland and a top bloke, feature some of my peers combining to deliver a kindly script. So far, so flattering.

But I think I know what's coming next so I cut Paul off at the pass: 'You're not going to ask me to retweet that?'

He smiles. He's known me long enough. I'll help them push the product where I can, but I draw the line at giving myself a big-up.

He moves on to the next part of the campaign proposal. 'Someone in England came up with this one,' he says, by way of an apology. The idea is to make a pair of limited edition Predator boots, put #thankyoubrian on the side – *and ask other players to actually wear them in my final Test match.*

'Don't even contemplate it!' I tell him, totally appalled.

The idea of Paul O'Connell – and whoever else they might have had in mind – being asked to go along with that makes me shudder. Adidas have been very good to me, but the relationship works because they understand that not all of their ideas are going to fly.

The next one is arguably worse – it has me holding up a sign saying #thankyouireland.

'What? Thank you – *my whole country*? That makes me look like an absolute dick!'

I'm a lot more comfortable with the idea for a pair of my own custom-made boots for my final home game. They suggest stitching some personalized touches in gold on the side, replicating my own handwriting. On my iPad I write the number 13, so that it also looks like the B in BOD. Above it on the instep, I write A & S for Amy and Sadie. Alongside one of the Adidas stripes they stitch LEINSTER and AD ASTRA, the Latin motto on the UCD crest that means 'to the stars'.

On the side of the boot that isn't shown in the publicity pictures, I ask for a single word that's for my eyes only, a small tribute to a departed friend: 'Face'.

Gone, but never forgotten.

*

By the time the Heineken Cup comes round again, I'm still waiting for a performance that really satisfies me, something that's better than solid. I don't pay too much heed to how they rate me in the papers, the ubiquitous marks out of ten that a lot of players are drawn to, particularly in the early days when being mentioned in a newspaper still has a little novelty value.

I know when I've gone well and when I haven't. If I come

off feeling happy and the verdict in the paper is less than complimentary – *6/10 – Never really imposed himself on the game* – I'm not going to let it bother me.

Screw you – I had a great game! I did a lot of stuff that went over your head!

I've got my own rating system and I like to think I'm honest with myself.

Ireland v. Samoa: 6/10.
Ireland v. Australia: 4/10.
Ireland v. New Zealand: 7/10.

We travel to Northampton and everything falls into place – a grubber kick that bounces nicely for Lukie's first try; a pass through my legs that opens up the space for Kearns to hit Lukie for his second; an intercept try of my own – our fifth – after good line speed in midfield. We're on fire, it's easily our best game under Matt. We hold them scoreless on their own ground for sixty-seven minutes and at the end – once Lukie runs in his hat-trick – it's 40–7. For me the satisfaction is all the greater because it's been a while since I've been so effective in both attack and defence: I give myself 8.5/10 and the buzz after a good game doesn't feel any less than it did in my first season as a pro.

'We've got to keep playing at that level, we've got to keep getting better,' Matt says, which is exactly what we want to hear. But one of the beauties of the Heineken Cup in December is that a team beaten out of sight one week gets a chance to put things right the next. Northampton, embarrassed in front of their own supporters, turn up at the Aviva and win 18–9.

This time, it just doesn't happen for me: 5.5/10.

We make the quarter-finals as pool winners and I play four more times in blue before the Six Nations, but my best game is a 6/10.

I leave off the newspapers, because there's nothing in them for me.

On the way to Ireland camp, I'm wondering if I'm going to be under pressure for my spot, hoping I can kick on to the next level.

*

You can tell how coaches are feeling about you without them saying anything. You know from how much they're bringing to you: the questions they ask, or don't ask.

At Carton House, I look at our defence coach, Les Kiss, and try to guess what he's thinking about my recent form — *You're a bit hit and miss with your reads at the moment* — but once I'm out on the pitch I train well. I feel the confidence rising again. When Les comes to me to discuss defensive issues before presenting to the rest of the backs, I take it as a good sign.

The first game up is at the Aviva against Scotland, my 129th Ireland cap — one more than Rog, the record-holder. I'm put out in front of the media in the week of the Test, which suits me fine because it means I won't have to sit there and take questions the following the week, when Wales — and Gats — are in town and the Lions thing gets dragged up again. When they try to squeeze a Wales question in, I bat it straight back: 'Look, we've got a big game this weekend. I wouldn't disrespect Scotland by talking about Wales.'

Against the Scots, we're the better team by 22 points and I'm solid, defensively at least — effective enough for Joe to say some encouraging things and give me the confidence that I've got every chance of being there for the duration, form and fitness permitting.

*

Saturday, 8 February 2014, Aviva Stadium, Dublin. Ireland v. Wales.

Game clock: 11 min, 50 sec. Score: 3–0.

Rory Best delivers a lineout thirteen metres inside the Welsh half. Peter O'Mahony takes it cleanly and finds Conor Murray in the same movement. It's a training-ground play we've run against Scotland. As Murr moves it to Sexto, Darce runs a blocking line and I know I'm the next receiver.

So does Scott Williams, the Wales 13.

He reads the play and comes up like a train. I'm about to shift it to Kearns: my body is open. I'm at my weakest, Williams at his strongest.

He absolutely ends me. He catches me full square in the sternum with his right shoulder. It's the biggest collision of my career, by far – 27 g on the GPS unit. If he'd hit me a couple of inches left or right, I'd have broken ribs.

As I hit the floor every last ounce of breath has gone from my body. I've been badly winded before, but nothing like this. I'm barely aware of any pain, but it feels like the closest thing to dying – unable to breathe, panicking.

I roll over onto my knees, head on the ground. James Allen, our physio, rushes over. Then Éanna Falvey. He leans into me, he's in my ear: 'What is it?'

I want to talk. I want to shout – *Get your hands off me! Just leave me!* – but I can't get any words out, so I just try to beat the two of them away.

I can hear them talking, picking up information over

the radio system from another doctor who has seen the hit on TV.

'Blow to the head? Okay!'

For another while I can't find the breath to tell them they're wrong. Eventually, I get it out: 'I just can't breathe.'

'They're worried about your head,' Éanna says.

'It's not my head – it's my sternum!'

'Come on – we need to go off for the concussion protocol.'

'That's not happening – I'm perfectly fine.'

'We just need to make sure you – '

'It's three-nil, Johnny scored last and we're in the Aviva.'

Éanna smiles. Once he's satisfied there's been no bang to the head, he lets me back in the game.

I get back in position and try to catch Scott Williams's eye, to send him my compliments on an unbelievable shot. I'm oblivious to the fact that in making the hit he has hurt his shoulder badly, so when he walks off three or four minutes later I'm thinking he's picked up a knock after another tackle.

With Sexto controlling the game and our lineout maul making serious inroads, we're good across the board and we want it more. It ends 26–3.

Afterwards, Scott Williams comes into our dressing room in a sling, looking to swap jerseys, telling me he's had a scan and he's probably out for the season. I tell him I'll be looking forward to watching him in the future – 'and by the way, that was some hit, it was insane!'

At the dinner, I have a good chat with Rob Howley and Neil Jenkins. Howlers, a real thinker of the game, talks about the different plays his backline ran in the match . . .

'What did you think of that one?'

'Yeah, good – nearly got me!'

On the way to the toilets, I see Gats walking in the opposite direction. He stops, smiles, offers his congratulations. He shakes my hand and we go our separate ways.

*

England at Twickenham, and I feel for Paulie. A week after having to deal with the questions about Gats and me, he's hit with more painful stuff. I'm equalling George Gregan's record of 139 Test appearances and as captain he's in the firing line again.

When he comes back from the press conference we have a laugh.

'Well,' I say, 'did you get me out there? Did you big me up?'

God help him.

I struggle during the build-up, reduced to limited training after hurting my calf on the Monday. The game is an attritional contest summed up by the half-time scoreline: England 3, Ireland 0. It's still a three-point game when the calf tightens up and I limp off with a minute to go. I hate heading off when we're still pressing hard for a winning score but I know I haven't got the legs if I need to go the length of the pitch. It ends 13–10, the end of our Slam hopes; but we'd come into the tournament thinking 'championship' and after three rounds we lead the table on points difference.

Before I even step on the training pitch on the Monday before the Italy match I know the calf is going to be a problem for the rest of the week. I pull up in the session and walk off. I can feel Joe's eyes on me, wondering.

Robbie Henshaw, a fast-rising talent, fills in for me again on the Tuesday and I resist the idea of a new scan, in case something shows up.

The next match, against Italy, is my last home game. I'm getting the world record for caps. In my head, there's not a chance in hell I'm not going to play.

After training, Joe comes up to me in the team room and it's obvious he's concerned. 'How is it?' he asks.

I know how his mind works in these situations. If I put a reasonably positive spin on it – 'Yeah I'd be hopeful – very hopeful!' – I won't be doing myself any favours. Because 'hopeful' doesn't cut it with Joe. He likes definitives. 'Hopeful' doesn't inspire confidence in him – he needs more. So I give it to him.

'I'll be fine – I'll be perfect.'

'If it's any way doubtful –'

'No, it's going to be fine.'

He's not fully convinced: 'I think we'll have enough for this game. But we'll need you for France.'

But I can't countenance missing this game: 'No, I'm good. I'll train on Thursday for definite.'

I spend Wednesday at home, with a Game Ready machine working non-stop on the calf, worrying about the nightmare of not being able to play, texting Mum so that she and Dad are prepared for the worst. I'm painfully aware that there's a plan in place for the end of the game – like my family coming down onto the pitch. It was a conversation I didn't really want to have a week beforehand – you prefer these things to happen spontaneously. I tried to avoid most of the details but Mick Kearney explained that a little knowledge was a necessary evil because it called for some advance planning.

On the Thursday morning before training, good-luck texts arrive from Sue and from Jules, who says she has barely slept with the worry. From my very first cap in Brisbane, back in the days when people sent faxes, my sisters have been pulling for me on every step of the journey and their support means more than ever on the last couple of laps. I know all I have to do is get through the session and I'll start the game – and even though it feels a little sore for my liking, I get by.

Before it ends, our strength and conditioning coach, Jason Cowman, comes onto the pitch after tracking my metres covered on the GPS. 'You've hit three K now, that's enough – we need to pull it,' he says.

Ordinarily when I've got a niggle and the coaches are try-ing to get me off the training pitch, I'm liable to put up a protest – 'One more!'

Not today. I walk off, as relieved as I've felt in a very long time. I know I'm not 100 per cent, or even close to it. But then again, I probably haven't been 100 per cent for the best part of ten years, because – no more than anybody else who plays the game for a living – there's always something that could feel better.

There's a cut-off point – a level of fitness you want to be at so you won't feel like you have the potential to let down the team. In years gone by, 80 per cent did it for me, but as I got older and closer to the end, the number started rising.

Now, I figure I'll be somewhere around 70, 75 if I'm lucky.

It's not ideal, far from it. But for the day that's in it, it's enough. I'll just have to play smart.

*

Once I'm confident in my head that I'll be playing, I sit down for another chat with Shaggy, to be screened in the build-up to the game on RTÉ. As before, I've got my guard down 100 per cent, totally relaxed in his company.

He recalls what I told him last August, when he asked if my final year was only going to be about trophies.

'Yeah, it is,' I agreed then. 'It's not about the waving goodbye to everyone, it's about being able to do laps of the pitch with a trophy and share those great moments with team-mates.'

Six months on, he throws out his follow-up question: 'You're now nine days away from holding the Six Nations trophy. Have you allowed yourself to think about that? Because I *know* you'll concentrate on the Italy game, but you must at some stage have had a little think – a visualization of yourself in Paris with the trophy.'

There's a default answer to a question like this, if it's asked by a journalist. There has to be: anything else would be madness.

No, not at all. It's about the next game.

This isn't a press conference, it's a real conversation. But it just so happens that my response amounts to the same thing.

'Honestly, I can say I haven't.'

The answer surprises him, but it's true. He presses the point. 'People watching this, they'll think, *How possibly can you not?* Because I know I was guilty of it many times.'

'I've been in this situation a good bit,' I say. 'There's nothing to be gained from doing that. Thinking about the outcome will get you nowhere. It will be about the function and the process of every situation you find yourself in – and doing the best you can to create that outcome.'

What I can't say, with the Italy match looming, is that I've enough to be worrying about with the calf.

'*You* keep thinking about process,' he finishes, 'and *I* – like the rest of the country – will think about the end result in Paris.'

I try to keep fully focused on the job at hand – two more wins, the first against a side that beat us in the previous campaign – but it's not easy to shut out the distractions. Outside the bubble of camp, it's hard to escape the fuss being made about my final home game and impossible not to be touched by the good wishes coming my way.

Last time to stay with the team at the Shelbourne – and there's a beautiful cut-glass decanter with glasses and a bottle of whiskey left in my room, along with bathrobes for Sadie, Amy and me, and a card signed by the entire staff.

Last captain's run at the Aviva – and a woman I've never met before comes up with her elderly father and says, 'Here's a little gift – thanks so much for the last fifteen years.' When I open it later there's a sharp intake of breath from Mike Ross, who knows a very expensive bottle of whiskey when he sees one.

Last time in an Ireland team bus on a journey to our national stadium – and the warmth of the supporters I see when I look out the window makes me happy.

Business.

We begin brightly. Six minutes in, after another training-ground play, a hole opens when I get a nice pop pass on the run to Sexto and he zips through it to score. It's a relief to have an early involvement because the calf doesn't feel too good and I can't get above 70–75 per cent pace. I'm out of my comfort zone in open-field running – I can't wait to get rid of the ball.

Someone, anyone – take this thing off me!

We lead 10–7 close to half-time in a good contest when I manage another assist without needing to step on the gas. Three of their defenders buy a dummy pass to Sexto in close quarters and I get the ball out to Andrew Trimble on the left wing. Trims, having a big season, forces his way over.

By the sixtieth minute, I'm starting to think my race is

almost run. The calf isn't getting any better and Joe has already made it clear that if we're far enough ahead he's likely to take me off, with the France game in mind.

From a breakdown close to their 22, we call one of the oldest plays in the book – Brumbies. It's been around since the best days of Stephen Larkham.

Their defensive line is set. Redser fires it across, and as Sexto hits me, Darce's defender sticks on him and there's a little gap. I'm thinking I might get it out the back door to Darce, running short, but they cut that off and I carry on.

Leonardo Ghiraldini, their hooker, wraps himself around me but I manage to stay on my feet and float it, one-handed with my leftie, over the top to Kearns. He moves it to Dreamboat and then Sexto comes charging up behind, in for his second try.

With a 20-point lead, I'm pretty sure it's game over for me. Ferg is on the touchline, having a word, as he'll tell me later, in the ear of the fourth official, Alain Rolland: 'Wait until you hear the reception for me when I run on this pitch.'

He high-fives me as he comes on and we embrace. There's no way I'm milking it as I jog to the touchline because I know there's something planned for full-time. I walk the last bit and I enjoy it. Mick Kearney is waiting with a handshake and Dave Revins with a jacket.

Sexto is off a couple of minutes later and he sits down beside me. It's a lovely feeling on the bench when the job is done and there's the prospect of more tries to come. The camera picks me out a couple of times and there's a decent cheer. I give it the old thumbs-up at the exact moment when my face disappears from the big screen, so for half a second it looks like I'm trying to milk it, with my thumb in the air, as if I'm waiting for the camera to come back.

I'll just take that down . . .

I'm named man of the match for my sixty minutes. Some of the lads are scarlet about the attention being paid to the bench and they scarper.

It ends 46–7 – a big, big result when it's likely the championship will come down to points difference.

An enormous banner with my picture on it starts drifting across the pitch. I'm interviewed for TV and there's a brief moment when emotion rises up inside but it's not something I want to encourage if it's not really there, especially with a game the following week. Somebody starts up another 'One more year' chant but it dies down after a while, thank God, and then the boys have a little tunnel for me – laughing and messing and slapping me wherever they can get me.

Touchingly, very few people leave. Amy comes down onto the pitch with Sadie, Mum, Dad, Sue, Jules and all the nieces and nephews. Talking to Mick, I hadn't wanted all of that, but when I see them there I just go with it, gladly.

Amy hands me my little girl – beautifully dressed for the occasion in her green jacket and Ireland jersey – and the best part of the day is taking her onto the pitch with me. Sexto gives her a big 'Aaaaagh!' as we pass him, but she's completely unfazed as she takes it all in, in her own little way. They were never going to get me to hold up a banner, but there's no harm in a few grateful waves to show my thanks and appreciation for an unforgettable day in my life.

Back near the tunnel, I see two of my aunties – Clodagh and Anne – and two of the Clontarf boys. Dunny's loving it, out front and in no way drawing attention to himself as he shoots some footage on a camera phone. Redser is mortified, tucked away at the side, but still smiling.

When I follow Paulie and the boys down to the dressing

room, our minds are already moving towards the Stade de France.

*

Tuesday at Carton House. Skiddy pays a visit. He's got his little boy Paddy with him, and there aren't many better ways of escaping the hype of the big-match build-up than spending time in this kind of company.

As they head away, Skiddy hands me a letter. Later I start reading it in my room – *It seems a very long time ago when we were kicking a ball around as young lads without a worry in the world* – and by the time I've reached the end there are tears in my eyes.

A beautiful email arrives from Felipe – more emotion.

All of a sudden I'm getting sentimental in my old age.

The good-luck messages come from everywhere: it's like my first cap all over again. Timmy Horan, a childhood hero and one of the centres opposite me in Brisbane that day in 1999, sends a text: *Make sure you get a picture of the jersey hanging up on the peg.*

In Paris, on Friday morning, a bunch of us have coffee on the Champs-Élysées. Later, at the Stade de France for the captain's run, we run a few defensive sets. These days, with so many cameras around, you can't risk showing anything from the playbook.

In Rala's room later that night – one final time – I pick out a particular pen-knife he carries, the one I've always used to get my boots just the way I want them, scraping away any remnants from the training pitch while his easy chat settles me.

There was a time when it went missing and I gave him no end of grief . . .

387

'Where's my knife, Paddy?' For most he's 'Rala', but I always call him by his given name.

'I can't find it, Brian! I dunno what I did with it! Here – what about this one?'

'But it's not the same!'

There's a plastic container he brings to each game and my name is written on a bandage taped to the blue cover – 'DRICO'. The writing is fading now after all these years but inside the box he keeps the special studs that I like, the laces I thread into my boots on the eve of the big day.

A few months later, I find out he intends to keep putting my container out on his hotel-room table after I've gone – a little relic of bygone days. It's a thought that makes me happy and proud at the same time.

Rala started out with the team five years before me; he's the last man standing from the mid-1990s, before some success came Ireland's way. He has seen any number of players come and go and stayed friends with so many.

Five years on from the Grand Slam game against Wales, only six of us from that twenty-two in Cardiff – Kearns, Darce, Paulie, Jamie, Rory, me – are in the match-day squad at the Hôtel du Collectionneur, close by the Arc de Triomphe: Rob Kearney; Andrew Trimble, Brian O'Driscoll, Gordon D'Arcy, Dave Kearney; Johnny Sexton, Conor Murray; Cian Healy, Rory Best, Mike Ross; Devin Toner, Paul O'Connell; Peter O'Mahony, Chris Henry, Jamie Heaslip. Replacements: Sean Cronin, Jack McGrath, Marty Moore, Iain Henderson, Jordi Murphy, Eoin Reddan, Ian Madigan, Fergus McFadden.

In the early kick-off, England win 52–11 in Rome – good, but not enough to put their noses in front of us on points difference. It means that when Rémi Talès kicks off for France, a one-point win gets us the championship.

*

It's a fast game and they score first and second: 6–0. They've got Mathieu Bastareaud at 13, a total handful, impossible to take down one on one. I'm giving him ten years and four stone in weight – I need at least one other guy with me to stop him in his tracks, preferably two and ideally three. For what seems like a long time, there's a lot of containing, a lot of hanging in there.

Twenty minutes in, Sexto takes a good pass from Chris Henry, gets a step on Bastareaud and puts us right back in it.

My calf feels fine, I can run full tilt. Five minutes later I get across the gain line in midfield, place it for Murr, and when I turn around he's over the 22 and putting Trims in for a second try, under the posts: we lead 12–6.

It's nip and tuck. They get a seven-pointer, we come back at them after the break with one of our own – Sexto again after Maxime Médard nails me a couple of metres short.

We lead by six. Then it's nine. One more score and we break them.

Pressure, pressure, pressure: we keep soaking it up.

Bastareaud rumbles forward: havoc stations. It takes four to stop him a metre short.

Their hooker Dimitri Szarzewski knocks on in the act of scoring. Nobody notices.

France 20, Ireland 22.

Ferg comes on for Darce, then Bastareaud runs straight at Sexto and knocks him out cold.

Ten minutes to go. They win a scrum penalty, very kickable.

Wide.

Ninety seconds left. Talès steps off the 22 and takes a pass from Brice Dulin, who has four men and an acre of space outside him. I can see it all unfolding as Yoann Huget comes onto the ball, with options wide. I've got Jack McGrath, a prop, alongside me in a defensive line that's already stretched. We're too vulnerable to play a soft defence so I shoot onto Huget, but I go a fraction late and he gets it away.

If there's a back outside him, we're dead.

But it's Pascal Papé, a second-row forward. He takes one step forward and winds it up.

If he makes his pass, we're dead.

The man in the scoring position is Damien Chouly, the number 8 – he's on the touchline with nobody near him.

Dreamboat is the last line of defence: it's all on him now. In the end, these games come down to the tiniest, most imperceptible margins. It's often about a guy making a right decision, or a wrong one, under the most severe pressure possible. It's about still being mentally and physically sharp enough after eighty punishing minutes, which is what all the training and all the sacrifice are for. And it's about trust – trust in the guy alongside you, so that your first instinct is to back him up when it's all on the line.

As soon as he sees me go to Huget, Dreamboat needs to come up hard on Papé. We defend as a team and I'm his trigger. If he hesitates – if he sits tight for even one fifth of a second – it's over.

But he doesn't. Papé sees him coming and the ball is like a hot potato in his hands. He rushes the pass.

Forward, definitely.

Out on the wing, Chouly gathers it and touches down.

France are celebrating as I'm walking past the referee, Steve Walsh.

'That went forward.'

'Mmmm,' he says.

He goes upstairs, but we don't hear what's said – we just stand there and wait. As the decision drags on and on, we don't feel the same kind of tension – the same helplessness – that family and friends tell us about later on. For us it's different, because we are living the game and we have a say in the outcome. It's so much easier to be involved than it is to watch. In the dying minutes, our entire focus is on doing our jobs to the absolute best of our ability and not being the cog in the wheel that lets the side down.

Finally, justice is done and we only need to win the scrum and end it.

We lose the scrum.

Sébastien Vahaamahina takes it on but Chris Henry hits him hard. Then Devin Toner. Then Paulie jumps in and wraps him up. I know the clock is red and I know there's no way the ball is coming back from here.

Vahaamahina hits the deck and three seconds later Walsh blows his whistle in our favour.

All over.

Ferg is the nearest guy to me. He jumps into my arms and this time there's no relief or stress to get out of my system – it's just full-on joy.

You watch people in other sports react in a moment like this and it's those who show dignity and respect who leave the deepest impression – like Paul Scholes of Manchester United, commiserating with every Chelsea player directly after the penalty shoot-out that decided a Champions League final.

I see my opposite number, Mathieu Bastareaud, and we embrace.

'*Bien joué,*' I say. Never a truer word.

'*Bien joué,*' he says back.

They make me man of the match – a laughably sentimental call. I feel like telling them I'd have given the TV interviews anyway – no bribe was necessary.

I'm grabbed for French television and I hit the guy with my Leaving Cert best.

'How do you feel?'

'*Je suis* très *content.*'

'Everybody asks for one more year. Is it right?'

'I can promise you, it's the final – the last time here in Paris.'

The realization that it's all over, the incredible satisfaction over what we've achieved, the stresses of the game I've just played – it all combines and comes rushing up on me. I couldn't allow myself to feel it a week earlier in Dublin but now I have to dig deep to stay in control of my emotions.

Talking to Claire McNamara, of RTÉ, I mention the emotional power of Joe's team talk and it's the thing that sends me over the edge. I have to step away to collect myself again, but pretty soon the crazy happiness of being among my team-mates takes over completely.

With the lights out in the Stade de France, I'm alongside Paulie as he lifts the trophy. We are double Six Nations winners and it's all the sweeter when you feel like you've earned it.

In the dressing room, I remember Brad Thorn after his last game for Leinster, telling us he didn't want to take the blue jersey off, and I feel the same way about the green. Eventually, though, I hang it on the number 13 peg and stick the boots up there, too, for good measure. I take a photo-graph on my phone and send out a tweet that sums up how I feel about it all.

Phew! Worked out ok! Thanks for all the messages of support. Unreal feeling.

*

At the post-match dinner in the Stade de France, I'm deeply moved by the unbelievable words Paulie has for me in his speech. Out on the balcony, a little later, Maxime Mermoz pulls out his phone, and as he takes a selfie of the two of us, seven or eight French players pile in around me. I'm given a France jersey with my name on the back, signed by all the team – a serious touch of class.

When we get back to the hotel, the place is thronged with Ireland supporters and the level of their excitement is like 2009 all over again. It feels great to have given them some-thing else to shout about. It's mayhem when the boys lift me up as we walk in and chair me across the lobby, with fans all around and my family there, too, loving every second. The sheer craic of that – I know I'm never going to get it again, but just having it at all is a memory for life.

Back in Dublin, the smile barely leaves my face all day or all night. There's a huge welcome at the airport. After four mostly frustrating years with the national team, it's nice to have the Six Nations trophy back in Irish hands and we pass it around to anyone who wants to get hold of it.

Katie, Aoife and Sean, Julie's kids, rush up as we're walk-ing through. Sean gives me a massive hug around the waist. He's four now, growing up fast. It's a couple of years since I changed his nappy, and there are high hopes for him in a certain household at Park Lawn, where a certain proud grandfather is already getting carried away by the next generation: 'He's going to be a very good footballer – just look at his hand-to-eye co-ordination! Well done!'

The homecoming party at Sam's Bar, Dawson Street, is one for the ages. I walk out of there at 6.20 a.m. on St Patrick's Day in the company of Willie Bennett, feeling like I could murder a burger and chips. At the nearest McDonald's they're serving the breakfast menu only, so we jump into a cab and I ring ahead to order room service back at the team hotel, the Four Seasons in Ballsbridge.

Amy's fast asleep when my club sandwich is brought up, but they've given us a big suite – so me and Willie sit happily in the second room, talking about the good times.

*

In the weeks that follow, the kindness that comes my way is overwhelming. To sit alongside the great Fr Peter McVerry, a tireless campaigner for the homeless and the disadvantaged in our country, and be awarded the Freedom of Dublin with him, is an unimaginable honour and a deep privilege.

Paris felt like the perfect ending, but there's another lap before retirement and I dig in as best I can. In my last game against Munster, with a full house at the Aviva, I score the final try of my career, running onto an offload from Jenno.

The victory pushes us five points clear at the top of the Pro12, but we don't have it in us the following week in France, and Toulon knock us out of the Heineken Cup.

We pick ourselves up. We win our last five of the season and see it out with another trophy, a second successive Pro12 title in front of our own supporters, and the first under Matt.

In a short span of time, our supporter base has grown to a level we couldn't have imagined when we were togging out for training from the back of our cars. In every county in Ireland, there are more kids playing the game than ever before. It's nice to think that some of the young lads watching us at the RDS or the Aviva will grow up to be the stars of the future, when all of the boys I shared my rugby days with have hung up their boots. It's a special life that happens for only a few, but even the thought that you've helped in a small way to foster a love for the game among the kids who play at any level makes you smile.

Dear Brian O'Driscoll

My name is Alexander and I go to Willow Park School (St Paul's) in Blackrock. I have been your biggest fan ever since I was a little toddler.

I wasn't really good at rugby at the start of the year but when I saw you playing, you just wowed me with confidence and skills. After a few weeks later a miracle had sparkled upon me. On that very day I was told to move up to the Cs. It was a great opportunity for me because it was my biggest dream of all.

So all I'm really trying to say is thanks for inspiring me in becoming a good rugby player and congratulations for u and your team-mates for winning matches in the last number of years. And I hope that you and your family will live happy and healthy.

Your number 1 fan
Alexander

*

When you're gone, you're gone. You move on to the next part of your life, staying in touch with some of the lads – the ones who'll always be friends – and you try to find your feet in the big world beyond the game.

It's nice that there are people out there who think you've still got something to contribute to rugby, albeit in a different way. Nicer again when some of them are prepared to go to the trouble of putting it in writing . . .

Dear Brian,

My team-mates insisted a lot to have me writing and I couldn't say no. I'm playing in a Swiss women's rugby team. We were wondering if you've already planned something for next year – and if you would be interested to come to live a few years in Switzerland and become our trainer. Ours is regrettably leaving us at the end of this season.

As you may know, Switzerland is one of the best countries in the world to live in and you'll surely enjoy our life's quality. Rugby is not played at a professional level here and therefore we can't pay you to coach us, but we can all help you to find a good job, pay the costs, find some new sponsors. It would be absolutely great if you come.

I wish you all the best. Even my mum enjoys watching rugby when you are on the pitch.

Regards,
Stéphanie Galloni (player of the Rugby Club Bern)

When all's said and done, it's good to be wanted when you're an ex-player. In early summer, I sign on for two part-time roles as a guest presenter on radio for Newstalk and an analyst for BT Sport. It gives me the chance to stay involved in the game without it dominating my life. I've also got ongoing business interests in the Ultimate Rugby app and Ikon Talent, a sports management agency, and I'm keeping my eyes open for other possibilities.

When pre-season begins there isn't even the suggestion of a pang for the life I've left behind. Driving by the Leinster training ground I wonder what's going on inside, but it no longer feels like a second home for me. I don't need to feel that attachment any more, because what I have inside is more than enough: memories of the great days, the tough days, the shared experiences with so many good people who lived it alongside me.

I know that when the season starts and I'm watching on just like any other supporter, I'm going to feel something different, especially when the bigger games start coming and the TV cameras follow my former team-mates off the bus and into the dressing room. I won't know what that emotion will be until it hits me, but I'm sure that a part of me will feel envious.

Everywhere I go, people ask the same questions and I can totally understand why, because I've been there myself – wondering how it was for other players when the time came for them to walk away, close enough to some of them to know what they felt deep down …

'How are you going to feel watching Ireland next time they play?'

'Will you be going to the games now you've retired?'

Not unless I'm working, I tell them – at least, not for the first couple of years after retirement. But I like to think that, in the seasons ahead, I'll be taking my kids along to support Leinster and Ireland, because my heart will always be with these two teams and I'm so glad to have had the chance to represent them. I feel grateful for the opportunity, for the journey, for the test. And now it's over I'm in a good place, enjoying the summer and the chance to do different things, ready for the next chapter.

In August, I look at the Leinster fixture list and notice that the first game of the season is a friendly against Northampton at Franklin's Gardens, the ground where I produced my best performance of the one more year.

When the boys turn up for a 5.30 p.m. flight to London on the day before the game, I've already been through Dublin airport before them, with Amy and Sadie by my side, bags packed for Portugal.

Our plane touches down shortly before 5 p.m. The family holiday is all in front of us and we cannot wait.

Acknowledgements

Brian O'Driscoll

The problem with acknowledgements is where to start and how to avoid forgetting important contributions. So many people have helped me on my way that it would be impossible to name them all without leaving some out. Many – though by no means all – are mentioned in different parts of the book. I'm truly grateful for the help and support I have received from coaches at all age levels, and not just in rugby. My gratitude also to the unsung heroes in the support staff, the physios who performed wonders against the odds, and the doctors and surgeons who put me back together, and who always had my best interests at heart.

Over the course of fifteen years as a professional – and before that as somebody who never even dreamed of being paid to play a game I love – I had countless great team-mates, and I feel very fortunate that some of them will be close friends for life. Elsewhere in these pages I've reflected on the camaraderie of the dressing room and I'd like to thank all those who I played with along the way.

I took great pride in representing the different teams I played for over the years, and supporters of Leinster, Ireland and the British & Irish Lions have always been good to me. As a result, I've been fortunate to meet so many special people during my rugby journey, as well as some great characters.

From my first international cap to my last, people had the kindness to send cards and other messages wishing me luck, and the neighbours in the street where I grew up, Park Lawn in Clontarf, were always very support-ive. The late RTÉ sports broadcaster Colm Murray was one of them, a truly nice man who is missed by us all.

For helping me to tell my story I'd like to thank Alan English, who did a brilliant job of conveying my voice and my sensibility in print. He is not just a great journalist and rugby writer; he is a great writer full-stop, and I was extremely lucky to have him on board in the making of this book. Thanks also to another great sportswriter, Paul Kimmage, who was my first collaborator on this project.

Thanks to Michael McLoughlin and Brendan Barrington at Penguin Ireland for their key contributions to the book.

Mick Kearney, the Ireland team manager, provided excellent advice and input, as did my great friend Denis Hickie. My wife, Amy – a more experienced author than me – was also a huge help throughout the whole process.

Billy Stickland has been present with his cameras since my earliest days as a pro – thanks to him and all at Inpho Photography for many of the photos in *The Test*.

As readers of the book will know, my family is incredibly important to me and words couldn't do justice to the support they have always provided. Huge thanks to Amy and my daughter Sadie, my parents Ger and Frank, my sisters Julie and Susan, and all the extended family for everything.

Alan English

I'd like to thank Brian and his family for trusting me to help tell his story. It was both a big responsibility and a privilege.

The task was made easier by the readiness of people close to Brian to help in any way they could. It's probably very unfair to single a few of them out, but I was particularly grateful to Brian's sister Sue and his wife, Amy, for their encouragement. His oldest friend, Donovan Rossi, was extremely supportive. Thanks, Dunny.

I benefited greatly from the transcripts of detailed interviews provided to me by one the best sportswriters in the business, Paul Kimmage, my former colleague at the *Sunday Times* and Brian's original collaborator on this book.

The first of my own interviews with Brian were diligently transcribed by my son, Jack, and he was succeeded in the task by Trish Davis. Thanks also to Ryle Nugent for providing DVDs of material from the RTÉ archives and to Brian's mum, Ger, for letting me borrow from her phenomenal collection of scrapbooks covering his rugby days.

Thanks to Michael McLoughlin and Brendan Barrington at Penguin Ireland for their professionalism and sound advice.

My brother, Tom, has written about Irish rugby since before Brian exploded onto the scene. His help and encouragement from day one were immense. One of the nicer legacies of the experience is that Tom English Junior is now the undisputed number 1 Brian O'Driscoll fan in the Bridge of Allan district of Scotland, and perhaps another star centre in the making.

Last but not least, I'm hugely grateful to my own children – Aisling, Holly and Jack – and to my wife, Anne, for their love and support.

Index

(The abbreviation BOD stands for Brian O'Driscoll)

INDEX